Here's what the critics say about Frommer's:

"Amazingly easy to use. Very portable, very complete."
—*Booklist*

♦

"The only mainstream guide to list specific prices. The Walter Cronkite of guidebooks—with all that implies."
—*Travel & Leisure*

♦

"Complete, concise, and filled with useful information."
—*New York Daily News*

♦

"Hotel information is close to encyclopedic."
—*Des Moines Sunday Register*

Suzy Gershman

BORN TO SHOP

HONG KONG, SHANGHAI & BEIJING

1st Edition

HUNGRY MINDS, INC.

New York, NY • Cleveland, OH • Indianapolis, IN

This one is for Peter Chan, who took such good care of me in my time of need—with double thanks for double happiness.

Produced by:

HUNGRY MINDS, INC.
909 Third Ave.
New York, NY 10022
www.frommers.com

ISBN 0-02-863671-6
ISSN 1531-7552

Editor: Alice Fellows
Production Editor: Cara Buitron
Photo Editor: Richard Fox
Design by Michele Laseau
Cartographer: Roberta Stockwell
Production by Hungry Minds Indianapolis Production Services

SPECIAL SALES
For general information on Hungry Minds' products and services, please contact our Customer Care department; within the U.S. at 800-762-2974, outside the U.S. at 317-572-3993 or fax 317-572-4002. For sales inquiries and reseller information, including discounts, bulk sales, customized editions, and premium sales, please contact our Customer Care department at 800-434-3422.

Manufactured in the United States of America.

5   4   3   2   1

CONTENTS

MAP LIST

ABOUT THE AUTHOR

Suzy Gershman has been named "the world's greatest shopper" by amazon.com and "Super Shopper Suzy" by Oprah Winfrey. She has been a contributing editor—on the subject of international retail, of course—for *Travel & Leisure* and now *National Geographic Traveler.* Gershman also writes for www.BonjourParis.com, *Where Paris, Porthole,* and assorted other travel destination sources. Her updates to city shopping can be found at www.born-to-shop.com. Suzy currently lives part-time in Paris, part-time in Boston, and part-time at the airport.

TO START WITH

This book was meant to be named *Born to Shop China* to show you just how hip we are, but zillions of shoppers and pals in Hong Kong told me that they don't associate their visits to Hong Kong with being in China. In principle, they know that Hong Kong is governed by China, but they don't think of Hong Kong as part of China and they wouldn't look for a book about Hong Kong in the China portion of the alphabet in a bookstore.

Therefore the new title: *Born to Shop Hong Kong, Shanghai & Beijing*. Rest assured that the *Born to Shop Hong Kong* book you've relied on for more than a dozen years has been reworked, revised, and updated. New sections on Shanghai and Beijing have been added, to give you just a taste of China. Naturally, in no time at all you'll be hungry for more.

Hong Kong has long been the door to the Orient. Many go on to Bangkok and deeper into the Pacific Rim, a few try Vietnam, or depart for cruises that'll navigate the South China Sea and the areas between Hong Kong and Singapore. But, more and more, people have decided that seeing all of China—or at least making their first trip into China—and getting to know it, is a multidecade task.

Research for this edition took about three years, with many trips into China. I went in different seasons (forget it in August); I went under different travel conditions. I went as a press guest of the Chinese government; I went on my own as a tourist. All along, I shopped until I thought SwissAir might kill me or I'd go broke on excess baggage charges rather than purchases.

I must thank all the people who made the trips possible and who taught me how to cope and how to shop better. I was lucky enough to have old friends in Beijing and to make new ones along the way.

Thanks go to Peter Chan and my whole team in Hong Kong; to Peter Finnamore and Chet Sharpe, formerly of Beijing, and to Chet's husband, Kevin, a champion shopper. Hugs, kisses, and dozens of Prada zipper makeup bags to Carole Klein at the Regent Hong Kong, and all "the girls" who make up my network in Hong Kong, and to Glenn and Lucille Vessa, part of my Hong Kong family. Special thanks go to Maggie Sheerin, who went on one of the research trips with me and who lends her expertise in collectibles (and life lessons) to this edition. She is Maggie the Maven.

In Shanghai, the whole support team at the Ritz Carlton Portman helped me out, as did my many friends at the Palace Hotel in Beijing, especially my adorable Flavia Caponi, whom I knew from London! (Small world or what?) Marion Darby in New York motivated the Shangri-La teams all over China to help me out, and they were all fabulous—with special thanks to Kelly Sum, who put me in touch with Sandra Walker and the wonderful artwork that now graces my walls.

In Zurich, thanks to Thomas Schmid and my dear Michel Rey, my hosts at the Baur au Lac who keep me up to date on Zurich and ensure that the China Passage through Zurich is always smooth. God bless SwissAir and the luxuries of Zurich.

To one and all, my heartfelt thanks—Chinese this Sunday?

Chapter One

....

THE BEST OF HONG KONG, SHANGHAI & BEIJING

According to the Hong Kong Tourist Authority, most visitors to Hong Kong stay only 3 or 4 days and then go on to another destination in China or the Pacific Rim. This means you're going to be crazy busy, every moment packed with sights to see, treats to eat, and things to buy. While wonders may never cease, your visit will. If you're fighting a desperate struggle against the clock, I've created this chapter for you.

All resources mentioned here are covered in more detail later in the book and obviously not every resource in the book has made it to this section.

China has so many rich and varied shopping, dining, and sightseeing opportunities, it's pretty hard to come up with a single best of anything. Best is a very subjective thing. Each choice here is based on a weighted combination of location, value, and energy. I know I'm sounding Zen-like on this one, but it's important to me that you get the right feel in your few free moments. Believe it or not, there isn't that much crossover in merchandise in the cities that are covered in this text.

THE 10 BEST STORES

....

Along with my list comes the usual disclaimer—these choices are based on my research visits. China is changing fast. As soon

Airports & You

Many businesspeople are in such a great hurry getting from meeting to meeting that they save up their shopping errands for the airport duty-free shops as they're leaving town. While I understand this inclination (I've fallen prey to it myself) and the new Hong Kong airport, Chep Lok (also known as Hong Kong International Airport), may be a virtual shopping mall, note that prices are the same as in town. Even duty-free prices are high. I suggest shopping the gift shop at your hotel in Hong Kong if you're willing to pay top dollar.

The Beijing airport has a super duty free, excellent for last-minute shopping. I can't tell you that the prices are the lowest in town, but the selection is wide enough for you to accomplish all your shopping goals.

Best airport gift? Panda-shaped cookies.

as we go to press, a bigger or better resource might pop up. Cope.

YUE HWA CHINESE PRODUCTS EMPORIUM, HONG KONG
301–309 Nathan Rd. (MTR: Jordan Rd.).

A real Chinese department store, complete with grocery store in the basement—I never found a store like this one in mainland China, although I supposed there would be scads of them. Buy every possible gift or souvenir, and don't forget the lower level for the seal-penis wine or the booze with snakes in it.

SHANGHAI TANG, HONG KONG
12 Pedder St., Central (MTR: Central).

This is undoubtedly one of the must-see, must-dos of Hong Kong, even if you don't buy anything. In fact, there is a good chance you *won't* buy anything. Still, the store is gorgeous to look at and inspirational in its creativity. There are souvenirs and fashions, Mao-mania and original artwork by contemporary artists—all imported from China. Get a load of the gift wrap! Wander, drool, buy, have a cigar, sit down for tea, or shop 'til you're late for your next appointment. Clothes are a tad expensive, but there are plenty of giftable items in the $15 to $50 range. Bad news: The fabulous postcards are no longer free. If the store doesn't interest you in your 1 hour, you can be in and out in 5 minutes and then hit the mall across the street, The Landmark, or The Lanes—around the corner—for fun junk.

WAH TUNG
Aberdeen/Hong Kong (no MTR).

Although Wah Tung has branch stores around town, I vote for their multifloor factory. They have so much china that you will never want to leave, and yes, they will ship for you. Wah Tung is a wholesale resource; they supply many of their goods to department stores around the world. You too can lose your mind as you touch and drool over the ceramics, or even arrange a custom-made order. You can have lamps made from vases; you can have anything! I want everything!

KAI YIN LO, HONG KONG
Mandarin Oriental Hotel, 5 Connaught Rd. (MTR: Central) and Peninsula Hotel, Salisbury Rd., Kowloon (MTR: Tsim Sha Tsui, TST).

For those who have the budget and ability to splurge on an important piece of jewelry, this artist makes incredible pieces from many mediums. Most of them are one-of-a-kind pieces that will knock the socks off those who see you wearing them.

YU YUAN GARDENS, SHANGHAI
Yu Yuan, the number-one tourist destination of Shanghai, is a village that includes a botanical garden at its core and many buildings in traditional Chinese architectural style. This means, bring the camera! There's a medieval-style village of shops as

well as many mall-like structures and a flea market in the basement of one of the buildings. To complete the picture, there's a tea house in the middle of a lake.

OLD SHANGHAI STREET, SHANGHAI

Not actually part of Yu Yuan but just down the street, it completes the perfect 1-day shopping adventure. Old Shanghai Street, a sort of U.S. marketing idea applied to a once quaint street, is now being commercialized like mad. At the farthest end of this street is the Fu Yu antiques market—which is fabulous, especially on weekends.

HU-HU FURNITURE, SHANGHAI

If you aren't interested in furniture, then you can miss this resource. If you love to look at pretty things and adore high style with ultra panache, this is the most chic furniture store in all of China. The woman who runs it is American-Chinese and therefore speaks English like few others in Shanghai. Have your taxi wait . . . even if it's a few days.

THE FRIENDSHIP STORE, BEIJING

In the old days, the Friendship Stores were the Chinese equal to Russia's Dollar Stores—places where tourists could shop so the mother country could rake in hard currency. While there are Friendship Stores in many cities in China, the one in Beijing is the only one that's really, really good. It's virtually a department store, the size of a city block, with everything you can imagine and more—there's even a Starbucks inside.

THE PEARL MARKET (HONG QIAO MARKET), BEIJING

This sounds a lot more romantic than it looks, but if you can adjust to the notion that this is merely an indoor mall, you're on your way to heaven . . . and the Temple of Heaven is conveniently across the street. The first floor has watches and small electronics (including Mao lighters), then there's leather goods and fakes, a floor of pearls and pearl wannabes, and then a floor of Chinese arts and crafts. After that are two floors with antiques. One-stop shopping for everyone. Don't forget that there's a portion of the mall across the street with an outdoor strip of shops.

PUNYUANJMIN FLEA MARKET, BEIJING

Saturday and Sundays only: If you are a flea market person you owe it to yourself to arrange your trip so that you have a few hours here. The market includes some aisles of dealers under tin rooftops, and masses of real people with their goods laid out on the ground. Beware of fakes (duh). Best time is before 10am, when it gets very crowded.

GREAT INEXPENSIVE GIFTS

....

- **Tea mugs.** Chinese tea mugs (complete with lid) cost about $3 each in any Chinese department store. You'll have to wrap them yourself (pack with care), but they are marvelous gifts.
- **Chinese tea.** From high-end brands and makers (such as Fook Ming Tong, Hong Kong) to any old brand in a great-looking package sold from the street or at a Chinese department store, tea makes a very traditional gift, and it doesn't break. Prices vary with brand and venue.
- **"Jade."** I buy "jade" donuts by the dozen at the Jade Market and then string each one individually as a gift. They cost about $1 each and are not real jade. If you're willing to move up to $10 to $15 per gift, you can purchase figurines of various animals.
- **Chops.** This is one of those great gifts that you buy—you know that no one has one. A chop—a Chinese signature stamp—costs about $25 and can usually be carved while you wait.
- **Perfume bottles.** Many like the kind of perfume bottles that are painted from the inside—I prefer the fake antiques that look like smoked glass from the 1920s. If you are

willing to spend a little more, you might actually find a real snuff bottle.

THE BEST SHOPPING EXPERIENCES

- Trolling for bargains on Granville Road or Fa Yuen Street, Hong Kong
- Having a garment made to measure, Hong Kong
- Any flea market, Hong Kong and China
- Any wet market, Hong Kong and China

THE BEST SOURCES FOR ANTIQUES

Antiques are very tricky in China—you simply don't know what's real and what isn't.

With that caveat, I rely on Honeychurch Antiques at 29 Hollywood Rd. in Central Hong Kong because I know and trust the American expatriate owners, Glenn and Lucille. Hollywood Road (and nearby Cat Street) is packed with antiques dealers.

Hollywood Road is an excellent stroll, both for antiques shopping and for getting an overview of what is available, and what the prices might be—but don't buy anything serious from a dealer who is not known in the trade.

Macau is an excellent source for antiques. That is, if they haven't made them right there!

Both Shanghai and Beijing are filled with shopping ops for smalls and antiques, real and fake. Prices can be half those in Hong Kong. But then, reliability can be, too.

THE BEST TAILORS

While prices in China for custom-made clothing may be less than in Hong Kong, don't be tempted. If you want top-of-the-line quality that competes with the best of Savile Row, you want a Hong Kong tailor (whose family probably came from Shanghai anyway).

There is no one best tailor in Hong Kong—there are three. They stand head and shoulders above all the others for one simple reason: They are the only tailors with their own workrooms who do not send their piecework across to China.

A-MAN HING CHEONG
Mandarin Oriental Hotel, 5 Connaught Rd. (MTR: Central).

H. BAROMAN
Swire House, Connaught Rd. (MTR: Central).

W. W. CHAN & SONS LTD.
92 Nathan Rd., 2nd Floor, Kowloon (MTR: TST).

While all good tailors also make shirts, there are two incredibly famous names in shirt making who specialize in men's shirts, shorts, and pajamas only:

ASCOT CHANG
Ascot Chang, Regent Hotel, 18 Salisbury Rd., Kowloon (MTR: TST); Prince's Building, Chater Rd., Hong Kong (MTR: Central).

DAVID
Mandarin Oriental Hotel, 5 Connaught Rd. (MTR: Central); 33 Kimberley Rd., Kowloon (MTR: TST).

Chapter Two

....

HONG KONG & BEYOND

I've been a Hong Kong person for well over a decade; I've seen good times and bad times and . . . well, I've seen it all. And if one more person asks me if Hong Kong has "lost it" I may karate chop him or her. Hong Kong has not lost it. Hong Kong has found it.

On the other hand, I think that it's time you got past Hong Kong and saw some of China. China, especially the big cities like Shanghai and Beijing, is now ready for prime time, and you are going to have the time of your life.

Shoppers: on your marks.

There's no question in my mind that China intends to blind Hong Kong someday with Shanghai's reflection. Until that day comes, however, Hong Kong will be, and is still, fabulous, with plenty of things to buy and even some bargains.

No, Hong Kong hasn't been ruined since the Chinese takeover. Retail sales were up 9% in 2000; tourist visits are up, and room rates are low. Hong Kong leads Asia in the great comeback and you cannot really consider Hong Kong as part of China in terms of the feel of the place.

The way I see it, Hong Kong will always be a little bit of shopping paradise—the tease that leads you beyond the gates and into the temples of heaven.

Sure, Hong Kong has the hotels and the fancy bathtubs and the shopping malls, but it also has the phone lines, the infrastructure, and everything that global business needs for expansion. Hong Kong isn't about what flag is flying; it is about the future; it serves as merely the stepping-off point to more shopping, more sightseeing, and more wonders. But China is the future of market share, of tourism, and, for the time being, of bargains.

Enter the Dragon.

WELCOME TO CHINA

I try to put politics aside when I write about China; after all, my mission is to shop. After spending a week in Russia each of the last 3 years, I can't help but wish that the Russians could be as good "communists" as the Chinese, because whatever you call it, my God, it's impressive.

Beijing and Shanghai are masterworks of marketing, in all senses and subtexts of the word. To market to market to score some fine buys. To market, to market, to influence the world.

If you're expecting a dull, gray world filled with tired people in lookalike clothing and a bunch of 1950s-style posters with enormous red letters, you can try some other place. Color is everywhere; the public areas and those sights most likely to be visited by mainstream, international tourists are clean, paved, often covered in marble, and planted with bright flowers—pink flowers, not even red ones.

Shanghai hardly even feels like China; it certainly looks a lot more like Hong Kong. Or is this what the new China will look like? Beijing, thankfully, still has a Chinese taste to it, but if you are hungry for more, you'll have to go to other cities in China.

In fact, there's an element of "get there now" just because China is changing so fast.

PRC VERSUS SAR

Before I launch into the nitty-gritty that will hopefully save you time and money and make your trip easier, let me clarify the

China

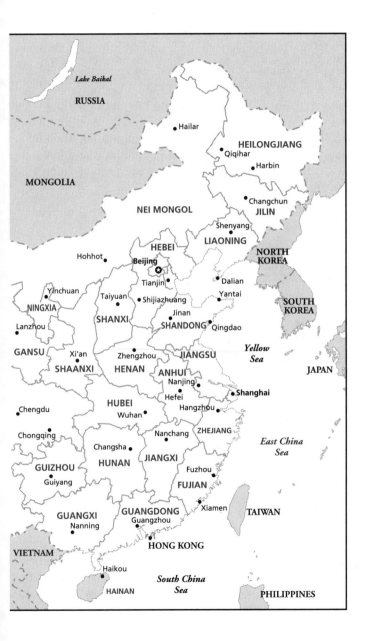

difference between the PRC (People's Republic of China) and Hong Kong, which is a Special Administrative Region of China (SAR). This is what China calls the "One China, Two Systems" theory in practice. Therefore travel information (and much shopping information) is different for the PRC than for Hong Kong.

Hong Kong is an old hand at tourism; China is not. While things have relaxed enormously in China, the mainland does not enjoy the same freedoms as Hong Kong and you'll be wise to mind your P's and Q's.

Getting a Visa

U.S. citizens do not need a visa to enter Hong Kong. They do, however, need a visa to enter the PRC, even if it is a day trip from Hong Kong. There are several ways to get the visa:

- Contact a visa service. Send them your passport and the paperwork, which they will fax you, along with the number of passport-size photos they ask for. Send these things by FedEx or some sort of mail system that can be traced. I use Zierer Visa Service (☎ 212-265-7887); they charge $50, but you have very little to do. You are paying for convenience and you will have your passport back, with hologram visa, in about a week.
- Get your visa in Hong Kong. This is doable; they even have a visa office right at the border in Shenzen (and probably in every border town). This can be time consuming and nerve-racking, as you may not be treated like the VIP you are. There are also travel agencies in Hong Kong—not at the border—that can get you the visa; your hotel concierge may also have connections. These visas can be issued anywhere from instantly to within 24 hours.
- Go to the Chinese Consulate and Passport Office nearest you. You are limited here, but I went into Manhattan to get my visa and found it worth doing. If you do it in person,

you can fill out the paperwork while you are in line. You will need one passport photo of yourself and you must pay in cash. This is a tad tricky because the amount differs with what services you ask for. I've paid extra for express service—the total was $60 once and $75 another time. The visa itself is about $30 but how quickly you get it depends on how much more you're willing to pay.

OK, now this part's none of my business, but here goes. They'll ask you the purpose of your visit and your occupation. Do not say journalist or photographer if you can help it.

Arrival Details

While you are standing at the luggage carousel you may indeed read the rules and regulations about entering China. That could be a little late, so herewith some of the broad strokes:

1. There is no limit to the amount of foreign cash you can legally bring into China. However, if you have amounts over US$5,000, they must be declared.
2. The first 100 CDs can enter the country without duty.
3. No pornographic materials, guns, bombs, and so on.
4. No motorcycles.

Booking China

There aren't as many great guidebooks to China as there should be, although once you are in China you will find more guides, in English. Airport book stores in Hong Kong and other Chinese cities have a surprising amount of special-interest books, going way beyond normal guidebooks. Even books that may surprise you are sold, and there's a large amount of fiction, both by Chinese authors and by international writers who use a Chinese setting. Nonfiction accounts of life in China at the turn of the 19th century and in the years leading up to World War II are fascinating. Try: *When We Were Orphans,* Kazuo

Electronically Yours

More Web sites will be given in each chapter, but here's some basics to get you started:

- Reports from *Asiaweek,* CNN, and *Time* magazine: www.Asiaweek.com
- HKTA (Hong Kong Tourist Authority) site: www.hkta.org
- Hong Kong Airport Authority: www.hkairport.com for flight schedules and information, terminal maps, special needs facilities, and so on.

Ishiguro, *Bound Feet & Western Dress* by Pang-Mai Natasha Chang, *Shanghai* by Harriet Sergeant, and *The Boxer Rebellion* by Diana Preston.

Screening China

To get more of a visual and cultural sense of China, a trip to a video store can garner a wide range of choices—from the well-known *The Last Emperor* to the esoteric, such as *Raise the Red Lantern,* a film about women in the past that is upsetting, but fascinating. Films that give us a glimpse into the more recent past and contemporary China are *To Live* and *The Story of Qui Ju.*

FLYING TO HONG KONG, SHANGHAI & BEIJING

With China opening up, demand has created more air routes into China and more and more airlines are fighting for hubs and the loyalty of both business and leisure travelers. They are also working to make the trip more comfortable, which is related to the long flying time, and therefore, to routes. The air wars will really launch in spring 2001 when many new routes from the United States right into China are inaugurated.

Chicago is now making a bid to become the U.S. hub for flights to China, although New York has its share of flights as well. Delta is now putting in for New York–to–Beijing service. Meanwhile, American Airlines is flying from Chicago to Shanghai. While there are flights from the major West Coast cities (LA, San Francisco, Seattle, and Vancouver), many of them connect through Narita or even Seoul. There are non-stops with flying time about 13 hours.

Since I've been going to Hong Kong at least once a year for a dozen years, I've developed my own ways to cope with the enormous time change (12 hours from the U.S. East Coast) and with the long haul, which can be 17 to 26 hours of travel time, depending on many factors.

First off, I have to say that I am a nervous flyer and only fly on a few airlines that I think are the safest in the world. Therefore, because of my own neurosis and no well-founded reasons, I do not fly Chinese carriers except for Dragon Air, which is a division of Cathay Pacific. This will become an important fact to consider when I start explaining Chinese travel laws to you.

I also confess that I have terrible jet lag when I go to the Far East; as much as a week of my trip can be ruined by it. As I get older, the jet lag becomes more and more of a problem— one that can no longer be denied.

Sooo, I have devised a genius system whereby I fly to China on the transatlantic route, taking SwissAir and booking a layover in Zurich or any European city within any hour's flying time of Zurich.

For me, this totally eliminates jet lag. You are dealing with two 9-hour flights (if you depart from New York) and two 6-hour time changes. Try it—I promise it will change your life.

If you lay over on the West Coast, you can make the flying time more manageable, but will not cut the jet lag as well, because flying time is still about 13 hours and the time change is ten hours. For more on transatlantic routes and jet-lag-beating techniques, see below.

Big Announcement

For those of you who will book all or part of your trip through Beijing, there's something major you need to know—in most airline parlance, Beijing is known as Pekin: This is the city's official airline designation. When checking for flights that are listed in alphabetical order, don't give up when you get to the letter *C* thinking you have passed *B* for Beijing; look under *P* for Pekin.

European Connections
SwissAir

Note that American Airlines flies to Zurich also, so you can get yourself there on miles and then go to a code share or buy a SwissAir ticket to China as a round-trip through Zurich.

British Air & KLM

KLM is always merging or going into business with a new partner, so it's hard to know who's on first. However, they are a terrific airline and have been selling Far East travel via Europe for many, many years. From Amsterdam they now offer service to Hong Kong, Beijing, and Shanghai (separate flights to these cities).

Austrian Airlines & Singapore Airlines

Austrian Airlines   If you are looking for the furthest western city in Europe in terms of getting more than halfway to China from the East Coast and having a layover to spare the jet lag, think Vienna. Austrian Airlines flies to Shanghai, but not every day of the week, so coordinate carefully.

Singapore Airlines   Flying to Singapore via Hong Kong from London.

TRANSPACIFIC FLYING

You can take United Airlines nonstop from San Francisco to Beijing or fly United to Shanghai via Narita. For more on Narita, see below. I find that I can get to Narita just fine; it's the layover and the ongoing travel that kills me. United also flies nonstop from Narita to New York.

If you can get nonstop flights from Los Angeles or San Francisco, consider your layover in one of these cities in order to beat jet lag.

If you're going to Hong Kong, you can also lay over in Hawaii.

Narita Connections

No one has a shorter connection time through Narita (Tokyo) than Northwest; with the mere legal connection of 1½ hours you hardly have time to wander Narita or feel foggy—you simply stretch your legs, pop back into your seat, and you're off. Arrivals are timed to create minimum effects of jet lag. It's also a rather social kind of thing in the hub at Narita—people meeting up with colleagues, people connecting on to all sorts of destinations in Asia, not just Hong Kong. And yes, Northwest flies to mainland China, Shanghai, and Beijing—even from the United States.

Also note that technology, trade, and diplomacy efforts will continue to revise the situation and offer different gateways. American carriers now have rights to fly over Siberia that had never been granted before; United Airlines has recently begun nonstop 747–400 service to Hong Kong from Chicago! This is the longest route segment in history, some 7,788 miles.

Other U.S. airlines have deals with Canada that allow them to offer nice routes from the United States with quickie refueling stops on Canadian soil. Canadian carriers are also looking at code shares to increase this marketing effort.

Unusual Connections

OK, so most people fly transpacific and connect through Narita. I depart from the East Coast of the U.S., fly transatlantic, and connect through Zurich. But there are two other choices I have discovered that are, uh, creative.

Hawaii: Believe it or not, service from Hawaii to Hong Kong has just been initiated by Cathay Pacific and can be done as a code share with American Airlines. This means that those who want to break up the flight, and avoid Narita, can make a stopover in Hawaii.

Tel Aviv: This is quite unusual, but it works. El Al uses Tel Aviv as the hub city and has ongoing service to Beijing and Hong Kong as well as other major cities in the Far East. The flying time from New York to Tel Aviv is about the same as New York to Tokyo, so it's not as strange as it sounds. This makes a layover in Israel completely kosher and will go a long way in eliminating jet lag once you get to China. Furthermore, El Al now has a code share with American Airlines so you can use miles, book through American, or probably also connect an around-the-world deal with American, El Al, and Cathay. Call American Airlines at ☎ 800/882-8880.

Detroit: Northwestern flies from Detroit right to China.

Ticket Deals

Flights on all airplanes to Hong Kong, especially from the West Coast, are packed. One of the reasons for this is that there are lots of businesspeople flying these routes. With China opening up, there are even more of them. Add to that the fact that there are wholesalers who buy blocks of tickets, knowing they will be able to resell them to travel agents and tour groups, and you can see why it may be hard to get the flights you want. Because they buy in bulk, wholesalers often get a better price. And these wholesalers or ticket brokers pass their savings on to their customers. Enter Lillian Fong, my personal secret weapon.

Call or fax Lillian Fong, at Pacific Place Travel, 1255 Corporate Center Dr., Suite 203, Monterey Park, CA 91754 (☎ 800/328-8778 or 213/980-8138; fax 213/980-8133; e-mail: pacplace@worldnet.att.net).

Other thoughts:

Don't be afraid of business and first class. The long-haul trip is a lengthy one; you will be much more comfortable in business or first class. For travel within China, prices on higher classes of services may not be much more than coach.

Furthermore, there are more business-class seats than any other class of seat (you aren't the only person who really doesn't want to do this trip in a coach seat), so there is the possibility of more deals than in coach or first class.

Talk to your travel agent about coupons or deals that can get you into first class on an upgrade basis. Lillian offered me first-class upgrade tickets if I paid the full fare for business class; this is a pretty good deal.

Don't accidentally compare apples to oranges. If you are pricing airfares on several carriers, it is imperative that you understand the quality of the service and what you are getting. Don't assume anything. Virgin has made quite a splash with their extra perks and great entertainment system, but they only offer real value to those travelers willing to fly economy at promotional prices or to those willing to pay extra for their upper-class service. The chitchat of the entire Pacific Rim is whether American carriers compete with Asian carriers on a service level.

- There are so many code shares these days that you can have seamless ticketing; however, you may want to know which carriers are taking you on which legs.
- Code shares are great for mileage travel; also check out partner promotions. SwissAir and Sabena had a mileage promotional deal with a free coach ticket for 80,000 miles from Zurich to either Beijing or Shanghai. Check it out at www.qualiflyer.net

- There are often air miles wars; recently you could fly to Hong Kong (coach) for 40,000 miles on a promotional deal.
- There are new gateway deals—as China opens up and technology allows airlines to fly farther distances, all things become possible. Watch for flights like Detroit-Shanghai or Minneapolis-Beijing, and so on.
- Around-the-world fares will always offer you the best price, especially in business and first class. See chapters 5 and 7 for around-the-world deals to Hong Kong and Shanghai.
- Circle Pacific prices may give you the best deal on a multiple-city trip when the stops are in the Far East.
- Airline miles are a great way to get to an exotic destination that you thought was out of reach.

Promotional Deals

All airlines have promotional deals; Americans have become accustomed to the regular airfare wars, which offer great domestic and European airfares during certain times of the year. Promotional deals to Asia are sometimes harder to find.

I was quite amused to read that many of the national carriers of Pacific Rim area airlines offer deals that aren't advertised in America, but you can find them by calling the airlines' toll-free number in the United States. For example, Air India (☎ 800/442-4455) offers "shopping rates" with a 33% discount for women flying between the major shopping cities of the Far East.

If that strikes you as too complicated, there's the offer that Virgin had, round-trip economy fare, London–Hong Kong for HK$4,700—about US$600! This offer was through American Express and had to be booked through them, but it pays to call them and ask what else they have. Oh yes, it's a long distance call to the Amex office in Hong Kong (☎ 852/2532-6060).

As for more easy-to-find promotions, I found a terrific deal that was advertised in the United States: Northwest offered a first-class ticket for the price of a business-class ticket; there is a little bit of fine print to this deal, but basically, it's not a bad offer. Call ☎ 800/447-4747 (www.nwa.com). In another Northwest ad, there was a terrific deal for an economy seat for $650 round-trip (!!!), but here's the cute part, if you brought a friend, the seats were $600 each. This was a winter promotion: Tickets had to be bought by the end of November and travel had to be completed by January 15. Still, it was a great deal!

Note that all airline mileage programs have sales and promotions at various times of the year or on certain routes. I was dumbfounded to read recently that American's frequent-flier program was offering round-trip economy-class tickets to Hong Kong on promotion for a mere 40,000 miles!

Cyberdeals

Cathay Pacific was one of the first airlines to go on-line and actively recruit travelers. They have many innovative programs, including mileage awards and auctions. They suggest you look at their site: www.cathay-usa.com and then use a travel agent for ticketing or finalizing plans.

Travel Within China

The Chinese government does not yet allow intra-Chinese flights by carriers that do not fly the Chinese flag. There are a few connecting flights that run once or twice a week, such as an Austria Air flight that flies from Shanghai to Beijing before heading back to Vienna. For the most part, travel between mainland Chinese cities must be done through Chinese-owned and regulated transportation.

Chinese airlines are coming on strong to convince you that they know their home skies better than anyone. I'm old-fashioned when it comes to picking a carrier, but businessmen in China often say several of the regional carriers have pilots trained in the United States and brand-new craft.

China Southern Airlines (CSA) has come on very strong in the market, with long-haul flights from the United States as well as intra-China flights. If you have a credit card from China Merchants Bank you can even do e-ticketing (www.cs-air.com). This is not their only new technological advance, the airline has what they call PASS (Passenger Assistance Service System), electronic kiosks to help travelers. In fact, these CSA guys are big on marketing flair. They had a deal whereby if you paid economy from Los Angeles to Guangzhou (Canton), you got an automatic availability upgrade to business class at check-in.

Frankly, I make my travel choices based on using the train within China. It's not as exciting as Paul Theroux would have you believe, and it's easier on my nerves. But then, I am a sissy when it comes to flying. For more on train travel between Shanghai and Beijing, see chapter 7.

Tours to China

I have never gone on a tour, but I know that especially with China travel, many people like to do this because they want to see a lot in a short period of time and they are afraid of language and political problems. Many also want to book Yangtze River cruises before it's too late.

Tours seem to be rather easy to find through travel agents and airline packages. I happened on an ad from a firm called Pacific Bestour, with such incredible prices that I was really impressed. The tours included airfare on United for the long haul, transportation within China, daily breakfast, some city tours, an English-speaking guide, and more. Beijing tours began at $729; Hong Kong was $699. There was a 9-day tour that included Beijing and an Eastern Yangtze cruise for $999.

Cruises

More and more cruise ships are offering stops in China; these are usually winter sailings from October through March. Some use Beijing as the turnaround city and then bus you to the port (about 2 hours away); others turn around in Hong Kong or even Bangkok. Often there are several ports in Vietnam on the cruise as well. Those lines with China ports include Seabourn, Silver Seas, and Sea Goddess.

MONEY MATTERS

....

Hong Kong has a different currency from China; in major cities in eastern China you can use Hong Kong dollars, but they are usually accepted at par although they are 10% more valuable.

As we go to press, the yuan—Chinese national currency— is not currently a convertible currency and is pegged to the U.S. dollar. That is expected to change; when the yuan floats it may devalue by 10%. Stay tuned. As we go to press, there are about 8 yuan to each U.S. dollar.

Many guidebooks refer to Chinese money as RNB; this technically refers to a system no longer in practice. When China was a closed country, foreign visitors were not allowed to use local currency and were therefore issued special script, called RNB. This is similar in the theory to "dollar stores" in Russia (which have disappeared).

You are now allowed to have paper currency and may even remember (from school) that the Chinese invented paper money. You can change money at your hotel or get it from the wall via ATM (but not the Great Wall). However, there are more and more ATMs, especially in Shanghai, so as long as you see the Cirrus sign, you're in business and can withdraw local currency at the best rate possible.

Since the best shopping in China is done in markets and on the streets, you will want to have access to cash, which also offers you the best bargaining position.

About Those Tips

In mainland China, a communist country, tipping is frowned upon and internationals who live in China, trying to preserve their own status quo, will tell you that it is wrong to tip. I disagree. When you are asking people to become capitalists, the most persuasive argument you have is cash. I tip 10%; more for a job well done or for enthusiasm and helpfulness.

Am I spoiling the old China? I hope so.

Exit Tax

There is an exit tax from Hong Kong and one from China too. Sometimes it is in the price of your air ticket, most often it is not and must be paid in cash, in local currency. Ask before you blow your last yen.

Chapter Three

....

A DICTIONARY OF CHINESE CRAFTS, STYLE & CUSTOMS

TALK THE TALK

Nothing tells a merchant you're an insider faster than your ability to "talk the talk." Mention a few buzzwords that immediately convey the message that you are not a fool and are, therefore, a force to be reckoned with. While nothing replaces true expertise, herewith is a short dictionary of local customs, products, and practices that'll give you some inside knowledge and, I hope, a little extra power at the bargaining table.

Entire books have been written on almost all of these subjects, so if you really want to learn more, stop by your local library or bookstore. You'll also find that major booksellers in Hong Kong have lots of books on local subjects that you might not find at home. Books are not cheap in Hong Kong, but the selection on specialty topics may be worth the price differential.

And now a story to remember about Maggie, who went to the Jade market with me in Hong Kong (and many other markets in China). We separated to do our own thing and when we met up, Maggie was in possession of a Ming dynasty vase for which she paid US$30, truly the find of the trip. How did

25

Maggie make such a score? Well, first off, she knew what she was doing. She found a dealer who had "antiques" and when he tried to tell her that his tiny horse was genuine, Maggie not only said "no way" but volunteered to flick away the antique finish with a finger nail. Now she had the dealer's respect. Then she saw a vase with the three ring decorative motif that she knew meant genuine Ming dynasty. So she pounced.

Now it's your turn.

AN ALPHABETICAL GUIDE
....

Alphabet

Mandarin is now the official Chinese dialect. It is now taught all over China and used in the legal system; people still speak their regional dialects, but can often understand Mandarin. Mandarin is called *guoyu,* meaning "the national language." The written language, however, is the same, whatever dialect is spoken, and it is one of the few things that unites some 90 million people. It's an ideographic language based on symbols, not sounds; there are four tonal systems of pronunciation to help differentiate meaning (although context is also important).

There's a recorded inventory of 50,000 pictograms; you need an acquaintance with 2,000 to 3,000 characters to read the newspaper. The average person can recognize about 8,000 characters.

The standard Romanization used in China today is called *pinyin.* There are a number of transliteration systems, and texts often cite which system they are using. Wade-Giles was the system used everywhere in the first part of the 20th century, and it was the changeover from Wade-Giles that changed Peking into Beijing.

Ancestor Paintings

Available on paper scroll or canvas scroll, these large paintings—most often family portraits—are called "ancestor paintings" in English and represent a very specific art form. Naturally they are widely copied and reproduced, so that fakes abound. The best one I ever saw, translated for me by my guide that day, was of two women—twins—with the inscription about what venerable old ladies they were in that, their 42nd year on earth.

Reproduction ancestor paintings on paper scrolls cost about $200 each in Hong Kong; paintings on canvas bought in China cost about $250 each, but are much harder to transport because they tend to be larger than their paper kin. Note that canvas scrolls can easily stretch to 10 or 12 feet in length, so your walls better be high enough!

When I bought my two ancestor paintings, I had traded myself up over the course of a week from paper imitations to the real thing on canvas. Although I was hurting when I paid about $500 for two, now that I have them home, I realize they were an incredible bargain.

Antiques

According to the U.S. government, an antique is any item of art, furniture, or craft work over 100 years old. The reason the U.S. government cares is simple: You pay no duty on genuine antiques. However, with the Chinese takeover, laws about the export of antiquities from Hong Kong are expected to change, so there's a whole new world of definitions of what's an antique and what isn't, and an even grayer area in which you can be cheated, especially if illegal activities are taking place. Watch it!

True antiques are a hot commodity, and unscrupulous dealers take advantage of the demand by issuing authenticity papers for goods that are not old. To make matters worse, Hong Kong does not require its dealers to put prices on their goods. Depending on the dealer's mood, or assessment of your pocketbook, the ginger jar you love could cost HK$100 or US$150; it could be 10 years old or 10,000. If 1,000-year-old eggs, sold in all markets, aren't really 1,000 years old, imagine what they do to antiques.

Mainland China is even more strict. Genuine antiques cannot be taken out of China unless they have a government wax seal on them.

Only you can determine if you're getting a good deal. Pick a reputable dealer and ask a lot of questions about the piece and its period. If the dealer doesn't know and doesn't offer to find out, he probably is not a true antiques expert. Get as much in writing as possible. Even if it means nothing, it is proof that you have been defrauded if later you find out your Ming vase was made in Kowloon, circa 1995. Your invoice should state what you are buying, the estimated age of the item (including dynasty, year), where it was made, and any flaws or repairs done to the piece.

I've noticed that there is a characteristic particular to most quality antiques shops, which is never even imitated in bad shops. In good shops, the dealers want to tell you everything they know about a piece or a style you have expressed interest in; they're dying to talk about the items and to educate you. They take pleasure in talking about and explaining the ins and outs of entire categories of goods. If you don't find these free lessons readily offered, don't spend a lot of money in that shop.

The center of international trade in Oriental antiques is actually London; all the big dealers come to Hong Kong to buy. Hong Kong is the crossroads for goods coming out of China (usually illegally) and for those goods already brought out. Grave robbing has been going on like mad.

There's also a business in antiques that are newly made out of old wood or from repaired pieces, so that dealers will certify that they are 100 years old for U.S. shoppers but in fact the items are not old at all.

Expect most, or many, of the antiques in markets in Hong Kong, Macau, and mainland China to be fakes.

Blue-and-White

Blue-and-white is the common term given to Chinese export-style porcelain, which reached its heyday in the late 17th century, when the black ships were running "china" to Europe as if it were gold. After 1750, craftspeople in both England and continental Europe had the secret of bone china and were well on their way to creating their own chinoiserie-styles and then manufacturing transfer patterns for mass use.

In those years before westerners were on to the secrets of the Orient (and still believed porcelain was created from baked eggshells), there was such a huge business in export wares that European shapes and styles were sent to Canton for duplication. Thus, a strong knowledge of these forms is required by the shopper who wants to be able to accurately date a piece.

Glenn Vessa of **Honeychurch Antiques** tells me that after you've handled a few thousand pieces of blue-and-white, you will have complete confidence in what you are doing. I can only tell you that I flunked the test he gave me, and I had studied beforehand.

The untrained eye needs to look for the following: pits and holes that indicate firing methods; the nonuniform look of hand drawing versus stencils; the shades of blues of the best dyes; the right shades of gray-white as opposed to the bright white backgrounds of new wares. Marks on the bottom are usually meaningless. Designs may have European inspiration (look at those flowers and arabesques), which will help you determine what you are looking at.

Be careful that you aren't looking at English-made blue-and-white passed off as export wares. I saw some in an antiques shop in Macau, and while it was nice, it wasn't what I came to China to buy.

Bound Feet

Since a woman's place was in the home and woman should be kept barefoot and pregnant, the feet of aristocratic women were bound during infancy so that the women could not walk—meaning they had to be carried, were most comfortable prone, and certainly couldn't work.

The binding process brings the toes underneath the foot toward the heel and results in a permanently deformed foot.

Special shoes were needed; these are still available in flea markets and are highly collectible. Make sure you don't have reproductions, however.

Bronzes

Antique Chinese bronzes are featured at several Hong Kong museums, making them an easy art form with which to commence your education in Chinese art. Visit several local museums to sharpen your eye so you can understand the difference between what will cost you thousands of U.S. dollars and what you can buy for a few hundred. The lesser price indicates a fake. As with all Chinese art, you must be able to recognize subtle changes in style and form that indicate time periods and dynasties in order to properly date your fake.

Glenn Vessa says that Japanese bronzes are still a good investment; bronze incense burners begin around $3,000 and go up. Stop by **Honeychurch** to talk to him about it.

Cameras

Can we tell you about cameras? You probably don't want to know everything that we can tell you about cameras.

First off, we have to deal with fantasy. For some reason, every shopper who comes to Hong Kong thinks he's going to get a great deal; that this is *the* place to buy a camera. Wrong! Unless you are a pro, you may not even want to bother with the exercise. But if you insist on playing the game, pay attention.

Start by doing research at home as to what equipment you need. *Do not* allow a Hong Kong camera salesperson to tell you what he thinks you should buy, or what is a good deal. Once you feel comfortable that you know what you are looking for, visit several shops (and not all on Nathan Road) comparing prices. Try the stores on Kimberley Road off Nathan Road. We've discovered that prices can vary by as little as $10 and as much as $200 before negotiations even begin.

Be sure to ascertain that the price for the camera includes a manufacturer's worldwide guarantee. The store's guarantee (even if printed on fancy paper) is worthless; the manufacturer's guarantee may prove worthless, too, but at least get it.

As soon as you start serious negotiations, examine the camera very carefully. It should still be in its original box, complete with the original packing material that holds it tightly. Remember that camera boxes can be repacked to look like new. Check to make sure yours was not. Look at the guarantee to verify that it is a worldwide guarantee and is authentic.

There must be a stamp from the importing agent on the registration card. The dealer will add his stamp upon conclusion of the sale. If you're really careful, you will call the importing agent and verify the sale. Check the serial numbers on the camera and lens with those on the registration card to make certain that they match. Take out the guarantee before the camera is repacked and ask to have it packed in front of you. This way the merchandise can't be switched. Ask to have the following information included in the store receipt: name and model of camera, serial numbers of each part, price of each item, date of purchase, itemized cost of purchase with total sum at the bottom, and form of payment you are using.

Carpets

As the Persian carpet market has dried up, the popularity of Chinese carpets, both new and old, has escalated. China still has a labor pool of young girls who will work for very little money and sit for long periods of time tying knots. There's also a newer business in needlepoint carpets.

Carpets come in traditional designs or can be special ordered at carpet factories. Price depends on knots per square inch, fiber content, complexity of design, how many colors are used, and city or region of origin. Any of the **Chinese Arts & Crafts** stores is a good place to look at carpets and get familiarized with different styles and prices ranges. You can visit the **Tai Ping Carpets** showroom in Hong Kong; many mainland tours have visits to carpet factories included. Of course your guide gets a kickback—what a silly question!

When considering the material of the rug, consider its use. Silk rugs are magnificent and impractical. If you're going to use the carpet in a low-traffic area or as a wall hanging, great. Silk threads are usually woven as the warp (vertical) threads, and either silk or cotton as the weft (horizontal). The pile, nonetheless, will be pure silk. Wool rugs are more durable.

Chinese rugs come in every imaginable combination of colors. No one combination is more valuable than the next. Some older carpets have been colored with pure vegetable dyes; more modern ones use sturdier synthetics in combination with vegetable dyes. Avoid carpets that were made with aniline dyes, since these are unstable. These dyes were used on older rugs that were crafted at the beginning of the century. To test for aniline dye, spit on a white handkerchief and then rub the cloth gently over the colors. If only a little color comes off, you're safe. If the carpet has been dyed with aniline dyes, a lot of smudgy color will come off on the handkerchief.

I bought needlepoint carpets on the last trip to China; they were not cheap—I've seen them for less in the United States at TJ Maxx—but the quality was good, the colors were perfect for my home, and the designs were classical English garden style. Because the price was so high, and I had to carry the carpet in my luggage, I bought a small rug, measuring about 120cm by 180cm (hmmm, I think that's 5 feet by 7 feet) for $250.

Ceramics & Porcelain

Ceramic and porcelain wares available in Hong Kong and China fall into three categories: British imports, new Chinese, and old Chinese. For a short lesson in buying blue-and-white, see above.

New Chinese craft pottery and porcelain is in high demand. Although much of the base material is being imported from Japan and finished in Hong Kong, it is still considered Chinese. Most factories will take orders directly. There are numerous factories in Hong Kong where you can watch porcelain wares being created and place your personal order. In fact, the better wares are coming out of Hong Kong while the mass market stuff is more likely to come from China.

Porcelain is distinguished from pottery in that it uses china clay to form the paste. Modern designs are less elaborate than those used during the height of porcelain design in the Ming dynasty (A.D. 1368–1644), but the old techniques are slowly being revived. Blue-and-white ware is still the most popular. New wares (made to look old) can be found at the various Chinese government stores, including **Chinese Arts & Crafts,** in zillions of little shops on and off Hollywood Road, in **Stanley Market,** in Macau and just about everywhere else. Fakes abound; buy with care.

Cheong Sam

You really already know what a cheong sam is; you just don't know the word so you're temporarily thrown. Close your eyes and picture Suzie Wong. She's wearing a Chinese dress with Mandarin collar and silk knot buttons that buttons from the neck across the shoulder and then down the side, right? Possibly in red satin with a dragon print, but that's an extra. The dress style is called a cheong sam. Really touristy ones come in those silk and/or satin looks, but you can buy a chic one or you can have one custom made. **Irene Fashions** made me a drop-dead elegant one in navy wool crepe. It was inspired by the dress Demi Moore wore in *Indecent Proposal.* Even though I don't quite look like Demi in it, I'm still amazed at the curves the tailor was able to cut in the garment. The cheong sam is the native dress from the Shanghai area and one way to get a good fit is to use a Shanghai tailor.

Also called a quipo.

Chinese New Year

During the Chinese (Lunar) New Year, most stores will close. For a few days preceding the festivities, it is not unusual to find prices artificially raised in many local shops, as shopkeepers take advantage of the fact that the Chinese like to buy new clothing for the new year.

Chinese Scrolls

Part art and part communication, Chinese scrolls are decorative pieces of parchment paper, rolled around pieces of wood at each end. They contain calligraphy and art relating to history, a story, a poem, a lesson, or a message. Some scrolls are mostly art, with little calligraphy, but others are just the opposite. Being able to identify the author or artist makes the scroll more valuable, but it is usually not possible. Chinese scrolls make beautiful wall hangings and are popular collector's pieces.

Chinoiserie

Exports from Asia were so fashionable in Europe in the late 18th century and again in the Victorian reign, that they started their own trend. Western designers and craftspeople began to make items in the style of Asia. Much was created from fantasy and whimsy; there is also a mixture of influence of Indian and other styles with the purely Chinese. Decorative arts and furniture in Asian style, made in Europe, are considered chinoiserie. Chinoiserie is not actually made in China.

Chops

A chop is a form of signature stamp on which the symbol for a person's name is carved. The chop is then dipped in dry dye and then placed on paper, much like a rubber stamp. The main difference between rubber stamps and chops is that rubber stamps became trendy only in the 1980s, whereas chops were in vogue about 2,200 years ago. Since chops go so far back, you can choose from an antique or a newly created version.

Cloisonné

The art of cloisonné involves fitting decorative enamel between thin metal strips on a metal surface. The surface is then fired

China Post

No, it's not the newspaper—it's the mail system!

To address outgoing mail from China, place the postal code portion of the letter in the appropriate six little boxes in the left-hand corner.

If you're trying to send out a package (ha!), you should not seal it before arrival at the post office, since it must be inspected. Start at the international desk, fill out the proper forms, go to the customs window at the post office, then go back to the international desk. It will be sealed by machine after inspection and voilà, it will be mailed.

under just the right temperatures, and the finish is glazed to a sheen. It sounds simple, but the handwork involved in laying the metal strips to form a complicated design, and then laying in the paint so that it does not run, is time-consuming and delicate and is an art requiring training and patience.

Antique works by the very finest artists bring in large sums of money. Most of what you'll see for sale in Hong Kong (outside of the finest galleries) is mass-produced cloisonné and is very inexpensive—a small vase sells for about $20; bangle bracelets are $3. You can also find rings, mirrors, and earrings for good prices at most of the markets. These make good souvenir gifts to take home. Frankly, I prefer the Hermès version.

Computers

All the famous brands, makes, and models of computers can be found in Hong Kong, but you had better be computer literate to know if you are getting a better deal than you could get back home. Be sure to check the power capacity, voltage requirements, guarantees, and serial numbers of every piece you buy. Clones are also available and at very good prices. However, "buyer beware" applies doubly in this category.

Various software programs are also available; prices are not much less than in the United States, but can be substantially less than in the United Kingdom. The biggest problem is that you simply must know what you are doing and what you are buying; the more you rely on the sales help, the more likely you are to be taken.

There are several office buildings that specialize in computer showrooms: try the **Silvercord Building** in Kowloon and **Golden Arcade Shopping Center** in Sham Shui Po.

Dim Sum

Dim sum is a Hong Kong specialty and an old custom. It is easily ordered in any western-style restaurant where someone speaks English or the menu is printed in dual languages. If you go for a more adventurous meal, you may need a few basic tips. You may also buy a book on the subject or carry around pictures with you. Some people show photos of the grand-children that they carry in their wallet; I have, in my wallet, a picture of my favorite dim sum. The best bet is to learn what you like at home, under western-style conditions, then learn the names of the items in Chinese or have them written out for you. Of course, that's too easy. It's much more fun to go someplace where they will allow you to stand next to the dim sum cart and point.

Embroidery

The art of stitching decorations onto fabric by hand or machine is known as embroidery. Stitches can be combined to make abstract or realistic shapes, sometimes of enormous complex-ity. Embroidered goods sold in Hong Kong include a variety of items: bed linens, chair cushions, tablecloths, napkins, run-ners, place mats, coasters, blouses, children's clothing and robes—all of these items are new. There is another market in antique embroidered fabrics (and slippers), which is, of course, a whole new category in terms of price. Antique embroidery items can be very expensive.

Traditionally, embroidery has been hand sewn. However, today there are machines that do most of the work. Embroidery threads are made from the finest silk to the heaviest yarn. Judge the value of a piece by whether it is hand stitched or machine stitched and what kind of thread or yarn has been used.

One of the most popular forms of embroidered work sold in Hong Kong is white work, or white-on-white embroidery. Most white work is done by machine, but the workmanship is very good. Hand-embroidered goods are hard to find today and very expensive. Try **Chinese Arts & Crafts.** Most of these goods come out of Shanghai and may be competitively priced in your hometown. Don't assume you're getting a bargain.

Feng Shui

Feng shui (translates as wind, water) is an important cultural concept related to keeping the spirits happy. It has to do with the positioning of human-made objects—especially buildings—that must remain in harmony with the earth and not disturb the spirits that inhabit that space. Harsh angles upset the spirits; the building, its doors, its windows, and its core must be in alignment so the spirits can flow. This means that before any project is built or any room designed, a feng shui expert must be called in for advice.

Furniture

Chinese styles in furniture caused a major sensation in the European market. Teak, ebony, and *padouk* were all imported from the Far East and were highly valued in the West. Yet the major furnishing rage was for lacquered goods, usually in the form of small chests of cabinets that were placed on top of stands, which were built to measure in Europe.

True Chinese antique furniture is defined by purity of form, with decorative and interpretive patterns carved into the sides or backs. Antique furniture is a hot collector's item. Dealers and collectors alike are scouring the shops and auction houses.

It is better to find an unfinished piece and oversee its restoration, than to find one that has already been restored. If it has been restored, find out who did the work and what was done. Some unknowing dealers bleach the fine woods and ruin their value. Others put a polyurethane-like gloss on the pieces and make them unnaturally shiny.

If you do decide to buy, decide beforehand how you will get the piece home. If you are having the shop ship it, verify the quality of their shipper and insurance. If you are shipping it yourself, call a shipper and get details before you begin to negotiate the price of the piece.

Happy Coats

One of the hottest-selling tourist items is the "happy coat," a padded jacket with a stand-up mandarin collar, usually made of embroidered silk with decorative flowers, animals, and birds. They make great souvenirs of Hong Kong, but all too often are the kind of thing that you can't (or don't) wear in the real world. When picking fabric, try for something classic that works with a western-style wardrobe.

The Lanes in Hong Kong is your best bet for these coats. In fact, I've hardly ever even seen them in China, although they could just be seasonal there.

Ivory

One word of warning: No. It's that simple. Articles made from ivory will not be allowed into the United States. It is not smart to try to run them. Only antique pieces with proper paperwork will be allowed in.

Carvers in Hong Kong are currently using dentin from walruses, hippopotamuses, boars, and whales as substitutes for elephant ivory. If you want to make sure you are not buying elephant ivory, look for the network of fine lines that is visible to the naked eye. If the piece you are buying is made of bone, there will not be any visible grain or luster. Bone also weighs less than ivory. Imitation ivory is made of plastic, but can be colored to look quite good. However, it is a softer material than real ivory and less dense.

There are very few antique ivory pieces left in Hong Kong. If someone claims to be selling you one, be very wary. Should you snag one, you'll want provenance papers.

Jade

Jade was originally used solely in rituals for the dead. In the late Chou dynasty it became a source of delight acceptable for the living to appreciate; interest in intricately carved jade ornaments, sword fittings, hairpins, buttons, and garment hooks took off.

The term *jade* is used to signify two different stones: jadeite and nephrite. The written character for jade signifies purity, nobility, and beauty. It is considered by some to be a magical stone, protecting the health of one who wears it. The scholar always carried a piece of jade in his pocket for health and wisdom. Jade is also reported to pull impurities out of the body; if you buy old jade that is red-brown in color, it is believed that the jade absorbed the blood and impurities of its deceased former owner.

Jadeite and nephrite have different chemical properties and, indeed, are written differently in chemical equations. Jadeite tends to be more translucent and nephrite more opaque. For this reason, jadeite is often considered to be more valuable. Furthermore, really good jade—imperial jade as it is sometimes called—is actually white, not green.

If you are shopping for jade, you need a quick lesson in Chinese: *chen yu* is real jade; *fu yu* is false jade. Jadeite comes in many colors, including lavender, yellow, black, orange, red, pink, white, and many shades of green. Nephrite comes in varying shades of green only. The value of both is determined by translucence, quality of carving, and color. Assume that a carving that is too inexpensive is not jade. "Jade" factories work in soapstone or other less valuable stones. Poor quality white jade can be dyed into valuable-looking shades of green. Buyer beware.

Jade should be ice-cold to the touch and so hard it cannot be scratched by steel. I always produce my trusty Swiss Army knife and ask the dealer if I can cut into a sample. If he nods yes, then his merchandise is real.

Some shoppers make it common practice to quick touch or lick-touch a piece. This is not a real test of good jade, although stone will certainly feel different to the tongue than plastic. You may also want to "ring" a piece, since jade, just like fine crystal, has its own tone when struck.

The **Jade Market** (Hong Kong) is a fun adventure and a good way to look at lots of fake and real jade. Test your eye before you buy. If you are determined to buy a piece of genuine jade, I suggest that you use a trusted jeweler or other reputable source; you'll pay more than you might in a market or a small jewelry shop, but you'll be paying for peace of mind. Please note that jade (real jade) is very, very expensive. Fake jade may be what you really have in mind. Don't be shy.

If you are interested in carved jade figures, bring out your own jeweler's loupe and watch the dealer quake. If the carving is smooth and uniform, it was done with modern tools. Gotcha! A fine piece and an old piece are hand cut and should be slightly jagged on the edges.

What are those green circles you see in the market and often in the street? They are nephrite and should cost no more than $1 per circle. They make fabulous gifts when tied to a long silken cord and turned into a necklace.

I've been buying brown jade over the last few years—I don't know if it's real or not; dealers claim it is "antique." I pay between $10 and $20 per piece and am happy with what I've got. What's it's really worth is anyone's guess. I've been attaching my jade pieces to the zippers or straps of various handbags— very chic. But heavy.

Joss Sticks

Although there is a method of telling fortunes with joss sticks, these long, thin, skewerlike pieces of wood are meant to be

An Alphabetical Guide   41

burned in a Buddhist temple with prayer or thanks. You buy
them in the temple. There are various methods—I plant all of
mine in one clump of sand in a chosen area.

The concept of joss is related to luck; it is proper to wish
a person good joss.

Kites

On one of my trips to China I bought two very similar kites,
one cost $26—bought at a hotel gift shop—and one cost $2,
bought at Tiananmen Square. If you are buying the kite for a
child who will most likely destroy it, this is a rather madden-
ing consumer problem.

It is believed that kites first appeared about 2,400 years ago,
first made of wood and bamboo and later refined in silk or
paper, which had better draft. While kite flying is a hobby and
an entertainment, it is also a science based on aeronautical engi-
neering. In fact, early kites were used for military purposes,
but around the year 784 and the start of the Tang dynasty, people
began to fly kites for entertainment.

Among the most common folk motifs in kites are dragons
and bats—bats being a figure for good luck, based on a pun
with the Chinese word *fu* which means "bat" and "blessing."

The value in a kite is based on the construction of the
frame, the fabric it is made with, and the artistic merit of the
designs.

Lacquer

No, I don't mean nail varnish. I'm talking about an ancient
art form dating as far back as 85 B.C. when baskets, boxes,
cups, bowls, and jars were coated with up to 30 layers of lacquer in order to make them waterproof. Each layer must be
dried thoroughly and polished before another layer can
be applied. After the lacquer is finished, decoration may be
applied. Black and red are the most common color combinations. (Black on the outside, red for the inside.)

You may date an item by the colors used; metallics in the decorative painting were used by the Han dynasty. Modern (post-1650) versions of lacquer may be European inspired chinoiserie; beware.

Monochromatic Wares

You may adore blue-and-white porcelains, but please remember they were created for export because locals thought they were ugly. The good stuff was usually monochromatic. Go to a museum and study the best and brightest before you start shopping because, again, fakes abound.

Celadon is perhaps the best known of the Chinese porcelain monochromes. It is a pale gray-green in color and grew to popularity because of the (false) assumption that poisoned food would cause a piece of celadon pottery to change color. The amount of green in the piece is based on how much iron is in the glaze.

Opals

Hong Kong is considered the opal-cutting capital of Asia. Dealers buy opals, which are mined mainly in Australia, in their rough state, and bring them to their factories in Hong Kong. There they are judged for quality and then cut either for wholesale export or for local jewelry. Black opals are the rarest and, therefore, the most expensive. White opals are the most available; they are not actually white, but varying shades of sparkling color. The opal has minuscule spheres of cristobalite layered inside; this causes the light to refract and the gem to look iridescent. The more cristobalite, the more "fire." An opal can contain up to 30% water, which makes it very difficult to cut. Dishonest dealers will sell sliced stones, called doublets or triplets, depending upon the number of slices of stone layered together. If the salesperson will not show you the back of the stone, suspect that it is layered. There are several opal "factories" in Hong Kong. These shops offer tourists the chance to watch the craftspeople at work cutting opal and offer opal jewelry for sale at "factory" prices. It's an interesting and informative tour to take, but we couldn't vouch for the quality of any opal you might buy from a factory.

Paper Cuts

An art form still practiced in China, paper cuts are hand-painted and hand-cut drawings of butterflies, animals, birds, flowers, and human figures. Often they are mounted on cards; sometimes they are sold in packs of six, delicately wrapped in tissue. We buy them in quantity and use them as decorations on our own cards and stationery.

Pearls

Pearls have been appreciated and all but worshipped in eastern and western cultures for centuries. Numerous famous women in history have had enviable pearl collections—from Queen Elizabeth I to Queen Elizabeth II, to say nothing of Elizabeth Taylor, Coco Chanel, and Barbara Hutton, whose pearls were once owned by Marie Antoinette.

The first thing to know about shopping for pearls in Hong Kong is that the best ones come from Japan. If you are looking for a serious set of pearls, find a dealer who will show you the Japanese government inspection certification that is necessary for every legally exported pearl. Many pearls cross the border without this, and for a reason.

Pearls are usually sold loosely strung and are weighed by the *momme*. Each momme is equal to 3.75 grams. The size of the pearls is measured in millimeters. Size 3s are small, like caviar, and 10s are large, like mothballs. The average buyer is looking for something between 6 and 7 millimeters. The price usually doubles every half millimeter after 6. Therefore, if a 6mm pearl is $10, a 6½mm pearl would be $20, a 7mm $40, and so on. When the size of the pearl gets very high, prices often triple and quadruple with each half millimeter.

Most pearls you will encounter are cultured. The pearl grower introduces a small piece of mussel shell into the oyster, and then hopes that Mother Nature will do her stuff. The annoyed oyster coats the "intruder" with nacre, the lustrous substance that creates the pearl. The layers of nacre determine the luster and size. It takes about 5 years for an oyster to create a pearl. The oysters are protected from predators in wire baskets in carefully controlled oyster beds.

There are five basic varieties of pearls: freshwater, South Sea, *akoya*, black, and *mabe*. Freshwater pearls are also known as Biwa pearls and are the little Rice Krispies–shaped pearls that come in shades of pink, lavender, cream, tangerine, blue, and blue-green. Many of the pearls larger than 10mm are known as South Sea pearls. They are produced in the South Seas, where the water is warmer and the oysters larger. The silver-lipped oyster produces large, magnificent silver pearls. The large golden-colored pearls are produced by the golden-lipped oyster. The pearls you are probably most familiar with are known as *akoya* pearls: These range from 2mm to 10mm in size. The shapes are more round than not, and the colors range from shades of cream to pink. A few of these pearls have a bluish tone. The rarest pearl is the black pearl, which is actually a deep blue or blue-green. This gem is produced by the black-lipped oyster of the waters surrounding Tahiti and Okinawa. Sizes range from 8mm to 15mm. Putting together a perfectly matched set is difficult and costly. Mabe pearls (pronounced *maw-bay*) have flat backs and are considered "blister" pearls because of the way they are attached to the shell. They are distinguished by their silvery-bluish tone and rainbow luster.

Pearls are judged by their luster, nacre, color, shape, and surface quality. The more perfect the pearl in all respects, the more valuable. Test pearls by rolling them—cultured pearls are more likely to be perfectly round and will, therefore, roll more smoothly.

You needn't be interested in serious pearls, whether natural or fake. In fact, prices being what they are, I'm in favor of fakes. Hong Kong sells fake versions of cultured pearls rather readily; specialty items such as baroque style or gray pearls are hard to come by. Chanel-style pearl items may be found in fashion stores, but not at pearl dealers.

Silk

Anthropologists will tell you that silk is China's single greatest contribution to world culture. The quality of Chinese silk has always been so superior that no substitute has ever been deemed acceptable; thus trade routes to bring silk around the world were established—the same routes that brought cultural secrets from ancient worlds into Europe's own local melting pots.

The art of weaving silk originated some 4,000 years ago in China. Since that time it has spread throughout Asia and the world. China, however, remains the largest exporter of silk cloth and garments. Hong Kong receives most of its silk fabric directly from China. Fabric shops in the markets sell rolls of silk for reasonable prices, although silk is not dirt cheap and may be priced competitively in your home market.

When buying silk, be sure that it is real. Many wonderful copies are on the market today. Real silk thread burns like human hair and leaves a fine ash. Synthetic silk curls or melts as it burns. If you are not sure, remove a thread and light a match.

Snuff Bottles

A favorite collector's item, snuff bottles come in porcelain, glass, stone, metal, bamboo, bronze, and jade. They also come in old and new old-style versions. They are also hard to distinguish from perfume bottles, especially if they have no tops. In short, watch out; this is a category that has been flooded with fakes, due to tourist demand.

A top-of-the-line collectible snuff bottle can go for $100,000, and that is American moola; so if you think you are buying a fine example of the art form for $10, do reconsider your position. The glass bottles with a carved overlay are rare and magnificent; there are specific schools of design and style in snuff bottles that are especially valuable to collect. You can find more ordinary examples in any of the markets. If you just want a few ornaments for the house (or Christmas tree), the markets or shops on Hollywood Road will have plenty.

Spirit Money

Colorful fake paper money to be burned for the dead. It's sold in any of the old-fashioned paper shops, which are fast fading out. There are a string of such paper shops on Shanghai Street in Kowloon; you can also find them in Causeway Bay near Jardine's Bazaar and in Macau, in the antiques stores neighborhood.

Tea

The Museum of Tea Ware in Flagstaff House, Cotton Tree Drive, Hong Kong, is a good place to start an exploration into the mysteries of tea. Tea has been grown in China for more than 2,000 years and reflects the climate and soil where it is grown, much as European wines do. There are three categories of tea: unfermented, fermented, and semifermented.

It is customary to drink Chinese tea black, with no milk, sugar, or lemon. Cups do not have a handle, but often do have a fitted lid to keep the contents hot and to strain the leaves as you sip. Since Hong Kong was a British colony, you may also find many hotel lobbies and restaurants that serve an English high tea (a great opportunity to rest your feet and gear up for a few more hours of shopping).

Because tea is relatively inexpensive and often comes in an attractive package or tin, it makes an excellent gift. Your choices are wide—there are many fancy tea shops selling high-priced and well-packaged goods, but there are also many choices in grocery store and local herbal/medicine shops that are equally attractive. All the Chinese department stores have a wide selection of teas and tea containers.

Xiying Pottery Teapots

Tea utensils are a popular item to purchase in Hong Kong, with Xiying pottery teapots being one of the most popular and expensive. They are made from unglazed purple clay and are potted by hand to achieve different forms of balance. They often resemble leaves, trees, or animals. Proportion is achieved by changing the balance of the base, top, and handle. Xiying teapots are always signed by the artist who made them, and the more famous artists' pots sell for over $1,000.

Chapter Four

....

SHOPPING STRATEGIES

THE YIN & YANG OF SHOPPING
....

Two questions I am most frequently asked are "Are there any bargains left in Hong Kong?" and "Is Hong Kong still worth visiting for shopping, or is China or Bangkok better?"

Bargains, of course, are in the eye of the beholder. I see bargains in junk in bins and in street markets, and bargains in very high-end items, tailor-made clothing, and custom-made jewelry. Beyond that, I think it takes luck and a sharp eye.

I've been on the streets long enough to know two important yin and yang facts:

- The good stuff is often hidden. Either it's put away, or, in Hong Kong, it goes to those who have custom work done and know how to go after real value.
- You have to go back to the same places constantly and hope to get lucky. Or you have to hit it just right. It's just like shopping at an off-pricer like Loehmann's—hit or miss.

It's virtually impossible to go to Hong Kong and not find anything to buy, but the days of deals galore may be over. Savvy shoppers are off to China with empty suitcases. I get wet palms and itchy feet when I think about the deals I left behind in China. The only problem I have in China is that I really need a container to ship everything I want—and I have no more space in my home in the United States nor my apartment in Paris.

The best values in Hong Kong can be found at the extremes of the retail spectrum:

- High end: The tailor who custom makes you a $2,000 suit for the same price as an off-the-rack suit in the United States offers a genuine bargain as does the jeweler who creates one-of-a-kind jewelry for you at better-than-at-home prices.
- Low end: Anything from a famous-name shop or maker that sells for $10 to $20 and is reasonably well made is a bargain to me. That hand-knit cotton designer sweater with the intricate floral pattern that I bought for $22 was a steal. Ditto for the Gap shirt for $10 and the white linen dress for $20. I even consider certain items without a name or a label I've purchased in Hong Kong to be bargains. I recently bought a silk chenille sweater (gorgeous dark turquoise color) for $10. It's the most fabulous thing you've ever seen. Who cares if it has no label inside? It's deals like this that remind us that Hong Kong has not "lost it."

The deals in mainland China:

- antiques and junk, antiques and junk, antiques and junk;
- everyday objects at low, low prices—like the French brand of toothpaste that I use (Signal), which costs about $2 a tube in France and 12¢ a tube in China;
- fake pearls . . . and some real pearls too.

When a Buy Is a Good-Bye

A true-blue shopper has been known to lose his or her head now and again. And no place on earth is more conducive to losing one's head than China and Hong Kong. You can see so many great "bargains" that you end up buying many items just because the price is cheap, not because you need or really want them. Or you can fall into the reverse trap, seeing nothing to buy, getting frustrated, and then buying the wrong things. When you get home, you realize that you've tied up a fair amount of money in rather silly purchases.

To keep mistakes to a minimum, I've got a few rules of the game:

- Buy items that have been made in China or Hong Kong that will cost more in the United States once U.S. customs and duties have been applied stateside.
- Try to catch the sale periods: the end of August and right before the Chinese New Year, especially in Hong Kong.
- Travel with price lists and even catalogs that carry major designer brands so you can compare prices on the spot. Designer goods are outrageously expensive in mainland China and while prices are going down a little, don't expect any deal here.
- Let go. Saving money isn't always paramount among my concerns. The reason one shops in European designer boutiques in China and Hong Kong isn't to save money but to find goods that simply are not sold in the United States or have a huge waiting list. Some haven't made their American debut, others are, for various reasons, deemed inappropriate for the American market, and still others don't pass FDA regulations. It's selection, not savings. Don't want to wait 3 years for a Kelly or Birkin bag at Hermès? They have them right on the shelves in Beijing. Who cares if the price is 20% higher than Paris? A bag in the hand is worth 2 years on the waiting list. . . .
- Avoid buying cameras and electronics in China and Hong Kong. Period. If you are bound and determined to ignore this gem of advice, see pp. 30–33 on how to buy cameras and electronics in Hong Kong and hope you don't get taken.
- Figure the price accurately. Despite rumor to the contrary, the Hong Kong dollar does fluctuate and the yuan is expected to be devalued by 10% any day now.

- Try not to make decisions based on labels; let the quality of the item speak for itself. In Hong Kong I have seen a surprising number of British name-maker labels, the kinds of names most Americans would not recognize. Likewise, Brits may not recognize American designer names. Eliminate the name factor in decision making and go by the correlation between quality and price.

- If you ignore this advice and buy a gift by the label, make sure the person who is receiving the gift knows the value of the name or the brand. I've given many a gift to a variety of international friends who went blank when confronted with a label they didn't know. Also make sure they know it comes from China and therefore may not stand the test of time.

- Figure in the duty. U.S. citizens are currently allowed $400 duty free. If you are traveling with your family, figure out your family total. Children, even infants, still get the $400 allowance. If you have more than $400 worth of merchandise, you pay a flat 10% on the next $1,000; after that you pay according to various duty rates.

- Calculate what your bargain will cost you in aggravation. Will you have to schlep the item all over the world with you? If it takes up a lot of suitcase room, if it's heavy, if it's cumbersome, if it's breakable and at risk every time you pack and unpack or check your suitcase, if it has to be hand-held—it might not be worth the cheap price tag. Estimate your time, trouble, and level of tolerance per item. Sure, it may be inexpensive, but if it's an ordeal to bring it home, is it really a good buy?

- Likewise, if you have to insure and ship it, is it still a bargain? How will you feel if the item never makes it to your door?

- I'm ambivalent about the value of counterfeit merchandise and cannot advise you whether to buy it or to walk away from it. If you suspect an item to be a fake, you must evaluate whether this is a good buy or should be a good-bye.

Remember that fakes most certainly do not have the quality of craftsmanship that originals have. You may also be asked to forfeit the item at customs or pay duty on the value of the real object. But you may have a lot of fun with your fakes.

- My rule of thumb on a good buy is that 50% (or more) off the U.S. or British price is a valuable saving. I think that a saving of less than 20% is probably not worth the effort. If the saving is between 20% and 50%, judge according to the degree of your personal desire for the item and the ratio of the previous points. If the saving is 50% or better, buy several and whoop with joy. That's a good buy!

Be Prepared Culturally

Unless you're accustomed to traveling in China, you may find Hong Kong and mainland China extremely different from anyplace you've ever been before. Depending on how sheltered your life has been, you may even go into culture shock. I don't preach about politics or the poor, but I do suggest that you be mentally prepared for what you are about to experience. There are a few particularly important cultural details:

- Chinese street vendors and retailers may be rude to Anglos. I try not to generalize about a thing like this, but you'll soon discover it is a common thread of conversation among tourists and expatriates alike. There is a two-class system at work. Face it. Furthermore, it's gotten ruder out there ever since the handover.
- The world works best with "tea money"—tip everyone and anyone if you want favors, information, or even a smile.
- As a tourist, you will never get the cheapest price possible, so forget it. Even if you are an American-born Chinese (called "ABC" by locals), you will not get the local price. Speak Cantonese perfectly? Great, for Hong Kong. Otherwise brush up your Mandarin if you want the best price.

- You're a rich American (or Brit) and will never miss what you overpay, according to many vendors. Take heart, prices are highest for Germans and then for Swiss. Americans ranks about fourth or fifth on the local list of rich catches.

Made in China

There is a caveat about those famous words, "Made in China." Just because an item is made there does not mean you will find it in local stores or outlets. Many garments and giftables are shipped directly to the overseas stores, with only dust left behind in the warehouse.

Toys, which are made in Hong Kong, are sent out to be packaged and therefore are imported back into Hong Kong at prices pretty close to those at home. Don't expect any great deals.

Whenever I look in my closet and see all the "Made in Hong Kong" and "Made in China" labels, I wish I had bought those items in Hong Kong (on Granville Road in a bin, of course), yet the chances of making a match are pretty slim. Most of the needle trades have left Hong Kong anyway, so more and more garments are made in China—but don't expect to find them in China.

Seconds for Sale

I've heard that the first words a manufacturer learns in Chinese are "no problem," which is all that can be said when faced with samples that aren't quite right. What happens to these samples or all the items that just don't quite cut the muster? They hit the shelves and streets of Hong Kong.

In the industry, this merchandise is called seconds, irregulars, or imperfects. In Hong Kong and in China, this merchandise is sold on the streets or in factory-outlet stores and may not be marked with tape or tags to tell you it is less than perfect.

Depending on the brand, the "inferior" merchandise may not have anything wrong with it. With name-brand goods in particular, the quality controls are so incredibly strict that when a unit does not pass inspection, it still may *appear* to be perfect. Possibly only the maker could find the defect.

"Damages" almost always have something wrong with them, but often it's fixable or something that doesn't upset you considering how good the bargain is.

Here are some of the flaws that may send a unit to the seconds or damages bin; watch for them in your inspection of lower-priced name goods:

- A dye lot that does not match other dye lots
- Stripes that are not printed straight or do not match at seams
- Prints that are off-register
- Bubbles in glass or plastic
- Uneven finish
- Unmatched patterns at seams
- Broken or poorly set zipper
- Puckered stitching
- Belt loops that don't match

Remember, seconds aren't sale merchandise that hasn't sold; they are stepchildren. Most stores will not admit that they sell seconds. If you are shopping in a seconds resource or a factory outlet, remember to check for damages or slight imperfections. Some imperfections are more than slight.

Also note that items sold as "seconds" in China may indeed be fakes.

The Beijing Rule of Shopping

The Beijing Rule of Shopping is the Asian version of my Moscow Rule of Shopping:

Now: The average shopper, in pursuit of the ideal bargain, does not buy an item he wants on first seeing it, not being convinced that he won't find it elsewhere for less money. This is human nature. A shopper wants to see everything available, then return for the purchase of choice. This is a normal thought process, especially in Hong Kong and China, where every merchant seems to have exactly the same merchandise.

If you live in Beijing, however, you know that you must buy something the minute you see it, because if you hesitate it will be gone. Hence the name of our international law. If you live in Hong Kong, you know the guys from Beijing can come over the hills anytime soon and take it all away. So you buy it when you can.

When you are on a trip, you probably will not have time to compare prices and then return to a certain shop. You will never be able to backtrack in cities—and if you could, the item might be gone by the time you got back.

What to do? The same thing they do in Beijing: Buy it when you see it, with the understanding that you may never see it again. But since you are not shopping in Beijing and you may see it again, weigh these questions carefully before you go ahead:

- Is this a touristy type of item that I am bound to find all over town? Are there scads of shops selling this kind of stuff, or is this something few other vendors seem to have?
- Is this an item I can't live without, even if I am overpaying?
- Is this a reputable shop, and can I trust what they tell me about the quality of this merchandise and the availability of such items?
- Is the quality of this particular item so spectacular that it is unlikely it could be matched anywhere else or at this price?

The Beijing Rule of Shopping breaks down totally if you are an antiques or bric-a-brac shopper, since you never know if you can find another of an old or used item, if it would be in the same condition, or if the price would be higher or lower. It's very hard to price collectibles, so consider doing a lot of shopping for an item before you buy anything.

The Tiananmen Square Rule of Shopping

This is a very simple and very important rule for all shoppers in Hong Kong: When things get violent—run. You think I'm kidding? I wish!

I had a very difficult experience in one of those electronics stores on Nathan Road in Hong Kong, during which much drama was enacted—there was yelling and screaming, laying on of hands and attempts to physically threaten and bully me. When I told *Born to Shop* British correspondent Ian Cook of the encounter, he looked at me as if I was utterly stupid and said simply, "Why didn't you just run?" Indeed.

I have also been jostled in China and had vendors who tried to frighten me into making an immediate purchase. Do not be threatened!

Vendors know how to make it even more difficult by putting the screws to you. For example, you want a camera. You have done your homework and know that the camera you want costs $275 from 47th Street Photo in New York. You decide to go to a few shops in Hong Kong to find out how prices compare and what's available before you make the big purchase.

You walk into Shop A, which you have chosen at random, since there are several million such shops within shouting distance. The marked price on the camera is $300. You begin to bargain because you know that $275 is the U.S. price. You finally get the price down to $250. You think this is a pretty good price, but you want to try some other shops. You thank the vendor and say you want to think about it. He says, "If you buy it right now, I'll make it $225. No one else would take this loss, but I've spent all this time with you already, and my time is valuable. If you come back later, the price will be $250."

How to Spot a Scam

Hong Kong is the original Scam City, but plenty of people in mainland China are catching on—especially taxi drivers. If you think you are street smart, you can still learn a trick or two in Hong Kong. If you know you are naive, get smart now.

The wise man asks, "How can you tell if you are being cheated in Hong Kong?"

The philosopher answers, "How can you tell how much you are being cheated in Hong Kong?"

I list only shops we have done business with or that readers have recommended. But I don't guarantee anything, and it doesn't hurt to be on the ball.

Markets and street vendors are more likely to con you than established retail outlets that are members of the Hong Kong Tourist Association (HKTA) or have a reputation to lose. Whatever the source, here are a few basic tips you can take to protect yourself when making a purchase:

- Feel the goods and carefully inspect any item wrapped in plastic—even go so far as to open the plastic. There is a good chance that the item you have been given is exactly like the sample on display in every way—except that the silk is of an inferior quality. Not everyone will cheat you. But many will try.
- Pick the skins for shoes or leather goods that are being custom made, and make it clear that you expect the skins you pick to be the skins in your garment. Have them marked with your initials. If you go for a fitting, before the linings are added, check your skins to make certain they are the same.
- Jade is very difficult to buy. A true test requires scientific measurement of hardness, specific density, and light refraction. If it's not incredibly expensive and guaranteed, walk away.
- Never trust anyone, no matter how much you think you can. Murphy's Law of Chinese Shopping: If you can be taken, you will be.

I can tell you that I was cheated on the purchase of a fax machine in a very elaborate con and that there are times when the bargaining and the shopping aren't fun, and you have to listen to that tiny voice within you, especially if it whispers, "Run."

If you are verbally or physically threatened in the bargaining process, leave at once.

If you are frightened, if things don't seem kosher, run.

Who Ya Gonna Trust?

Trust being such a desirable commodity (since it's also so elusive), I've developed a few simple guidelines for those who are concerned and don't know whom to trust in Hong Kong.

- The Chinese System of Trust: The Chinese know that you can't trust anyone except family. As a result, nepotism reigns supreme. Rich people in China do their business within a small cadre of those they trust, most of whom are interrelated. On high-ticket items, they never take risks on outsiders or unknown vendors.
- The HKTA System of Trust: The Hong Kong Tourist Association is a heavy-duty presence in Hong Kong and is uniformly referred to as the HKTA. Because rip-offs are so common in Hong Kong, the HKTA put together a merchants' association. They make merchants swear to be honest when they join. In exchange, the merchants get a little red Chinese-junk sticker (it's about 8 inches high) to put in their window, signifying that they are approved by the HKTA and, therefore, honest.

This is nice in theory, but let's face it, honesty can't be policed. However, if you have problems in one of the HKTA-approved shops, you have recourse. If you have a problem, call the HKTA. They have set up a special shopper's hot line for consumers with questions or complaints. Call the main number (☎ 852/2524-4191) and ask for the Membership Department. If the shop is not a member of the association, there's little that can be done.

TAXI SMARTS

··

While there's no such thing as general rules about cheats and/or taxi drivers, I have been cheated in just about every taxi I have ever taken in Beijing. By cheated I mean that the driver purposely chose the long way to the destination or the more trafficked route in order to get the fare up. When I discover an honest driver, I tip him. When I know I have been cheated, I do not tip. Of course, they weren't expecting a tip anyway, but capitalism works slowly in some towns.

Chapter Five

....

HONG KONG

WELCOME TO HONG KONG
....

When my buddies in Honkers, as some lovingly call Hong Kong, discovered that *Born to Shop Hong Kong* was being expanded and that China was being added on, yet Hong Kong included, they were a tad upset.

"But we don't think of ourselves as part of China!" they said. "When people come to Hong Kong they don't think they are coming to China!" they said. "That will be really confusing for readers!" they said.

But I have confidence; I don't think you're so easily confused. You already know that Hong Kong is officially part of China, you already know that the experiences of mainland China and Hong Kong are totally different and you already know that shopping in Hong Kong has changed over the years, but is still fabulous and does not at all compare to shopping in China. Besides, it's Hong Kong, not mainland China, that got the bid to build the new Disney park.

So welcome. The Tiger stood at the gates of Hong Kong, accomplished a smooth takeover, has given way to the dragon and let life slide. In the long run, Hong Kong may suffer another brain drain or lose talents to the United States, Canada, and even Mainland China, but right now—Hong Kong glitters in the roar of all its neon. There are more fancy hotels, amenities, fine dining, and fairly priced (or even bargain) merchandise than anywhere else, and yes, there are things to buy . . . and no, Hong Kong hasn't "lost it."

Hong Kong was, in fact, the first of the Asian markets to come back from the slump; last fall's auctions at Christie's and Sotheby's saw record prices set for specialty sales. There's also a reflection of the Wall Street and Silicon Valley philosophy of easy money and big spending. Stores report that they sell at least 75% of their merchandise at full retail price. More and more brands are coming into Hong Kong and opening shops. After all, Starbucks has arrived.

A SHORT HISTORY OF HONG KONG TRADE

Hong Kong and the South China Sea have always been a hotbed of commerce because China silk came out of either Canton (now Guangzhou) or Shanghai. You remember *Shōgun* and the Portuguese and their "black ship"? The black ship brought goods from Europe in exchange for silk from China. This was a lucrative business, and the Portuguese wanted it all to themselves. So did the British, the Spaniards, the French, and, later, the Americans.

The only problem was, the big British ships couldn't get into the shallow waters of Macau (the Portuguese port), which is somewhat closer to Canton. Happily, they soon discovered that the perfect port was on the island of Hong Kong. So for no other reason than deep water, Hong Kong became the "in" place.

Queen Victoria howled with laughter when in 1842 Hong Kong was given to the British as a prize of war. And it really was a laughing matter. You see, not only were silks and woolens being traded, the British had also initiated a thriving business in opium. The first Opium War ended with the British winning and getting Hong Kong, in perpetuity. The second and third times the British won, they got the rights to Kowloon and then certain mainland territories for 99 years.

Strangely enough, time flies when you're shopping and shipping. The 99 years ended with the handover on June 30,

1997. By that time, trade and commerce and money and real estate and infrastructure were all the soul of Hong Kong. Global firms wanted to be in Hong Kong to use her byways into China, and the Chinese wanted to take over, if only for the cash, the prestige, and the need to not lose face. The Chinese have made it clear that the future is Shanghai, but Hong Kong will remain a business and cultural (and shopping) destination for years to come.

GET THERE NOW

I don't expect anything radical to happen in the next few years. The handover is past us. The future is ours. I think Shanghai will take 10 years to fully get it together, although it sure is glam and fab now. I do think in the long run, Shanghai will overshadow Hong Kong. But the race won't even be run and Hong Kong ain't quittin' yet.

Nonetheless, knowing what will happen should put on the pressure to get to Hong Kong before it changes too dramatically. You want to be able to grasp what Hong Kong has been historically and to understand what all the fuss was about. See, we're talking sociology, not shopping!

Change/No Change

Briefly, in case you were wondering, here's what hasn't changed since the takeover:

- money, though the queen's image has come off of the coins;
- visa requirements (none).

Here's what's changing:

- everyday lives of locals;
- export laws on antiques;
- prices—going up!

Hong Kong Orientation

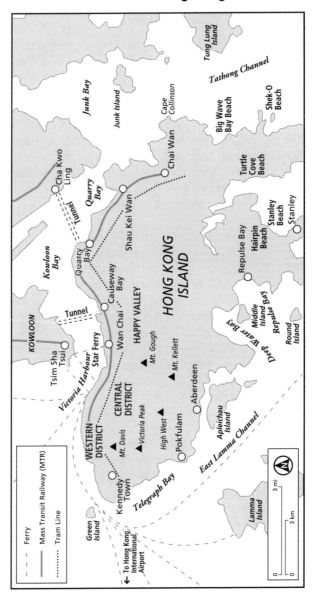

The Lay of the Land

With the new airport on the island of Lantau, shopping destinations spread across major land masses, and folks darting off to Macau, Malaysia, and mainland China at a moment's notice, you may find yourself asking, "Just what and where is Hong Kong?"

Hong Kong encompasses Hong Kong Island, of course, but also the city of Kowloon, the New Territories, and a few hundred islands. Technically speaking, what we commonly refer to as Hong Kong is now part of the People's Republic of China (PRC), but because it has separate but equal status, its address is written as "Separate Administrative Region," or "SAR."

When people discuss addresses in the Hong Kong area, they may cite a particular number on a particular street, but more often than not, you'll hear your fellow travelers oversimplifying these directions by just naming a building and the neighborhood in which it is located. And they play fast and loose with what constitutes a neighborhood. Some people call all of Victoria Island "Central" and all of the Kowloon Peninsula "Kowloon." While these terms are technically incorrect, everyone seems to understand this system, so don't knock yourself out trying to be absolutely precise.

Shopping in Hong Kong is concentrated heavily in two areas: Central, the main business "downtown" area on the Hong Kong Island side, and Tsim Sha Tsui in Kowloon. Central is very upscale, civilized, businesslike, and modern. Tsim Sha Tsui (often written TST) is more gritty and more active in a frenetic way.

Please see "Shopping Neighborhoods," below, for a more detailed discussion of Hong Kong's shopping and commercial districts. When you become an Old China Hand, you'll decide which side of the harbor is more "you" or more convenient to your business or shopping style. Smart visitors stay on both sides of the island and shop all corners.

BOOKING HONG KONG

The Hong Kong Tourist Association (HKTA) provides a great deal of very useful information for travelers at no cost. They publish pamphlets on almost every subject imaginable, many of which you can pick up as you exit passport control at Hong Kong International Airport.

The *Official Hong Kong Guide* is published monthly and contains general information about the city including a short description of Chinese foods, organized sightseeing tours, and a listing of festivals, events, and exhibits being held that month. The HKTA also publishes a weekly newspaper, *Hong Kong This Week*. It contains news of events and shows, along with the usual ads for shops and is distributed free at major hotels and in HKTA offices.

Inside the free packet you can pick up at the airport is the A-O-A Map Directory. Maps show both building and street locations. Since so many addresses include the building name, street, and area, it makes finding an address simple.

GETTING THERE

When it comes to booking your plane tickets, have I got news for you: There are a confusing number of possibilities and deals and routes and reasons to go with any number of different plans (and planes).

If you're going to Hong Kong via the Pacific Ocean, which is the cheapest and most common route, then what you are looking for is the right combination of ticket price and short layover time. Enter Northwest Airlines. I've now timed this with a variety of airline charts and connection tables and have it down to a science—a Northwest Airlines science. Northwest is part of a merger proposal, so watch this space.

No one has a shorter connection time through Narita (Tokyo) than Northwest, with the mere legal connection of

1½ hours. Arrivals are timed to create minimum effects of jet lag once you are home or on the ground in Hong Kong. (See chapter 2, p. 17, for more on Narita.)

Also note that different gateways continue to open. American carriers now have rights that had never been granted before to fly over Siberia; United Airlines has recently begun nonstop 747–400 service to Hong Kong from Chicago! This is the longest route segment in history, some 7,788 miles.

Ticket Deals

Flights on all airplanes to Hong Kong, especially from the West Coast, can be packed. Not only are lots of businesspeople flying these routes, but wholesalers buy blocks of tickets to resell to travel agents and tour groups. Because they buy in bulk, wholesalers often get a better price, and pass their savings on to their customers. In this situation, Lillian Fong is my personal secret weapon: Call or fax her at Pacific Place Travel, 1255 Corporate Center Dr., Suite 203, Monterey Park, CA 91754 (☎ 800/328-8778 or 213/980-8138; fax 213/980-8133; e-mail: pacplace@worldnet.att.net).

Other thoughts:

- If you're flying to Hong Kong from the West Coast, look into what is called a "Circle Pacific" fare. Most American carriers, and many international ones, offer you this chance to make your own itinerary, traveling to several cities in Asia at package-tour prices. You do not join a group; you set your own pace, but get a break on the price because you fly all legs with the same carrier.
- Don't be afraid of business class. The trip is a lengthy one; you will be much more comfortable in business class. Furthermore, business class has more seats than coach or first class, so there are more possible deals.
- Don't be afraid of first class. Lillian offered me first-class upgrade tickets if I paid the full fare for business class; this is a pretty good deal. There are all sorts of promotions out there—ask. Also, if you are traveling in and out of Hong

Kong, we found first class on Dragon Air was not that much more expensive than coach, and well worth the extra price when it came to changing tickets and planes and coping with extra luggage.

- If you're pricing airfares on several carriers, it is imperative that you understand the quality of the service and what you are getting. Don't assume anything. Virgin has made quite a splash with their extra perks and great entertainment system, but they only offer real value to those travelers willing to fly economy at promotional prices or to those willing to pay extra for their upper class service.
- Consider unusual routing, especially if there are promotional fares. Even if you don't get a price deal, you may end up saving time. For example, the flying time from the U.S. West Coast to Hong Kong is approximately 17 hours. From Toronto to Hong Kong is also 17 hours, but you may save time or aggravation if you fly from an East Coast city to Toronto and then catch the Cathay Pacific flight from Toronto to Hong Kong.
- Consider unusual time flights; Cathay now offers a flight that leaves New York rather late at night but gets to Hong Kong first thing in the morning, the day after (you do pass the international date line, remember?). This is great for jet lag.
- Package tours often offer you the best deals financially, especially if they include airport transfers and some extras. Check them out, especially when you can stay at luxury hotels. Likewise, add-on tours offered by cruise-ship lines sometimes have fabulous prices that include promotional events and benefits. More and more cruise ships offer in or out add-ons in Hong Kong.

PROMOTIONAL DEALS

All airlines have promotional deals. Promotional deals to Asia are sometimes harder to find, and often aren't advertised in America, but you can find them by calling the airlines' toll-free numbers in the United States.

Cathay Pacific, one of the first airlines to go on-line and actively recruit travelers, has many innovative programs, including mileage awards and auctions. Their Web site is www.cathay-usa.com. They also offer a 25% discount for senior travel.

AROUND-THE-WORLD DEALS

The deal of the century happens to be an around-the-world ticket on British Airways (BA). An around-the-world coach ticket on British Airways is good for 1 year and needs to be bought 14 days before departure. The cost is about $3,000 but can be as low as $1,600 if bought during a promotion!

A business-class ticket on British Airways, which routes you from New York to London and London to Hong Kong, is about $4,000 with 14-day advanced purchase. To put that into perspective, please note that a round-trip business-class ticket from London to Hong Kong is approximately $4,000. Do you smell a bargain or what?

It gets better. A first-class, around-the-world ticket is about $6,000, and a Concorde ticket—you fly Concorde from New York to London only—comes with an add-on price: $863 for first-class passengers; $1,719 for business-class passengers. Since the ticket can be used over the space of a continuing year, this means that you can book yourself one hell of a deal.

One of the catches is that different price tickets have different perks: The basic cheapest ticket allows you six stops with use on any of six partner airlines affiliated with BA. You must always travel in one direction, but you can make side trips, which few other round-the-world tickets allow you to do. The number of miles you can travel on the basic ticket is 28,500. Not bad, huh?

Other airlines do offer round-the-world fares and deals, but in most cases, you will code share with two or more combinations. I trust BA and usually use them to get around. I personally find the transpacific trip from New York to Hong Kong to be punishing; I'd much rather go around the world or fly in and out of London or Paris.

Do consider using Cathay Pacific, which can get you to Hong Kong from the United States transpacifically and then, from Hong Kong, put you into any major city in Europe (try London or Paris). All you have to do after that is connect on another carrier for the European-U.S. leg of travel. Or, even better, use a Northwest/KLM code share to go completely around the world and get the benefit of the many Northwest gateway cities that serve various European destinations. You simply connect out of Hong Kong to a chosen European destination on KLM.

TRANSATLANTIC TRAVEL

For me, the secret is often that transatlantic is the way to go—even come and go! This is true not only if you live on the East Coast, but also if you live in Chicago, the Midwest, or Texas. Detroit, Minneapolis, and Cincinnati are now hub cities that offer choices in either direction. Don't be blind to the possibilities.

The day I found out that Hong Kong was a mere 10-hour flight from London was the day I converted. (*Note:* It takes 11 hours from Hong Kong to London!) A few months after my discovery, I noted that several airlines, led by Singapore Airlines, began advertising their transatlantic routes. Even Delta now has a code-sharing plan with Singapore so that they, too, can offer passengers transatlantic service.

British Airways doesn't have to advertise; they've had the London–to–Hong Kong and the New York–to–London business sewn up for years. Virgin also flies from London to Hong Kong, so there is some competition going on here. Meanwhile, by looking at a map, I realized that going deeper into Europe would help beat jet lag, so I turned to SwissAir, the first western carrier flying into China, and now with more than 50 years' experience in China.

I now fly only on SwissAir to Asia, going into Zurich with a layover in Europe for 2 nights to combat jet lag. From New York, I am making a 6-hour time change. When I go on to Hong

---

Electronically Yours

- HKTA (Hong Kong Tourist Authority) site: www.hkta.org
- WW Chan Tailor site:www.wwchan.com
- Hong Kong Stock Exchange site:www.sehk.com.hk
- Wah Tung China site:info@wahtungchina.com; wahtung@ hkstar.com

---

Kong or mainland China, there is just another 6-hour time change to cope with. This is far easier on the body than being assaulted with a 20-hour trip and a 12-hour time change followed by a week of recovering.

ARRIVING IN HONG KONG

Hong Kong's Chek Lap Kok International Airport is fabulous—landing is glorious and while you are farther from downtown than before, you get to go over a very nice bridge (one of the world's longest) and have a pleasant ride through some hills. And soon, when you're there, you'll be right near Disneyland.

There are several modes of transportation into town; each is marked in the grand entry hall. If you have arranged car service from your hotel, look for the hotel desks in the center of the Arrivals Hall. Find the appropriate desk and check in; someone will escort you through the rest of the process, taking your baggage and meeting you at your car.

Car Service

Traveling from the airport to your hotel in the swank car your hotel sends for you is a delightfully elegant way to arrive—if expensive. While public transport is simple and inexpensive, part of the fun of being in Hong Kong is settling into that Rolls or Daimler or Mercedes-Benz that your hotel has provided. Expect to pay about $100 (it varies from hotel to hotel) each way for the luxury, but do try to find it in your budget. *Note:* Most of the hotels have eliminated their fleets of Rolls Royces because the long journey to the new airport is too difficult for them.

While one certainly doesn't pick a hotel based on the cost of its luxury car service, do note that hotels in Central may charge more for this service.

Better yet, note that Shangri-La hotels include the transfer in the room rate when you pay rack rate—this is a real bonus and definitely pays for itself.

Airport Bus & Train

There is a new Central Terminal on the Victoria side of Hong Kong where you can check your luggage and then ride the train to the airport. This is particularly great for departures from Hong Kong. Arriving passengers can also take the fast train to this station and then taxi to their hotels.

AirBuses run every 15 minutes or so. Check to make certain that your hotel is on the list; up to 20 or 25 hotels may be served on one route. There is an enormous chart at the airport, which even the most jet-lagged can handle. There is also a transportation desk that will help you or you can call ☎ 852/ 2745-4466. The fare to Central is HK$40.

There are also regular old city buses that serve the airport and cost half the price of the special tourist AirBus.

Taxis

Taxi stands are near the arrival lounge. A large sign will give you approximate fares to different areas of Hong Kong and Kowloon. If you're confused, look for the transportation desk. Taxis usually charge a flat rate: approximately $45—it is a long drive to town.

Officially, the meter on a taxi begins at HK$15 and turns over at HK$1.30 per every 200 meters of travel. Drivers charge extra for rides in either direction through the tunnels, for additional pieces of luggage, waiting time, and radio calls. The charges for all of these extras are slight, amounting to less than $1 per item. You do tip, but just by rounding up the fare, not by a straight percentage.

GETTING AROUND

Hong Kong is an easy city to navigate because its transportation options are excellent. It's a good city for walking, true, but you'll also want to enjoy its ferries, kaidos (bigger ferries), trams, double-decker buses, and superb MTR (Mass Transit Railway).

Most rides on the MTR take under 20 minutes; you can cross the harbor in approximately 5 minutes. Crossing the harbor by car or taxi during rush hour is hardest, but it's a breeze doing it on the MTR or the Star Ferry, which takes almost the same amount of time. Don't ask me about the hour I spent in a taxi trapped inside the tunnel (!!!) when I was too lazy to take public transportation.

If you intend to sightsee, pick up the HKTA brochure "Places of Interest by Public Transportation" to get exact directions and bus routes throughout Hong Kong Island and Kowloon, or consult our Major Transportation Map.

MTR

Before I explain the workings of the MTR, the phenomenally convenient mass transportation system in Hong Kong, I want you to remember one basic rule: When looking up a listing in this book, the MTR stop at Central will get you to most locations in Hong Kong and the stop at Tsim Sha Tsui (TST) will get you to most locations in Kowloon. Unless otherwise noted in the addresses given, these are the MTR stops you want. Simple enough.

Hong Kong Regional Transportation

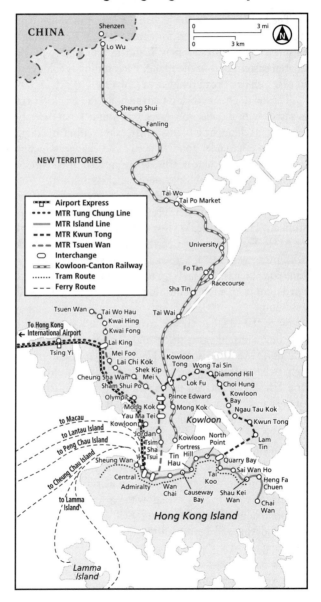

The MTR is half the fun of getting to great shopping. Three lines connect the New Territories to industrial Kwun Tong, to business Central, to shopping Tsim Sha Tsui, and to the residential eastern part of the island. Each station is color-coded in case you can't read (English or Chinese).

The longest trip takes less than an hour, and the ticket's cost is based on the distance you travel. Buy your ticket at the station vending machines by looking for your destination and punching in the price code. You will need exact change, which you can get from a machine nearby. There are also ticket windows where you can buy multiple journey tickets.

If you're visiting Hong Kong from overseas, the best value is a HK$20 tourist MTR ticket, which can be obtained from any HKTA office, MTR station, select Hang Seng banks, or MTR Travel Services Centres. You must buy your ticket within 2 weeks of your arrival and show your passport at the time you purchase it. This is for tourists; otherwise stored-value cards come in high denominations—HK$70, HK$100, HK$200.

Since the MTR is always crowded, you'll be happiest if you buy a stored-value ticket and consider it a souvenir if you don't use it. I also order HK$5 coins to use in the self-help ticket machines. One-stop journeys usually cost HK$4, and HK$8 can get you just about anywhere on either side of the harbor. Your ticket comes out of the machine into your hand; insert it into the turnstile and then retrieve it as you go through.

Remember to keep your ticket after you enter the turnstile because you will have to reinsert it to exit. If you get off at the wrong stop and owe more money, an alarm will sound, and you'll have to go over to a window to pay up. Unless you have a stored-value ticket, the turnstile will eat your ticket upon exit, and you will be denied that pretty souvenir you were counting on.

The MTR runs between 6am and 1am. If you need to get somewhere earlier or later, take a taxi.

Taxis

Taxis in Hong Kong are cheap, so go ahead and splurge. The meter starts at HK$15, and sometimes you simply pay the minimum fare. After that the charge is HK$1.30 per 200 meters. Taking the Cross-Harbour Tunnel will cost an extra HK$10 each way, making the total additional fees you pay HK$20. (As a result, I tend to avoid taking a taxi through the Cross-Harbour Tunnel unless I'm loaded down with packages and have had a long, hard day of shopping.) There are surcharges for luggage, waiting time, and radio calls.

If a taxi is in Central and has a sign saying KOWLOON, it means that the driver would like a fare going back to Kowloon and will not charge the extra HK$10 tunnel fee if he gets such a fare. Shift changes occur at 4pm, and it is sometimes hard to find a cab then. If a taxi doesn't stop for you on a busy road, it is probably because the driver is not allowed to stop.

Look for a nearby taxi stand where you can pick up a cab. Hotels are always good places to find a taxi. Even if you are not staying at that particular hotel, the doorman will help you. Tip him HK$5 for his services, however.

While English is still an official language, it's always nice insurance to have your destination written in Chinese. Hotels will do this for you on cards they have printed up; the flip side of the card tells the driver how to get you back to the hotel. I was quite shocked on several different taxi trips when the drivers simply put a map-book in my hand and asked me to find the address for them on a map page. If I didn't know my way around town, I would have been sunk. Save yourself the aggravation—get a card ahead of time.

Trains

The Kowloon-Canton Railway (KCR) services the areas between Hung Hom and the Chinese border. Since you can't get into China without a visa, chances are you won't be traveling as far as the border. But do hop on board because you should take this chance to get out into the New Territories and see some of the real world. If you have a visa (or want one) to visit Shenzen, step this way.

If you're expecting an experience out of one of Paul Theroux's books, you'll be disappointed. The KCR is modern, clean, and just like any big-city commuter train. The stations are modern poured concrete, and while some of the passengers may be worthy subjects for a photographer, the train itself is not a romantic experience. But it's cheap, it's fun, and it feels exotic just because there aren't that many tourists on board.

Ferries

The most famous of all the Hong Kong ferries is the Star Ferry, with service from Kowloon to Central and back. The 8-minute ride is one of the most scenic in the world. You can see the splendor of Hong Kong Island's architecture and the sprawl of Kowloon's shore. The green-and-white ferries have been connecting the island to the peninsula since 1898.

Billed as the least-expensive tourist attraction in the world, the Star Ferry is a small piece of magic for less than 30¢ a ride. First-class costs HK$2.25; tourist-class is HK$1.75. The difference is minimal except at rush hour, when the upper deck is less crowded. The difference is maximized if you want to take pictures, since you get a much better view from the upper deck, where the first-class passengers loll. The Central/Tsim Sha Tsui (TST) service runs from 6:30am to 11:30pm.

Please note: The different classes have different entries; on the Kowloon side, you get different shopping opportunities depending on which class of service you use!

Trams

Watch out crossing the streets of Central, or you're likely to be run over by a double-decker tram. Island trams have been operating for more than 85 years, from far western Kennedy Town to Shau Kei Wan in the east. They travel in a straight line, except for a detour around Happy Valley. Fares are HK$1 for adults, half fare for children. You pay as you enter. Many trams do not go the full distance east to west, so note destination signs before getting on. Antique trams are available for tours and charters, as are the regular ones.

The Peak Tram has been in operation for more than 100 years. It is a must for any visitor to Hong Kong—unless you are afraid of heights. You can catch the tram behind the Hilton Hotel, on Garden Road. A free shuttle bus will take you from the Star Ferry or Central MTR station (Chater Garden exit) to the Peak Tram terminal. The tram runs to the Peak every 10 minutes starting at 7am and ending at midnight. The trip takes 8 minutes. At the top you hike around to various viewing points or peek in on some of the expensive mansions and high-rises. The best time to make this trip is just before dusk; you can see the island scenery on the trip up, walk around, and watch the spectacular sunset, then ride down as all the city lights are twinkling.

Rickshaws

It's over folks. Rickshaws are fini, kaput, anachronistic, socially incorrect, gone with the wind.

Every now and then you can find someone near the Star Ferry terminal on the Hong Kong side to pose for a picture, the price for doing so is negotiable. The going rate is HK$70, however, sometimes you can put HK$50 in the driver's hand for a few quick snaps.

Car Rental

Avis, Budget, and Hertz have offices in Hong Kong if you want to drive. I do not advise renting a car in Hong Kong, unless you have a great deal of experience driving in foreign countries. It is far better to hire a car and driver directly from your hotel. Prices vary with the hotel but are approximately $65 an hour. If your hotel gives you a choice between a Mercedes and a Rolls Royce, the Mercedes will generally be less expensive. Remember that you may also make a deal with a taxi driver for several hours, or even a day.

Phoning Home

To avoid hotel surcharges on international phone calls, you have a number of options that let you use your credit card or call home collect. I almost always end up using AT&T's USADirect, but there are other games in town. On my last visit, I paid only $2 a minute from Hong Kong to home, which isn't bad considering it was AT&T.

Hongkong Telecom, the local service, allows you to connect to an operator and make a credit card or collect call. You can also buy a stored-value phone card and use a public phone—this is a good value. They are sold at HKTA offices, 7-11 stores, many foreign exchange booths, and all over town.

Otherwise, call these numbers for direct access:

- To call the United Kingdom, dial ☎ 800-0044 for an operator.
- To call the United States, dial ☎ 800-1111 if your long-distance carrier is AT&T; ☎ 800-1121, if MCI is your carrier; ☎ 800-1877, if Sprint provides your long-distance service; and ☎ 900-1115 if your long-distance carrier is TRT/FTC.

Various credit cards have world plans that allow you to make international calls. The savings are not sublime, but they are usually better than direct dialing from a hotel.

To get in touch with Hong Kong from the United States, dial ☎ 011-852 followed by the eight-digit number. Hong Kong does have a different country code than mainland China; Macau also has a different code.

SLEEPING IN HONG KONG

I can't think of any other city in the world, and that includes Paris, where your choice of hotel is a more integral part of your stay than in Hong Kong.

Although I'm incredibly picky about hotels, I've found several in Hong Kong that offer the most important factor in a shopping hotel—location—and still have all the luxury I lust after. Asian hotels are famous for their deluxe standards and fabulous service; enjoying these perks is part of the whole pleasure of staying in Hong Kong.

I recently read that grand hotels are where memories are made, and I think I believe that. Surely I've had memories made in stores, in restaurants, on street corners, and in alleys, but the right hotel is very much a part of the whole. Choose yours with the same care you would use in buying any precious memory or souvenir.

Hotel Tips

Many tour companies and large hotel chains offer shopping packages for Hong Kong, but few of these include the kind of five-star hotels I depend on. If you're a sucker for luxury, don't fight it—but shop around so you can get the most for your money. Hong Kong has a good base of luxury hotel rooms, and when things aren't too busy, there are big-time deals to be made.

I find official rack rates that hotels publish very irritating and refuse to quote them in these pages—few people pay the official rates; there are almost always deals to be made. Hong Kong is deal city.

Promotional rates can be as low as $149 a night at the Omni (Kowloon); I once saw an ad for Mandarin Oriental touting their Oriental Interlude Leisure breaks, with prices per room (not per person) at HK$1,100 ($142). Rates are on the rise in Hong Kong and rooms can be dear, especially when trade fairs are in town. It pays to shop around for rates and for the right time of year to visit, as rates do change with the seasons.

Tricks of the Trade

Some secrets that might make booking your hotel easier:

- Ask about packages that may include breakfast, airport transfers, and other items that are usually charged as extras.

Almost every luxury hotel in the world offers a honeymoon package. As long as you don't show up with the kids, you're on your honeymoon.

- Mileage awards can be used to pay for hotel rooms, to obtain discounts on rooms, or to accrue more mileage for your favorite frequent-flier account.
- Always ask the hotels if they're offering weekend or 5-day rates. Almost all hotels discount rooms during the off-season or when there is not a lot of business in town. Hong Kong has so many conventions that you may get a low-price convention rate.
- Peak season in Hong Kong is October and November; you'll pay top dollar for rooms during these months. Summer rates are usually the least expensive although there are often discounts beginning the first week in December.
- Watch out for Japanese holidays, which are usually not on U.S. and U.K. calendars; they fill up Hong Kong hotels.
- The Hong Kong Tourist Association (☎ 800/282-4582) publishes a brochure called *Hong Kong Hotel Guide*. This publication provides a comprehensive list of all possibilities, including addresses, phone numbers, room rates, fax numbers, and services offered.
- Check the big chains for promotional rates. Often you can prepay in U.S. dollars and save, or they'll have a deal in the computer that your travel agent doesn't know about. A telephone operator from Hilton told me about an exceptional value at The Conrad. Ask!

The Best Shopping Hotels of Hong Kong

There are several hotel enclaves on Hong Kong Island; one in Causeway Bay and two in Central. In the heart of Central, pick from those hotels right at the base of the Star Ferry in downtown or from those grouped slightly off to the side at Admiralty. How does one decide among them? It all depends on price, style, and location. Don't worry—you can't go wrong with any of the choices below.

CENTRAL

I've actually found three hotels that serve as one since all three are in the same location: **Pacific Place,** right above a mall of the same name. They all have entrances within the mall as well as front doors on the street.

ISLAND SHANGRI-LA
Pacific Place, Supreme Court Rd. (MTR: Admiralty).

The first time I visited the Island Shangri-La was for Richard Branson, who put me into the shopping tour business. I fell in love with this location and with **Pacific Place,** the mall, and the exotic architecture and style of the Island Shangri-La. Before understanding the hotel, I had thought that perhaps this location wasn't convenient—wrong! I found ease in getting around simply by hopping in a taxi or even walking, and loved being attached to the best mall in the city for shopping and dining options.

My room had a view of the harbor; the decor was so wonderful that I bought prints for my apartment from the hotel interior designer (Sandra Walters). The combination of excellent hotel eats plus being attached to a mall made all things not only possible, but easy. Furthermore, Shangri-La has so many additional benefits in terms of airport transfers, etc. that I felt pampered and privileged.

Note that the **Marriott** and the **Conrad** also have hotels in this cluster and are also connected to the mall. You may want to price all three hotels, if price becomes an issue.

U.S. reservations: ☎ 800/942-5050. Local phone: ☎ 852/2877-3838; fax: 852/2521-8742; on-line: www.shangri-la.com.

THE CONRAD
88 Queensway (MTR: Admiralty).

I tried to book the Island Shangri-La on one visit, but they were full. So I called Hilton's U.S. reservation number and immediately realized that the Conrad not only had space, but had a great deal. Not only are prices less, but the operator on the phone very quickly explained several price options in package deals, telling me where the best buys and values were. There was even a rate that included the limousine transfer to and from the airport—it was simply the best rate in Hong Kong.

Yet I found the best part when I got to my room—each room is provided with a complimentary teddy bear in the bed and a yellow rubber ducky in the bathtub. You can buy more ($3 each), but the first set is on the house.

The hotel also has a business-y atmosphere to it that I really like; it's a luxury hotel, but they are organized to help you get things done—they provide a booklet with the bus transport information right in your key card; the business center is open 24 hours a day; you can pay the airport departure tax when you check out. The hotel is structured to compete with fancier hotels by offering more business perks and conveniences; I'm hooked.

U.S. reservations: ☎ 800/HILTONS. Local phone: ☎ 852/2521-3838; fax: 852/2521-3888.

MANDARIN ORIENTAL
5 Connaught Rd. (MTR: Central).

If your motto is "location, location, location" and you also care for old-world service, fabulous hotel restaurants, power breakfasts, and sensational afternoon teas, rooms with a view, and an indoor pool, then it must be Mandarin. You'll pay for the privilege, but this is the single best shopping location in Central.

While Mandarin Oriental has a forbiddingly formal reputation that may lead you to believe you cannot afford their services, I beg you to reconsider. If you book during one of their promotional periods, they are practically giving away rooms. When you can stay in a Mandarin Oriental for less than $150 per night, they are giving away rooms.

U.S. reservations: ☎ 800/526-6566 or Leading Hotels of the World ☎ 800/223-6800. Local phone: ☎ 852/2522-0111; fax: 852/2810-6190.

Even if you aren't staying here, please come use parts of the hotel and check it out: Go upstairs for cocktails and a view; use the coffee shop for lunch; have formal tea (it's a meal unto itself), and shop the hotel's mall. There's a branch of Vong upstairs.

KOWLOON

REGENT HOTEL
18 Salisbury Rd., Kowloon (MTR: TST).

Still considered to be one of the most scenic locations in Hong Kong, the Regent occupies the tip of Kowloon Peninsula; the views from the lobby bar at night are nothing short of spectacular.

In addition to its spectacular views, I consider the Regent home because they have Hong Kong's best hotel shopping mall, which has now replaced the one at the Peninsula Hotel as the chic address. Every big-name European designer has a shop here, but so do other big names—from Chanel to Donna Karan! And I dote on the concierge. There's also a less fancy mall (New World Shopping Centre) attached to the Regent's three-level mall and a new underground road of dreams—the Palace Mall, right alongside the Regent and somewhat hidden by the fact that it's underground and will eventually connect the Regent and the Pen.

The Regent also has one of my favorite quick-bite places— the coffee shop (called Harbourside; it's downstairs). They have serious restaurants here, too, but this one is a great shopper's special because it is quick and well priced.

Part of what's so interesting about this hotel is that it is both formal and casual at the same time. The pool is great, but you'll come away raving about the hot tub. After a really stressful day, there's the spa, or even specialty baths that they will run for you in your own room. *Also note:* The Shanghai Club is a must-do for a drink if you aren't staying at this hotel.

There are always promotional deals, such as Suite-er Options, which earns you free stays at Four Seasons properties. There's also Great Breaks and a shopping package.

U.S. reservations: ☎ 800/545-4000. Local phone: ☎ 852/2721-1211; fax: 852/2739-4546; on-line: rhk@fourseasons.com.

PENINSULA HOTEL
Salisbury Rd., Kowloon (MTR: TST).

The Pen, as it is called, is the most famous hotel in Hong Kong and in Kowloon as well; it continues in its friendly competition with the Regent, as the two vie for international titles as the best hotel in town — or the world.

The only way to decide which deserves the "best" title is to stay in both of them—preferably during the same trip—so you can see how uniquely different the two properties are. (This is not as nutty as it sounds, especially if you are going to Macau in between for a few days.)

The Pen built a new tower with health club, pool, and view firmly in place, as well as a Philippe Starck–designed restaurant (**Felix**) to add to their galaxy of gourmet stars. And yes, there's a helicopter pad on the roof.

The Pen prides itself on its old-world charm and classy elegance; the crowd is much more dressed up than at the Regent. The lobby, where the tea is famous, is the best place for people watching.

Gaddi's is the single most famous French restaurant in town, and a living legend in its own merit. If food isn't your thing, not to worry—the hotel has one of the best hotel shopping arcades in the world.

Now then, in case you're tacky and care only about the bottom line, here's the dish you've been waiting for. Yes, The Pen is more expensive than the Regent and yes, they pride themselves on this fact. A deluxe harbor-view room will cost close to $500 a night.

U.S. reservations: ☎ 800/262-9467 or Leading Hotels of the World ☎ 800/223-6800. Local phone: ☎ 852/2366-6251; fax: 852/2722-4170; on-line: www.peninsula.com.

KOWLOON HOTEL
19–21 Nathan Rd., Kowloon (MTR: TST).

If you want the best location in town but don't feel up to spring-
ing for a five-star hotel, perhaps you should consider the
Kowloon Hotel, whose secret is the simple fact that it is owned
by the Peninsula Group. It is a four-star rather than a five-star
hotel and is more in keeping with an American-style big hotel
than a palace, but it's got advantages.

You're next door to the Pen (this means you are in the middle
of a shopping neighborhood), and the hotel is built in a slim
tower, so view rooms are available. In terms of location, I don't
need to get more explicit, do I?

Now let's talk about price. The rooms are half the price of
those at the Pen. Best of all, a suite here costs the same as a
regular room at the Pen or the Regent. A harbor-view double
costs about $150 a night. Also, because the clients are mostly
businesspeople, there are fax and computer terminals in the
rooms and all sorts of modern, up-to-date electronic gadgets.

U.S. reservations: ☎ 800/262-9467. Local phone: ☎ 852/
2369-8698; fax: 852/2369-8698.

GREAT EAGLE HOTEL
8 Peking Rd., Tsimshatsui (MTR: TST)

I discovered this hotel from the window of my airport transfer
as I was leaving Honkers, so I can't tell you that I have stayed
here. I can tell you that it has a very interesting shopping
location and as a four-star hotel is a little less expensive than
the palace hotels.

The hotel is relatively new to the scene, after a $30 million
renovation that made it a luxury property aimed at business
travel. It has almost 500 rooms, is modern and plush, and has
an unusual à la carte system: Rooms start at a base of about
$168, and you can add on whatever extras or amenities you
want—sort of like taking one from column A and one from
column B. There's also a Club floor with even more perks.

Located a short walk from the Star Ferry, the hotel is one block from the Pen, toward the Harbour City complex at the edge of the main Kowloon shopping area, so that within a minute or two you are able to get a shopping fix.

If you have never heard of Great Eagle, don't fret—you have, but don't know it. Great Eagle is the name of a holding company that owns many famous hotels including the Langham Hilton in London, one of my regular treasures.

U.S. reservations: ☎ 800/457-4000. Local phone: ☎ 852/2375-1133; fax: 852/2375-6611; on-line: www.gehotel.com.

DINING IN HONG KONG

If you think Hong Kong is most famous for shopping, think again. The international word is that the number-one attraction in town is culinary pleasures—from five-star restaurants in the most elegant hotels to Chinese restaurants somewhat off the beaten path. There are certain places in town that are so fabulous you just have to try them in order to complete your Hong Kong experience.

While I have developed my own list of favorites, I've also had a few whispers in my ear from Fred Ferretti, an editor at *Gourmet* magazine. I'm lucky enough to bump into Fred and his wife a few times a year—she's Eileen Yin Fei Lo, one of this country's well-regarded cookbook writers. They always are generous with their thoughts on best bets and best buys. Because Fred and Eileen spend part of each year in Hong Kong, be sure to check back issues of *Gourmet* for Fred's latest finds.

Legends & Landmarks

When I pick a restaurant for this category, my selection is based on a combination of factors: the length of time the establishment has been in operation, the quality of its food, location, and ambience. Some places so typify what is special about Hong

Kong, I consider them "don't miss" experiences. These establishments are designated with a shopping-bag icon.

JUMBO FLOATING RESTAURANT
Shum Wan, Aberdeen (MTR: taxi).

My first thought about Jumbo was that only tourists go here and, therefore, it wasn't worth my time. It took me years to get up the nerve to come here and, now that I've done it, I feel like a fool. Why did I wait so long? I can't wait to come back and bring my son! If ever there was a fantasy place to bring your kids, this is it.

Jumbo, as you may already know, is the most famous of the floating restaurants in Aberdeen Harbour. It is best seen at night when all the lights are aglow, but you can go for lunch and take advantage of the various souvenir vendors who set up shop in junks and on the pier that provides service from Aberdeen Harbour to the floating restaurant. (There's more shopping when you get into the restaurant, but all the prices are marked in yen.)

The place is enormous and has a fun, almost silly atmosphere. This is not intimate dining, but if dressing up in a mandarin's outfit and having your photo taken sounds like fun to you (or your kids), this is the place. Menus feature pictures, so you just point to what you want. Dinner for two with beer is about $40. The food is American-style Chinese. To get here: Take a taxi to Jumbo Pier and hop aboard Jumbo's tender. For reservations: ☎ 852/2553-9111.

GADDI'S
Peninsula Hotel, Salisbury Rd., Kowloon (MTR: TST).

From Jumbo to Gaddi's is surely going from the ridiculous to the sublime: Gaddi's is known to visitors and locals alike as the best French restaurant in town; serious foodies wouldn't consider a trip to Hong Kong complete without a visit. It's much like a private club of local and visiting professionals.

Lunch and dinner are both popular; lunch is less expensive. However, we have indeed found a deal: The house offers a set dinner menu of five courses, each with its own wine, for approximately $125 a person, an excellent value.

This may be the most elegant restaurant in Hong Kong; an evening spent here will send you home with delightful memories (be sure to dress the part). The maître d' is named Rolf; for reservations: ☎ 852/2366-6251.

THE PEAK CAFÉ
121 Peak Rd. Also: Café Deco, Peak Galleria (MTR: none, take the tram).

Although there are now two landmark restaurants atop the Peak (**Café Deco** is the other one), I prefer the Peak Café because it is not part of the tacky mall that houses Café Deco. It has a chic and accessible quality that makes it perfect for anyone and any occasion. The food is a mixed bag of continental with some Pacific Rim thrown in.

And yes, darlings, of course there's shopping up here. It's touristy, but the Peak Café logo souvenirs are tasteful and there's even an outlet store. Could I make this up? For reservations: ☎ 852/2849-7868. For **Café Deco,** ☎ 852/2849-5111.

LAI CHING HEEN
The Regent Hotel, 18 Salisbury Rd., Kowloon (MTR: TST).

Patricia Wells, food critic for the *International Herald Tribune,* has named Lai Ching Heen one of the top 10 restaurants in the world; this accolade alone should be your reason to book. The fact that every other food critic in the world agrees with her is your second reason.

Located downstairs in the Regent Hotel, this restaurant is so famous that it helps to book ahead. You don't get the same view of Central that comes with dinner at **La Plume** or **Yu,** but you do get a view of Causeway Bay. Last time we were there, we also got to watch a full moon rise over Causeway Bay. Talk about perfect!

But it's the food, not the view, that draws people from all around the world in droves. They are known for their fresh seafood and wide selection of dishes.

During hairy crab season (October to November) there was no hairy crab on the menu; nonetheless, at our request, the kitchen prepared them. Then the waiters gave us lessons in how to dismantle the crabs. For reservations: ☎ 852/ 2721-1211.

Snack & Shop

It's quite easy to get a snack while shopping in Hong Kong. It's simply a question of how adventurous you are. *Dai pai dong* is the Chinese name for the street vendors who cook food from carts in street markets or corners. Although I have pictures of my sister, the late great Dr. Debbie, eating from assorted dai pai dong, her advice to me on how to stay healthy has remained in the back of my head: *"Always eat lunch in the best hotel in town."*

Hong Kong has lots of great hotels and each has several restaurants, so you'll have no trouble sticking to this simple piece of advice. While I have also ferreted out a few more places in "Other Restaurants" below, those of you who dislike surprises should remember that a five-star hotel offers your best shot at happiness.

From a price point of view, hotels usually have a coffee shop or one restaurant with moderate prices amid their galaxy of four or five eateries. But, for a shopper's lunch, I'm often at:

MANDARIN ORIENTAL COFFEE SHOP
The Mandarin Oriental Hotel, 5 Connaught Rd. (MTR: Central).

HARBOURVIEW COFFEE SHOP
The Regent Hotel, 18 Salisbury Rd., Kowloon (MTR: TST).

THE LOBBY
The Peninsula Hotel, Salisbury Rd., Kowloon (MTR: TST).

Fast-Food Notes

If this kind of conservatism is not your cup of tea and you'd like to watch your purse (or you have the kids with you!), there are tons of franchised American fast-food joints in Hong Kong. You'll have no trouble finding a **McDonald's** or **KFC** anywhere you turn.

One night in Kowloon, we found a local diner where there were no other *gwailo* (foreigners) and then went for a stroll on Nathan Road and had dessert from **Häagen-Dazs**—and I didn't feel as though I'd sold out on the local experience in the slightest.

Other Restaurants

Below is a selection of restaurants outside the hotel circuit that are appropriate for lunch or even a quick dinner, listed by the shopping neighborhood in which they are located.

CENTRAL

TRATTORIA
The Landmark Shop 203A, Queens Rd. (MTR: Central).

This Italian restaurant couldn't be more convenient for shoppers—it's right inside the Landmark Mall. There's a buffet as well as menu service; the decor is nice and prices are easy to handle. The mall also has the Harbourside Café for a more casual meal. Reservations at Trattoria: ☎ 852/2524-0841.

LUK YU TEAHOUSE
24 Stanley St. (MTR: Central).

It's not the teahouse of the August Moon, but Luk Yu could be a movie set. It's located in the center of Central and is a landmark eatery. Order dim sum from the menu in Chinese, and try not to take pictures since that's what all the other tourists are doing. Go for an early lunch (locals eat between 1 and 4pm, so if you're there by noon, you should be able to get a table without much of a wait) or at teatime when you can get a table easily.

Dim sum is served until 5pm. A perfect location in Central makes this a good stop for shoppers; it's halfway to Hollywood Road and not that far from the Landmark.

Do note that waiters at Luk Yu make it a policy to be rude to Westerners. A recent attempt to order in Cantonese brought on scowls. For reservations: ☎ 852/2523-5464. Cash only.

BLUE
45 Lyndhurst Terrace (MTR: Central).

Blue is the newcomer you wish you were smart enough to open: It's chic, it's well located (at junction of Hollywood Road), and the food is terrific. The decorations are (duh) blue and ethnically minimalist and ever so chic; the food is Pacific Rim, imaginative, and comforting. Needless to say, you need reservations: ☎ 852/2815-4005.

WESTERN

YAT CHAU HEALTH RESTAURANT
262 Des Voeux Rd. (MTR: Central or Shueng Wan).

The gimmick is that you see a doctor when you enter; the doctor diagnoses you, and then you choose your menu according to your personal needs. Based on ancient Chinese medicine, the practice is sound to those who believe. The examination is free, but lunch or dinner can get pricey if you pick dishes with civet cat, ginseng, or even more exotic ingredients. Our rather bland meal was about $40, including a single glass of three-penis wine. Credit cards accepted. The English-speaking doctor is not in-house on Saturday. Conveniently located between Western and Central, a few blocks short of Western Market. Credit cards are accepted.

OK, so we know you're dying to know: What's the three penis wine for? Backache, of course. Ian has had a bad back since a car accident several years ago. Did it do any good? Well, no. But then he didn't drink every drop. If you are traveling with preteens, they'll eat this place up, and they'll never stop talking about it.

HOLLYWOOD ROAD/MIDLEVELS

PETTICOAT LANE & THE PAVILLION
2 & 3 Tun Wo Lane, Central (MTR: Central).

This place, with two different menus and two different names, is located in an alley right off Hollywood Road and is truly a find, if only because it's so hidden. But everyone knows how to get here, so ask any of the stores on Hollywood Road if you feel frustrated. The hole-in-the-wall eatery is adorable in a baroque-bordello fashion; it's a gay scene at certain times of the day but straight for lunch. Really a treat!

The two places have different types of formality to them— Petticoat is informal, whereas Pavilion has a fancy menu with salads, pasta, and main courses; reservations for Petticoat Lane: ☎ 852/2973-0642; the Pavilion: ☎ 852/2869-7768.

LE TIRE BOUCHON
9 Old Bailey St., Central (MTR: Central).

Right off Hollywood Road's antiques row is this very authentic little French bistro that will completely dissuade you that you are in China. Charming and intimate, with good food— you can even try out your high school French. This is a popular dinner spot but a real find at lunch. Reservations: ☎ 852/2523-5459.

STANLEY

STANLEY'S ORIENTAL
90B Stanley Main St., Stanley (MTR: None, take bus no. 6 from Exchange Sq. in Central to Stanley).

Part of my ritual when I visit Stanley is to have lunch at Stanley's Oriental. There is also Stanley's French, virtually around the corner, and Stanley's Fukashima, a Japanese restaurant; but

I like the Oriental because of its colonial feel, view of the beach, and quiet corner location. It has quick bites, salads, sandwiches, and more. Sometimes we go for a late lunch to avoid crowds; they'll take the last lunch order at 2:45pm. We don't usually reserve, but you can: ☎ 852/2813-9988. If you want to eat on the balcony, a reservation is a must.

KOWLOON

FELIX
The Peninsula Hotel, Salisbury Rd., Kowloon (MTR: TST).

So it's like this. You're only in Hong Kong for a few days, and you're faced with an overwhelming number of shopping and eating experiences. You want to take advantage of all of them, yet you can't quite get your priorities straight. Step this way. Felix should be high atop your priority list if you like the young and hip and can take a little bit of noise and a few out-of-towners staring out the windows. (Speaking of staring out the windows, be sure to do so from the men's toilet.)

Named after the former general manager of the Pen, Felix was designed by Philippe Starck and created atop the new Pen tower to offer view, view, view and something for everyone—which means a large menu, moderate prices, and casual dining. Felix is not intimidating, and it is a once-in-a-lifetime must-do; use the special elevators to the side.

TST EAST

SHANG PALACE
Kowloon Shangri-La, 64 Mody Rd. (downstairs), Kowloon (MTR: TST).

Fred Ferretti from *Gourmet* tells me that Shang Palace gets his vote for best Chinese restaurant in Hong Kong. It gets my vote just for decor alone. Eating in this restaurant is like being in an exquisite Chinese dream.

Meanwhile, Fred's wife, Eileen Yin Fei Lo, also votes for Shang. Note that if Fred's wife, one of the most famous Chinese cooks alive, gives the nod, the place has to be great.

The walls are made of the most beautiful carved and lacquered wood. The dining room features both small and large tables so, regardless of the size of your party, you can have a Chinese family style dinner and really get into it. For more intimate dining, ask for a private room. Extensive menu, quite moderate prices. Lunch and dinner. For reservations: ☎ 852/2721-2111, ext. 8401.

SHOPPING HONG KONG

Shopping Hours

Generally, shops open late in the morning and stay open until late in the evening. The majority of specialty stores open at 10am and close at 6:30pm. However, these are just general guidelines. Some stores open whenever they feel like it. Central tends to open later than Kowloon.

For the most part, stores close at 6:30pm in Central, 7:30pm in Tsim Sha Tsui, and 9pm on Nathan Road in Yau Ma Tei and in Mong Kok. In all honesty, I've been in the stores on Granville Road until 11pm at night. I think that as long as there is traffic, the stores are willing to stay open.

Mall stores are open during regular business hours on Sunday. Most shops in the main shopping areas of Tsim Sha Tsui and Causeway Bay are open 7 days a week. Those in Central close on Sunday.

Major public holidays are honored in many shops. Everything closes on Chinese New Year; some stores are closed for 2 days, others for 2 weeks. Do not plan to be in Hong Kong and do any shopping at this time. The stores that remain open charge a premium. The stores where you want to shop will all be closed.

Store hours are affected by the following public holidays:

- January 1 (New Year's Day)
- January/February (Chinese New Year)
- March/April (Good Friday, Easter Sunday, and Monday)
- June (Dragon Boat Festival)
- August 25 (Liberation Day)
- December 25 (Christmas) and December 26 (Boxing Day)

On public holidays, banks and offices close, and there is a higher risk of shops closing as well. Factory outlets will definitely not be open. Many holiday dates change from year to year. For specific dates, contact the HKTA before you plan your trip.

If you are planning a tour of the factory outlets, remember that lunch hour can fall anywhere between noon and 2pm, although 1 to 2pm is most common. Outlet shops will close for 1 hour, along with the factory. Because of this practice, you might as well plan to have lunch then, too.

Department store hours differ from store to store. The larger ones, like Lane Crawford and Chinese Arts & Crafts, maintain regular business hours, 10am to 5pm. The Japanese department stores in Causeway Bay open between 10 and 10:30am and close between 9 and 9:30pm. They're all closed on different days 1 day of the week, however, which can be confusing. Don't assume because one department store is closed, that they all are.

Market hours are pretty standard. Only food markets open very early in the morning. Food markets are sometimes called "wet markets." There's no point in arriving in Stanley before 9am. Even 9:30am is slow; many vendors are still opening up. The Jade Market opens at 10am every day and closes around 3pm; this includes Sunday. The weekend street market on Reclamation is a local market so it opens earlier; there's plenty going on at 9am.

Hong Kong Privilege

Born to Shop readers who would like some special perks on their next visit to Hong Kong can write to the HKTA for a Hong Kong Privilege card, a discount card that comes with its own little booklet and map, inviting you to discounts in participating stores and restaurants. Discounts are up to 20%, considerable savings. Get the package from the HKTA in the United States (☎ 800/282-4582) before you leave for Hong Kong.

If you are a senior citizen (age 60 or over) you qualify for Hong Kong Silver Plus, which also provides discounts.

The Privilege Plan also goes by the name Hong Kong VIP Card as part of the Best Buys events, a seasonal offering in the summer season.

For both plans, contact your nearest HKTA:

East Coast: HKTA, 590 Fifth Ave., 5th floor, New York, NY 10036; ☎ 212/869-5008; fax: 212/730-2605; e-mail: hktanyc@aol.com.

West Coast: HKTA, 10940 Wilshire Blvd., Suite 1220, Los Angeles, CA 90024; ☎ 310/208-4582; fax: 310/208-1869; e-mail: hktalax@aol.com.

Midwest: HKTA, 610 Enterprise Dr., Suite 200, Oak Brook, IL 60521 ☎ 708/575-2828; fax: 708/575-2829; e-mail: hktachi@aol.com.

Christmas in Hong Kong

Christmas decorations go up in Kowloon (it's hard to spot the neon from all the neon) in mid-November as the stores begin their Christmas promotions. Among the best deals in town at this time of year is the free shipping that many department stores offer, to either the United Kingdom or anyplace in the world, depending on the store.

Marks & Spencer sends Christmas hampers (gift baskets) to any address in the United Kingdom for free, as long as the hamper costs £50 or more. Chinese Arts & Crafts stores will ship items as long as they cost US$350 or more.

Christmas permeates the air; even street markets sell decorations—plastic wreaths, silk flowers, ornaments, and more. You'll also be thrilled to find those Victorian-style embroidered tree ornaments in stores in Hong Kong.

Better yet, Hong Kong is the perfect place to load up on inexpensive presents—what can you find at home that's fabulous for less than $1? Not much! Go to the Jade Market and you'll find plenty.

Even when I'm in Hong Kong in July, I start thinking about Christmas.

New Year in Hong Kong

I don't mean Western New Year and Auld Lang Syne; I mean Chinese New Year, and when it comes, you may go crazy if you want to shop. Stores close for days or weeks, depending. Expect most stores to be closed a minimum of 2 to 3 days. The date of the New Year varies because it is based on a lunar calendar; the danger zone falls somewhere between the end of January and mid-February.

Hong Kong on Sale

Hong Kong has two traditional sale periods: the end of August and shortly before Chinese New Year (January or February).

Everything else goes on sale during this same period. You'll find a lot of no-name merchandise that didn't interest you when it cost $50, but is looking a lot better now that it's marked down to $30.

The best thing about the sales in Hong Kong is that this is your best time to get regular retail merchandise at its lowest price. The real bargains in Hong Kong are not in retail stores; the real bargains in Hong Kong may not be in perfect condition. So if you insist on brand-new, clean, undamaged goods, you should feel safe buying them on sale. If you have teens or are on a limited clothing budget, shop Hong Kong during the sale periods. Check the advertisements in the *South China Morning Post* for special sale announcements.

Remember, the best buys in Hong Kong are not in retail shops. If you crave designer merchandise, about the only time to buy it in Hong Kong is during one of these big sale periods.

Typhoon Retailing

During the summer (from May to September), Hong Kong falls prey to typhoons. To best protect the population, the Royal Observatory now ranks the typhoons on a scale from 1 to 10. While each number has some significance in terms of the velocity of the wind, we will translate this to you only in terms of shopping habits.

- No. 3 typhoon: The Star Ferry might stop running.
- No. 8 typhoon: All stores are supposed to be closed; everyone is supposed to go home or seek shelter. Offices will not be open during a No. 8. However, hotel stores will stay open and may even jack up their prices.

Tourists are told to stay inside the hotel during a No. 8. The hotels circulate a brochure telling you what to do: Close the drapes, stay away from the windows, and so on. You can stay in your room all day reading a book, or you can drink Singapore Slings at the bar. Or you could do what any normal person would do: Go shopping. If you stay indoors, you'll find every shop in the hotel is doing a booming business. We were even offered "special typhoon prices."

Fakes for Sale

New York's streets are teeming with vendors selling faux Chanel earrings, T-shirts, and scarves. These goods are easily differentiated from the real thing. While Hong Kong doesn't have a lot of fake Chanel on the streets (it's hidden), there are many items for sale—especially at markets—that appear to be real. But they aren't!

I bought a canvas-and-leather book bag from a street market for the high (for Hong Kong) price of $20. It had a big and perfect Gap label on the front. It fell apart 36 hours later. Both buckles and one leather strap broke so quickly (in three different incidents) that I am convinced that real Gap labels were sewn onto rather ordinary canvas bags. Let the buyer beware.

The biggest change in the atmosphere comes from mainland China where locals and tourists alike are flocking to Shenzen (and beyond) to snap up fakes for bargain prices. See pp. 124–129 for all the details about Shenzen.

The Buildings System

Most of us are used to finding stores on street level, with fancy glass storefronts and large numbers identifying their addresses. There are many such stores in Hong Kong, but many more are operated high up, out of office buildings. You may arrive at an address and see only a cement building. Before you think that the address is wrong, go into the lobby and look at the directory. The store or business will probably be listed with a floor and room number next to it.

Because of this practice of "office shopping," the addresses in Hong Kong usually refer to a particular building. When getting the address of a particular shop, you are likely to be told that it is in the Sands Building, instead of being told that it is at 17 Hankow Rd. Luckily many maps are marked with the actual buildings and their addresses.

Cab drivers are so used to the system that you can usually give them the name of the building, and they will take you right there.

In planning your shopping expedition, work carefully with a map so that you determine all the shops in one building at one time. Remember that it is not unusual for a business to have a shop on each side of the harbor, so decide if you are going to be in Hong Kong or Kowloon before you make plans. Use the A-O-A Map Directory to locate a building before you head off.

Shipping

Shipping from Hong Kong is easy and safe. Container shipping is not inexpensive, but freight is moderate. Whether the item is as cumbersome as a giant Foo dog, as small as a few ginger jars, or as fragile as dinner plates, you can arrange to ship it home. All it takes is a little time and a little more money.

If you anticipate buying an item that needs shipping, do your homework before you leave the United States. You may need a family member to claim the item at customs if you will still be out of the country, or you may even need a customs agent (see "Bringing it all Back Home," below). You will also want to know enough about shipping costs to be able to make a smart decision about the expense added to your purchase.

To make shipping pay, the item, including the additional cost of shipping, duty, and insurance (and customs agent, and so on, if need be) should still cost less than it would at home, or should be so totally unavailable at home that any price makes it a worthwhile purchase. If it's truly unavailable (and isn't an antique or a one-of-a-kind art item) at home, ask yourself why. There may be a good reason—such as it's illegal to bring such an item into the country!

If you are indeed looking for a certain type of thing, be very familiar with American prices. If it's an item of furniture, even an antique, can a decorator get it for you with a 20% rather than 40% markup? Have you checked out all the savings angles first? Are you certain the item is genuine and is worth the price of the shipping? There are many furniture fakes in Hong Kong.

There are basically two types of shipping: surface and air. Air can be broken into two categories: unaccompanied baggage and regular air freight.

Surface mail (by ship in a transpacific transaction) is the cheapest. Surface mail may mean sending through regular mail channels—that is, a small package of perfume would be sent by parcel post. Or it may require that you fill an entire shipping container, or at least pay the price of an entire container. If you are doing heavy-duty shipping, look in the back of the *South China Morning Post* for shippers wanting to fill containers. Surface mail may take up to 3 months; I find 2 is the norm.

If you're shipping by container, but can't fill one, you might want to save money by using groupage services. Your goods will be held until a shipping container is filled. The container will then go to the United States, to one of only four ports of entry (Los Angeles, New York, San Francisco, or New Orleans), where you can meet the container at the dock, be there when your items are unpacked, and then pay the duties due. A full container is approximately 1,500 cubic feet of space (or $8'6'' \times 8'6'' \times 20'$) and will not be delivered to your door (no matter how much you smile). It will cost about $5,000 to ship a container by sea.

For small items, there are international overnight air package services, like Federal Express, UPS, DHL, etc., that deliver within a day or two. This part of the shipping business is growing just as fast as overnight U.S. services did over the past few years, so check out the latest possibilities. Crossing the dateline can make "overnight" deliveries seem longer or shorter. Local Hong Kong office numbers for overnight shippers are: Federal Express: ☎ 852/2730-3333; UPS: ☎ 852/2735-3535; and DHL: ☎ 852/2765-8111.

The U.S. Postal Service has international express mail, which is a 3-day service from U.S. post offices. Hong Kong post offices offer a similar program. Ask at the counter.

Do remember that whatever you are sending to yourself is subject to duty when it arrives home. If you've bought a special Hong Kong bargain, leave the price tag on it to prove the price to customs officers who may otherwise value an item at a higher price and charge more duty.

If you want to price a few local freight offices, try: Unaccompanied Baggage Ltd., Counter 330, Departure Hall, Hong Kong International Airport, Kowloon (☎ 852/769-8275), or Michelle International Transport Co. Ltd., 20 Connaught Rd.

West, Room 1002, Western District, Hong Kong (☎ 852/
548-7617).

You can have items shipped directly from shops. Many Hong
Kong stores, especially tailors, will ship your purchases to the
United States. Most people I know who have done this are surprised when their goods arrive by UPS. Ask about the shop's
shipping policies before you decide to ship—some stores will
charge you for their trouble (a flat fee), then add the actual
shipping rate and an insurance fee.

Try to pay for the purchase with a credit card; that way if
it never arrives, you'll have an easier time getting a credit or
a refund. Be sure to ask when the store will be able to ship the
goods out. I planned to send home some perfume so as not to
have to lug it around during a month's worth of touring. The
shopkeeper told me she was so backed up on her shipping that
it would take her at least 6 weeks to mail our order. Then it
would take several weeks or months for the package to arrive
by surface mail. I took it with me.

SHOPPING NEIGHBORHOODS
....

The island of Hong Kong (Central) and Kowloon (TST), on
the Kowloon Peninsula, are the most popular areas and your
two basic shopping neighborhoods.

Just because they are the best known and the handiest
doesn't mean you should stop learning your neighborhoods.
I will send you everywhere, from TST East to the New Territories; I'll also tell you how to get into some factory districts
and a lot of other neighborhoods outside the merely obvious.

The more I visit Hong Kong, the more comfortable I am
with getting away from tourists and the commercial main
streets of Central and Kowloon—define a successful visit to
Hong Kong as one in which you've spent at least a little bit
of time in the real-people neighborhoods. But I also have
to admit that during my last trip to Hong Kong, with only

4 full days in town, anything in a weird or out-of-the-way neighborhood quickly disappeared from my must-do list.

Getting Around the Neighborhoods

The MTR will get you almost everywhere, or at least into the main neighborhoods and basic shopping areas. Unless I specifically note otherwise in an address, the MTR stop at Central gets you to most locations in Hong Kong; the MTR stop at Tsim Sha Tsui (TST) services most Kowloon shopping areas.

There's also excellent bus service and ferries to outlying islands where you can just roam around upon arrival. Getting to specific addresses in the New Territories can be difficult without a car; consider hiring a taxi or a car (with driver) from your hotel.

I really think that if your time is limited and you want to see a lot, a car and driver is an economical luxury. The price ranges from $250 to $350 per day. If you can't afford the whole day, hire car and driver up until lunch, or half a day. Then, you can finish off on foot. The time you'll save with your own personal chauffeur will permit you to get to a number of out-of-the-way neighborhoods and enhance your enjoyment of the shopping time that you have.

Whatever you do, don't take a taxi through the Cross-Harbour Tunnel if you can help it. I once painfully sat in traffic for an hour trying to get through it!

A Word About Addresses

Although I have already warned you that the address you will be given is most often the name of the building and not the street address, I want to stress that when street addresses are written out, they may designate a specific door or portion of a building. So you may see different addresses for the same buildings, like the **Landmark, Swire House,** or **Prince's Building.** Don't freak out or assume it's an error. Simply check your trusty map. If an office building takes up a city block, as many do, shops can claim different street addresses on all four sides!

The same is true when cruising the boutiques in a shopping center like the **Landmark:** Often the shop's address will simply be the name of the building. The easiest way to find what you're looking for is to check the directory on the main floor of the mall.

Hong Kong Island Neighborhoods

The island of Hong Kong actually makes up only a portion of what most tourists refer to as "Hong Kong." While government, business, and "downtown" functions take place on the island, much of the local population live elsewhere in neighborhoods that do not seriously feature shopping and, therefore, are not included in these pages.

The island is divided by a ridge of hills topped by the famous Peak. The rich and famous live in villas lining the roadway up the Peak; the almost rich and famous (as well as the upper-middle class) live in what's called the "Mid-Levels," the area of the hills above Central but below the Peak.

To get to most other portions of the island you can either go through a tunnel under the hills toward Aberdeen, or take the tram or MTR along the shoreline to the housing estates, where middle-class people live in housing blocks and "mansion" or "estate" developments.

CENTRAL

Central is the part of Hong Kong that refers to what we used to call "downtown" when I was growing up. It's the main business and shopping part of town: It's the core of Hong Kong Island.

Shopping in Central is mostly Westernized and even glitzy, but wait, you round a corner and voilà—it's **the Lanes:** real people galore. You walk up Pottinger to Hollywood Road and, again—the real thing. Central seems to house the ridiculous and the sublime within the same city block; it's your opportunity to mix Westernized shopping with Eastern lifestyles.

Central & Western Districts

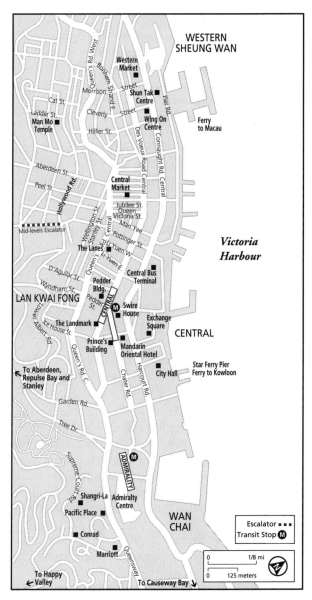

WESTERN
SHEUNG WAN

Queen's Rd. West
Bonham Strand E.
Morrison Street

Western
Market

Cat St.
Cleverly Street
Shun Tak
Centre

Ladder St.
Man Mo
Temple

Hillier St.
Wing On
Centre

Pier Rd.
Ferry
to Macau

Des Voeux Road Central
Connaught Rd. Central

Aberdeen St.

Peel St.
Hollywood Rd.
Central
Market

Jubilee St.
Queen
Victoria St.
Man Yee

Mid-levels Escalator
Wellington St.
Stanley St.
Pottinger St.
Queen's Rd. Central
Li Yuen W.
Li Yuen E.

The Lanes

D'Aguilar St.
Wyndham St.

LAN KWAI FONG
Pedder
Bldg.
Pedder St.
Central Bus
Terminal

Victoria
Harbour

Ice House St.
Lower Albert Rd.
CENTRAL
M
Swire
House
Exchange
Square

The Landmark
Prince's
Building
Mandarin
Oriental Hotel
CENTRAL

Queen's Rd. C.
City Hall
Star Ferry Pier
Ferry to Kowloon

← To Aberdeen,
Repulse Bay and
Stanley

Garden Rd.
Chater Rd.
Harcourt Rd.

Tree Dr.

Supreme Court Rd.
ADMIRALTY
M

Shangri-La
Admiralty
Centre

Pacific Place

Conrad
WAN
CHAI

Marriott

Queensway

Escalator ▪ ▪ ▪
Transit Stop M

To Happy
← Valley

To Causeway Bay ↓

0   1/8 mi
0   125 meters

The **Landmark** (see map on p. 105), a shopping mall of mythic proportions, houses five floors of shopping including stores in the basement, at street level, on a mezzanine above the street shops, and up in two towers that rise above the main floors of shopping. European designers have their shops here or across the street in **Swire House,** the **Prince's Building,** or the **Mandarin Oriental Hotel.**

The Lanes are two little alleys (Li Yuen West and Li Yuen East, see map on p. 105) half a block away from each other— they are lined with storefronts and then filled in with stalls so you have to look behind the stalls and poke into nooks and crannies to get the full flavor. Each is teeming with people and products. One lane specializes in handbags (most imitations of famous brands and styles, few of good quality); the other, underwear.

The **Pedder Building** (see map on p. 105) is a must: This one building is conveniently located across the street from the Landmark and in every shopper's direct path. There are enough outlets here to empty your wallet and keep you satisfied, even if you have no more time for stores. **Shanghai Tang** is also here, alongside the outlet building—this is the best one stop you will make, especially if you are in a hurry.

WESTERN

The Western District is adjacent to Central and can be reached on foot or via MTR. Take the MTR to Sheung Wan to get to central Western. Despite the decidedly touristy flavor in the renovation of **Western Market,** the Western District is a lot more Chinese, in both appearance and attitude, than Central. This is really the district to see before it is ruined; as the modernization continues, the Western as I know it will disappear within the next few years.

Here you'll feel less like a sightseer and more like a visitor to the Far East. Western used to represent the real part of town, but the high-rises and the glitz are encroaching quickly.

It's moving fast, so strike out to find the shops with snakes in cages and little restaurants where you're not sure if the snacks are snacks or snakes. There's an electronics district in Western, as well as old-fashioned Chinese medicine shops, and the terminal for heading off to Macau.

Going west from Central, the area begins shortly after **Central Market,** at Possession Street, and continues to Kennedy Town, where most of the local working people live. Western includes the famous **Man Wa Lane,** where you can purchase your own personalized chop (see p. 34), the **Shun Tak Centre** (off to Macau), and **Bonham Strand East,** where you'll find scores of Chinese herbalists. The farther west you wander, the more exotic the area becomes.

My best way of "doing" Western is to combine it with a trip to Hollywood Road; if you walk downhill from Hollywood Road, you'll automatically end up in Western. Then you can take in the **Western Market** before walking back to Central or hopping in the MTR station right there at Shun Tak.

HOLLYWOOD ROAD

Up above Central, and technically within the Central District, Hollywood Road is a shopping neighborhood unto itself. Hollywood Road isn't hard to get to, but it is not necessarily on the way to anywhere else you're going, so it's essential that you specifically plan your day or half a day to include this outing. You can reach it from either the Central or Sheung Wan MTR stops. It's within walking distance, if you're wearing sensible shoes and have the feet of a mountain goat; you can also tell your taxi driver "*By Fa Gai*" (meaning "white flower") and be dropped off in the core of the antiques area, in what used to be the neighborhood where the prostitutes plied their trade.

Or you can simply take the Mid-Levels outdoor escalator— a moving staircase to the heavens that moves pedestrian traffic from the Mid-Levels down into Central. Just make sure you get it during an "up" hour as the stairs only go "down" during rush hour in the morning. You shop your way right up to the top. Although I admit that I did it (and after Hollywood

Road), it sort of loses its zip, and you find yourself rather in the middle of nowhere, looking for a taxi. Still, you must ride up at least to Hollywood Road.

Hollywood Road is Hong Kong's antiques neighborhood. Because of the escalator, the arrival of the Chinese with new laws on antiquities, and the ever-rising rents in Hong Kong, the area has changed tremendously and will continue to do so. There are antiques stores elsewhere, but Hollywood Road is still a great place to get to know. The idea is to walk the 3 blocks of Hollywood Road from Wyndham to the Man Mo Temple. Then you'll hit Cat Street and the flea market before descending into Western.

As charming as this area is, I must warn you up front that much of what is in these shops must be considered imitation, or at least faux. If you are looking to do anything more serious than browse, I suggest you make your first stop **Honeychurch Antiques** (no. 29), where the expatriate American owners Glenn and Lucille Vessa are bright, honest, and always willing to help. They know who's who and what's what in their world of dealers and will tell you about their stock and everyone else's. Their look is an eclectic blend of antiques from around the Orient (kind of country chinoiserie); however, they know who has the more formal pieces. In fact, they know who has everything.

If you are spending big bucks, it is imperative that you buy from a reputable shop. Ask Glenn and Lucille for guidance.

The most visually arresting "store" on the street has a quasi–flea market feel and the name **Low Price Shop** written in scrawl across the door. Bird cages, beads, old clothes, new snuff bottles, all spill out onto the sidewalk at no. 47, where prices range from dirt cheap—about $3 for an American bestseller paperback, used but recent—to outrageous. Most of the so-called antiques are not so old, and the prices can be rather high. Old-looking postcards and photos (newly made, my friend) are sold here and make very popular souvenirs. Despite the fact that the place is of questionable authority, it's still a heap of fun. A great photo opportunity.

Many dealers sell what look like reproductions to me (although they swear this is the real stuff), and I get that empty feeling in the pit of my stomach as I work these stores, trying to discern real treasures from imagined finds. I must also tell you that Glenn Vessa gave me a blue-and-white ceramics test (after I read and studied four books on the subject) that I flunked outright. I could not accurately ID a piece that was 300 years old. Glenn says knowing what you're doing with ceramics is easy (that's what brain surgeons say about their job as well), but I beg you to be careful.

There are serious porcelain dealers on Hollywood Road, and then tourist traps that sell porcelains and then some factories. It all starts to look alike to me, and that's why I know you should worry. **Hwa Xia** sells only blue-and-white and looks very important (no. 56); **the Place** (no. 81A) is very western-looking in style and sells lots of porcelains, but also other objects and some furniture, too.

But wait! **Wah Tung,** my favorite porcelain shop in Hong Kong, has opened a showroom on Hollywood Road, and while nothing will replace the experience of being lost in an industrial flat, there's a lot to be said for convenience. Don't miss it: 148 Hollywood Rd. The entrance is small and not very warm; you may be put off. Go upstairs, relax.

LAN KWAI FONG

It's Food Street. Take the MTR to the Central station and you'll find Lan Kwai Fong, which is right in the heart of Central, beneath Hollywood Road in an alley right off D'Aguilar Street. This area is more of an eating neighborhood than a shopping neighborhood. Look carefully or you will miss it.

Lan Kwai Fong is where everyone goes to party and to see and be seen; where everyone wants to know which of the clubs or eateries you think is best so they can judge their own chicness (and yours). There are only a few boutiques. Jammed on Friday and Saturday nights.

WAN CHAI

Wan Chai these days means Convention Center. It means Hyatt hotel—one of the best in Hong Kong. It means great location between Central and Causeway Bay, and it means expensive real estate. It does not particularly mean shopping, despite a gigantic **Chinese Arts & Crafts** store.

The Star Ferry provides direct access from Kowloon Peninsula as it travels from Tsim Sha Tsui to Wan Chai Pier. Old Wan Chai has been pushed back from the waterfront and will continue to be developed. If you want to see some of the original architecture and shops, prowl Queen's Road East and the lanes connecting it to Johnston Road. Shopping in the convention center is decidedly unexciting, but if you move on to the Hopewell Building, there is a **street market** on nearby Fenwick Street that is fabulous—no other tourists in sight, and a great place for taking pictures.

CAUSEWAY BAY

This area is changing rapidly, so some of this information may be out-dated by the time you hit the streets. Causeway Bay features one deluxe hotel (the Excelsior) and many tourist package-style hotels. This area is far funkier than Central. The MTR stop is Causeway Bay. Bordered by Victoria Park on the east, and beyond that, Aw Boon Haw (Tiger Balm) Gardens, the whole area was once a bay until land reclamation turned the water into soil several decades ago. Home to the **Royal Hong Kong Yacht Club,** one of the most colorful parts of Causeway Bay is its typhoon shelter, where sampans and yachts moor side by side. You can have dinner on a sampan while cruising the harbor.

Shopping here breaks down into different categories:

- Funky street shopping, which includes plenty of medicine shops, snake soup cafes, a great market, and Jardine's Bazaar.

- Hip, young, and with-it Hong Kong boutiques, where new designers (who can't quite afford Central) open shops.
- **Times Square,** a relatively new giant mall that has taken the town by storm because it has four floors of local and western brands. Even if you don't want to shop here, you may want to visit to check out the scene and people watch—the young, hip Chinese yuppies who are cruising and shopping.
- The Japanese department stores, which are closing up shops and changing this neighborhood. Seibu is located in Pacific place Mall and is probably the best of the Japanese department stores.

Continue your shopping spree in Causeway Bay away from the modern stores and onto Lockhart Road—sort of a main drag down the backbone of Causeway Bay—for a good look at some lost Chinese arts. This street is crammed with herbal and medicine shops and, yep, snake shops. Pick your fave from the cage.

A great nearby photo opportunity is the fresh food market right before Jardine's. **Jardine's Bazaar** is alive with action from the early morning into the night. This is the Hong Kong I want you to see. It features a produce market; a clothes, fabrics, and notions market; and an indoor meat market (I only suggest a visit to the latter if you are very strong and not at all squeamish—I did it once and once was enough).

Many of the shops in Causeway Bay stay open until 10pm, due to the street action. Causeway Bay lacks the expensive sheen of Central, but still has a lot of glitter packed in with the grime. The **Excelsior Hotel**—the fanciest hotel in the area—has a huge shopping arcade that most would call a mall.

HAPPY VALLEY

Happy Valley is situated directly behind Causeway Bay (no MTR—take a taxi) and is well known for its racetrack, amusement park, and shoe shops. Horse-racing season lasts from September to June, and during this time thousands of fans stream in and out of the area.

I've only tried shopping in Happy Valley once because this is home to a number of infamous shoe shops, and I thought I should give it a whirl. Wrong. Cheap, ugly shoes. And no big sizes for my big American feet.

ABERDEEN

Say "Aberdeen" to most tourists, and they think of the floating restaurants this waterside community is famous for. Say "Aberdeen" to me, and I nod and smile and whisper "Wah Tung," my favorite pottery and porcelain factory. Plan your attack carefully. Consider going with a car and driver for several quick hits (then continue on to Stanley and Repulse Bay).

Wah Tung is one serious shopping adventure. Send the husband and kids off in their own taxi to play at **Ocean Park** at the edge of Aberdeen (see next listing) while you hop a taxi for china (not China). You may dash off to **Wah Tung China Company** in the taxi, but plan on needing a truck to get home—this is the place for pottery. There's some 30,000 square feet of breakables here. They claim to have the largest selection in the world, and they ship (see p. 100). Hours are 9:30am to 5:30pm from Monday through Saturday, and 11am to 5pm on Sunday. This happens to be a great Sunday adventure, by the way. You can even call **Wah Tung** (☎ 852/ 2873-2272), and they'll come and fetch you.

This is a fabulous way to shop. The showroom is in a warehouse; follow the signs to the elevator. There are four floors of glorious finds. Pay no mind to the price tags; negotiate for a discount.

STANLEY/REPULSE BAY/OCEAN PARK

It seems to be very "in" to bash **Stanley Market** and say it isn't up to the old standards. I have my own love-hate relationship with this tourist trap. Last trip, I loathed it. I actually had tears streaming down my face. It's very touristy, and I couldn't find anything to buy.

In my opinion, Stanley Market, in the heart of downtown Stanley (no MTR; take a taxi or bus no. 6), is an authentic tourist trap. However, when I spoke to some British first-timers a week later, they couldn't stop raving about Stanley. And my Hong Kong shopping friends still claim to find bargains here. Maybe it's a matter of perspective.

Part of the pleasure of a visit to Stanley is the drive across the island, especially the view as you go around some of those coastal curves. If you agree with me about Stanley, simply get back in the taxi, go to Repulse Bay, shop the snazzy stores, eat lunch, and then return to Hong Kong proper.

Stanley is exceedingly crowded on the weekends, but delightfully quiet midweek. Note that Stanley is not one of those markets where the early bird gets the worm. The early bird gets to sit and sulk until the shops open around 9:30am.

Now then, about Repulse Bay and Ocean Park. They are theme parks of different sorts. Repulse Bay is no longer a hotel but a very tony residential address with a fancy restaurant (the **Verandah**) and a minimall of very, very upscale shops. Ocean Park is a water park for the kids. Both are conveniently combined with Stanley, though it's unlikely that the same person will want to do all three in a day.

Kowloon Neighborhoods

The peninsula of Kowloon was ceded to the British during the Opium Wars, in one of three treaties that created the Royal Crown Colony of Hong Kong. We think it was the best gift Britain ever received; too bad they had to give it back.

Kowloon is packed with shops, hotels, excitement, and bargains. You can shop its more than 4 square miles for days and still feel that you haven't even made a dent. Like Hong Kong Island, Kowloon is the sum of many distinct neighborhoods.

Tsim Sha Tsui

The tip of Kowloon Peninsula is made up of two neighborhoods: Tsim Sha Tsui and Tsim Sha Tsui East. It is home to most of

Hong Kong's fine hotels, and the home of serious tourist-shopping in Kowloon. The Tsim Sha Tsui (TST) station on the MTR will get you into the heart of things. There's also the Jordan Road station for when you're traveling a bit farther into Kowloon and working your way out of the tourist neighborhoods.

At the very tip of Tsim Sha Tsui are the Star Ferry Terminal and the Harbour City Complex. This western harbor front includes Ocean Terminal, Ocean Galleries, Ocean Centre, the Omni Marco Polo Hotel, Omni the Hong Kong Hotel, and the Omni Prince Hotel.

The heart of Tsim Sha Tsui, however, is **Nathan Road,** Kowloon's main shopping drag; Ian says it's the equivalent of London's Oxford Street. Nathan Road stretches from the waterfront for quite some distance and works its way into the "real-people" part of Kowloon in no time at all.

The most concentrated shopping is in the area called the **Golden Mile,** which begins on Nathan Road perpendicular to Salisbury Road. Both sides of this busy street are jam-packed with stores, arcades, covered alleys, and street vendors. There are also some hotels here, each with a shopping mall and enough neon to make Las Vegas blush from embarrassment.

If you are walking north (away from the harbor), you'll pass the Golden Mile. Then you reach a mosque on your left and then the **Park Lane Shopper's Boulevard,** also on your left. To your right, across the street from the Park Lane, is **Burlington Arcade.** The next street on your right is **Granville Road,** which is famous for its jobbers, where brand-name goodies are sold from bins.

While Nathan Road is the core of Kowloon, my favorite part of Tsim Sha Tsui is actually a bit off the beaten path, although directly in sight. In the Golden Mile section of Tsim Sha Tsui, there are two streets that run parallel to Nathan Road and are centered between the Golden Mile and Ocean Terminal: Lock Road and Hankow Road.

If you have adventure in your soul, we ask that you wander this area with your eyes open. It's crammed with shops,

The Kowloon Peninsula

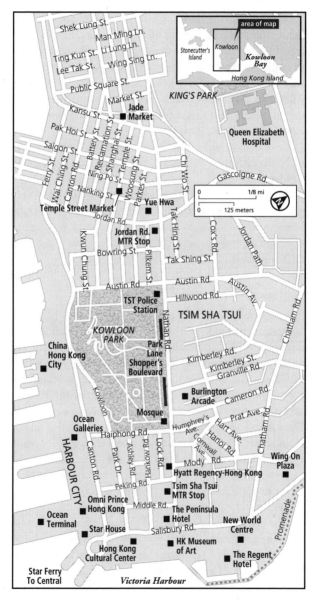

Shek Lung St.
Man Ming Ln.
Ting Kun St. Li Lung Ln.
Lee Tak St. Wing Sing Ln.
Public Square St.
Market St.
Kansu St.
Jade Market
Pak Hoi St.
Saigon St.
Battery St.
Reclamation St.
Shanghai St.
Temple St.
Woosung St.
Parkes St.
Ferry St.
Wai Ching St.
Canton Rd.
Ning Po St.
Nanking St.
Temple Street Market
Yue Hwa
Jordan Rd.
Jordan Rd. MTR Stop
Bowring St.
Kwun Chung St.
Pilkem St.
Tak Hing St.
Tak Shing St.
Austin Rd.
Austin Rd.
Austin Av.
Hillwood Rd.
TST Police Station
TSIM SHA TSUI
KOWLOON PARK
Nathan Rd.
China Hong Kong City
Park Lane Shopper's Boulevard
Kimberley Rd.
Kimberley St.
Granville Rd.
Cameron Rd.
Burlington Arcade
Mosque
Kowloon
Ocean Galleries
Haiphong Rd.
Humphrey's Ave.
Hart Ave.
Prat Ave.
Chatham Rd.
Canton Rd.
Park Dr.
Ashley Rd.
Hankow Rd.
Lock Rd.
Hanoi Rd.
Cornwall Ave.
Mody Rd.
Wing On Plaza
Hyatt Regency-Hong Kong
Peking Rd.
Tsim Sha Tsui MTR Stop
Omni Prince Hong Kong
Middle Rd.
The Peninsula Hotel
Ocean Terminal
Star House
Salisbury Rd.
New World Centre
Hong Kong Cultural Center
HK Museum of Art
The Regent Hotel
Star Ferry To Central
HARBOUR CITY
Promenade
Victoria Harbour

KING'S PARK
Queen Elizabeth Hospital
Gascoigne Rd.
Chi Wo St.
Tak Hing St.
Cox's Rd.
Jordan Path

0   1/8 mi
0   125 meters

area of map
Stonecutter's Island
Kowloon
Kowloon Bay
Kowloon
Hong Kong Island

neon signs, construction, and busy people and does not get so many tourists because it has the aura of being hidden. At the top of Lock Road, right before you get to Haiphong Road, look to your left, where you'll find a small alley that leads all the way through to Hankow Road. This is called the **Haiphong Alley,** and it is crammed with vendors. Many of these vendors do not speak English and will drive a very hard bargain, if they bargain at all. Who cares?

Once you become an Old China Hand, you'll note that prices on Nathan Road are for tourists, and you may disdain the whole Golden Mile area.

Near Jordan Road the atmosphere is more real. Be sure to get to the **Temple Street Market** (see map on p. 115). And, of course, you can't miss the **Jade Market.** If you have a true spirit of shopping and adventure, you'll also make sure you get to Fa Yuen Street (see below).

HARBOUR CITY

Although technically still part of Tsim Sha Tsui, I count the western portion of Kowloon as a separate neighborhood, since it is basically one giant shopping mall—or, actually, several giant interconnected shopping malls. I call the whole entire stretch of Canton Road—from the Star Ferry to China Hong Kong City—Harbour City. This definition includes the buildings across the street on Canton Road, like **Silvercord** and the **Sun Plaza Arcade.** Many *gweilo* big names have opened in this area including **HMV** and **Planet Hollywood.** This whole area has changed dramatically and will continue to do so.

Note: If you are arriving from the Hong Kong side, it's easier to get to the Harbour City part of Tsim Sha Tsui by the Star Ferry. You'll be right there when you land.

The denser shopping is on the Ocean Terminal side, where (walking away from the Star Ferry) the buildings, in order, are: **Star House, Ocean Terminal, Ocean Galleries, Ocean Centre, World Financial Centre, Omni Prince Hotel,** and **China Hong Kong City,** which is a mall-and-towers complex and ferry terminal. This entire stretch of shopping buildings also includes office space and residential towers, as well as some of the well-known tourist hotels in this area: Omni Marco Polo, Omni Hong Kong Hotel, and Omni Prince Hotel.

TSIM SHA TSUI EAST

If you have Hong Kong Harbour at your back, Ocean Terminal to your left, and the Regent to your right, you're looking at the heart of Kowloon, or Tsim Sha Tsui. As the Kowloon peninsula curves around the harbor and the land juts away from Kowloon and the Regent, the area just east of Tsim Sha Tsui but before Hung Hom and the airport is known as Tsim Sha Tsui East.

Because it's waterfront property, it has become known mostly for its string of luxury hotels.

Although the MTR does not come over in this direction, the walk to Tsim Sha Tsui station isn't unreasonable, even in the noonday sun. You may also get here via a specific routing of the Star Ferry.

Tsim Sha Tsui East has come to fascinate me as a miniature version of greater Hong Kong. You can find almost everything you need right here. Mobbed on weekends by local shoppers, its various buildings include **Auto Plaza, Houston Centre,** and, of course, the enclosed mall itself, which is **Tsim Sha Tsui Centre.** There is street-level shopping all along Mody Road, in the various buildings, inside the mall itself (of course), and then on street levels of the buildings behind the Nikko.

There is also some shopping inside each of the hotels; I often take a lunch break at the **Kowloon Shangri-La** coffee shop and hit the hotel stores before returning to the malls.

YAU MA TEI

Remember when I was telling you about Jordan Road and the area north of Tsim Sha Tsui? Well, this is it. Take the MTR to

Jordan Road. Above Tsim Sha Tsui, north on Nathan Road or Canton Road, is the district of Yau Ma Tei.

The most famous shopping site in the area is the well-known **Jade Market** at Kansu and Battery streets; look for the overpass of the highway, and you'll then spot the market right below it.

Here you can shop from 10am until 2:30pm, going from stall to stall, negotiating for all the jade that you might fancy (see map on p. 115). There are two different tents filled with vendors. The experience is just short of mind-boggling. You'll never be strong enough to do both tents.

Alongside the **Jade Market,** on Shanghai Street, is a "wet market"—real live Chinese green market worthy of exploration with or without camera.

At night you will want to visit the **Temple Street Market.** As you push your way through the shoulder-to-shoulder crowds you'll have the chance to buy from the carts, have your fortune told, or enjoy an open-air meal.

I went to the **Jade Market** on a Sunday last time and walked there via Reclamation Street, which was filled with stalls heaped with market goods, from fruits and vegetables to chicken feet and dried lizards, and finally cheap T-shirts and socks. I had a ball.

HUNG HOM

Home of Hong Kong's original outlets, this part of town will disappear once the real estate here goes up in value, due to the change in airports. Already the factory outlets here have gone downhill, and shopping visitors no longer feel compelled to visit. In fact, factories have already moved out, and the outlet scene is bad. If you have tons of time on your hands, maybe—but most agree with me, don't waste your time checking this out unless you are doing a dissertation on Hong Kong real estate.

The most famous address in Hung Hom is **Kaiser Estates,** an industrial development of factories and factory-outlet stores with a few fancy outlets—when you look at **JBH/Fashions of**

Seventh Avenue, you'll be seeing a boutique as smart as any-thing in Central. There's no MTR stop; you'll need to take a taxi.

PRINCE EDWARD & FA YUEN

Even though Fa Yuen is just a street and not a true neighbor-hood, (see map on p. 121) it's enough of an event unto itself that it should be considered as a separate destination. Fa Yuen is so great, I consider it my favorite new neighborhood in Hong Kong. On a recent visit, I bought so much I truly could not fit down the stairwell to the Prince Edward MTR in order to return to the Regent.

To put it in a nutshell, Fa Yuen is the newer version of Granville Road. It's farther "uptown," deeper into the real Hong Kong, and a good bit cheaper than Granville Road, while still offering much of the same style of shopping—storefront after storefront of racks and bins filled with no-name and designer clothing for as little as US$10 an item. Silk blouses cost a tad more, but not much.

Fa Yuen has been blossoming for several years now; no doubt it will become too commercial, and a new place will sprout. Until then, what are you waiting for? Bring plenty of cash because most of these stores do not take plastic. Consider bringing airline wheels with you or a donkey. It is time to shop 'til you drop, Hong Kong style.

When I study my shopping bags from Granville Road, I note that some of the jobbers who sell U.S. name clothing on Granville also have a store on Fa Yuen Street. But names and addresses are truly meaningless—you go, you see, you shop.

You must be prepared to rummage at Fa Yuen, but because you won't see guests from your hotel, you will feel like a real China Hand for having come here and outsmarted everyone else you know.

If you need a jumping-off place, head for **Come True,** 146 Fa Yuen St. Then there's **Kwong Shui Hong** at 190 Fa Yuen St. These 2 blocks are dense with great stores; just walk from one to the next. They truly all look alike, but by now, you're getting used to this kind of thing. Besides, after you've done Granville Road, this will come naturally to you.

From here, you can wander over to the nearby **Ladies Market** (see below). It's 2 blocks away on Tung Choi Street, which opens around 4pm. Don't confuse these two different shopping venues. This Ladies Market is mostly a street market with stalls on the road, while Fa Yuen Street consists of traditional retail with actual shops. Look at a map.

Also note that the new **Bird Market** is in this neighborhood, Yuen Po Street.

To get there: Take the MTR to Prince Edward.

MONG KOK

Mong Kok is very gritty but easier on the nerves than Sham Shui Po (see below). Clustered around upper Nathan Road, where the tourists thin out fast, the **Mong Kok Market** at Tung Choi Street is an afternoon market that is also called the **Ladies' Market** (see p. 121).

If you have evening plans and can't make it to the **Temple Street Market,** then Mong Kok is the afternoon market you should plan to visit. In addition to stands selling alarm clocks that cluck, blaring Canto-pop, and fake designer scarves, you'll find everything you could ever need.

To get there: Depart the MTR at Mong Kok station and find Hong Lok Street, which is more of an alley on the south side of Argyle Street. It's 2 blocks west of Nathan Road (if your back is to the harbor, then west is to your left).

SHAM SHUI PO

For more adventures of a very real kind, head out a little farther to hit the food markets in the streets just down from the Sham Shui Po MTR station, where Kwelin Street crosses Ki Lung Street. You can walk around this city block to see live fish wriggling in red plastic bins, heaps of bok choy, and cages of bound bamboo sheltering fowl of every type. Watch more

Mong Kok & Fa Yuen Street

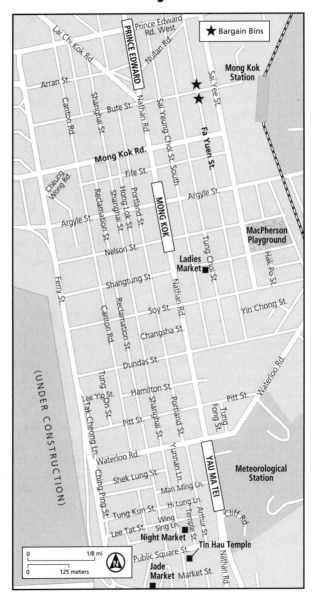

★ Bargain Bins

Prince Edward Rd. West

PRINCE EDWARD

Nullah Rd.

Lai Chi Kok Rd.

Mong Kok Station

Arran St.

Sai Yee St.

Canton Rd.

Shanghai St.

Bute St.

Nathan Rd.

Sai Yeung Choi St. South

Fa Yuen St.

Mong Kok Rd.

Cheung Wong Rd.

Fife St.

Argyle St.

Portland St.

Hong Lok St.

Shanghai St.

Reclamation St.

MONG KOK

Argyle St.

MacPherson Playground

Hak Po St.

Nelson St.

Tung Choi St.

Ladies Market ■

Ferry St.

Shangtung St.

Reclamation St.

Canton Rd.

Nathan Rd.

Soy St.

Yin Chong St.

Changsha St.

Dundas St.

Waterloo Rd.

Tung On St.

Lee Yip St.

Trak Cheong Ln.

Hamilton St.

Shanghai St.

Portland St.

Pitt St.

Pitt St.

Tung Fong St.

Waterloo Rd.

(UNDER CONSTRUCTION)

Ching Ping St.

Shek Lung St.

Yunnan Ln.

YAU MA TEI

Meteorological Station

Man Ming Ln.

Tung Kun St.

Hi Lung Ln.

Cliff Rd.

Lee Tat St.

Wing Sing Ln.

Temple St.

Arthur St.

Night Market ■

Tin Hau Temple ■

Nathan Rd.

Public Square St.

Jade Market ■   Market St.

0	1/8 mi
0	125 meters

N

carefully to see the true details of market life. This is not for young children or the squeamish.

Sham Shui Po is also headquarters to the wholesale computer world, where you can bargain for video games that cost anywhere from 25% to 75% less than U.S. prices. Head for **Golden Arcade Shopping Centre**, at 44B Fuk Wah St.; you'll see it from the MTR station.

In fact, Sham Shui Po is getting more and more socially acceptable, now that the fabric dealers and trim sellers are beginning to move in. Many relocated when Cloth Alley was abandoned; some went into Western Market, others not.

This is not a neighborhood I recommend for everyone, especially those with only half a day for shopping; but it is the kind of place the stouthearted, with 2 or more days to shop, will enjoy exploring. This is also one of the few remaining patches of the "old" Hong Kong.

Outer Island Neighborhoods

The more I visit Hong Kong, the more I need to get away from the touristy places and the malls and find the true spirit of China. Or at least of Hong Kong. Often this means a day trip to an island. However, I don't mean a day trip to the new airport!

The great thing about the outer islands—all technically part of the New Territories—is that they make fabulous little side trips. Since being on the water is so much a part of the Hong Kong experience, being able to take local ferries and *kaidos* (flat barges used as ferries) will add to the pleasures of your visit. Shopping, eating, and simply wandering these islands can make a perfect day trip; some hightail it to Lantau, especially for the beaches. I prefer to wander the little village streets on other islands and poke into the shops.

In addition to the islands below, **Lantau** is the airport island; soon to be the Disneyland island too.

LAMMA

Lamma doesn't have any shops that I've noticed, but there are a few vendors here and there to add to the colorful scene. They sell things like waxed parasols, plastic back-scratchers, and straw hats, but, hey, isn't that what you came here to buy anyway?

There are two main towns on Lamma, but the place you want to be is Sok Kwu Wan, with its view of the harbor (and the cement factory) and its stretch of outdoor cafes (everyone goes to Lamma to eat at one of the harbor-front dives where the food is fresh and the clientele is local). It's the second stop on the kaido from Aberdeen; there's direct service from Central.

CHEUNG CHAU

Don't go to Cheung Chau in May because of the famous Bun Festival (it's way too crowded). Do go when no one else wants to go, so you have the full glory of the place all to yourself. Take the ferry from Central.

This island has banned cars, so all you can do is walk the garden paths. There are temples, shops (lots of porcelain shops), and restaurants. There's also a market along the Praya (beach front) in Cheung Chau Village.

Chapter Six

. . . .

SHENZEN & MACAU

Although Hong Kong can keep you happily busy for weeks, a day or so out of town may give you a glimpse at the New China and widen your horizons enormously. You may also need to buy an extra suitcase for your widened horizons.

WELCOME TO SHENZEN

My friends in Hong Kong have been offering to take me to Shenzen for years and years; always it got postponed— obviously not a high priority to me. But when the *Wall Street Journal* and *The New York Times* did articles about Shenzen and the hordes of shoppers who come for the fake designer goods . . . well, then I knew it was important, and proceeded to apply for a double-entry visa to China.

I have to say right up front that I do not condone fake merchandise and for the most part I think you get what you pay for—fake is fake and won't last; it usually looks cheap and tarnishes your reputation. That said, I have to admit that many of the fakes I saw in Shenzen were remarkably good looking, and the ones from Guangzhou were ever better. Given as gifts with the understanding that they are what they are, fakes will amuse you and your friends.

And the day trip to Shenzen is as good as a trip to the far side of the moon—and a whole lot closer. For those with a little adventure in their soul, I highly recommend the trip. Princesses need not apply.

A Short History of Shopping in Shenzen

Shenzen became a Special Economic Zone in 1980—this was China's way of encouraging capitalism before they admitted they had found a way to mix communism and capitalism. As a result of this action, a nothing little town about 1 hour by train from Hong Kong began to boom.

Young people flocked to Shenzen for new opportunities; major hotel chains opened fancy western-style hotels for all the businessmen; investors flushed the city with money and the highrises rose.

With all this money and enterprise came a whole lot of shakin'—and shopping. Local Chinese people began to earn and spend in the western fashion; Hong Kong locals began to come on day trips to benefit from the low prices and atmosphere of adventure.

Although now filled with tourist attractions in order to earn extra income for tourist stays, the main reason people come to Shenzen is to do business—and shop till they drop.

But then, dropping is not a big problem in Shenzen where you can be revived by a massage, a manicure, and a pedicure for $10.

Getting There

While there are bus tours to Shenzen, the most comfortable way of getting there is by train. One of my friends taught me a fabulous trick—you take a taxi to the last city on the Hong Kong side, then get on the train for one stop (a 15-minute ride). Coming back, when you're tired and not in a hurry to get to the bargains, you take the train straight through, a ride of nearly an hour. A taxi costs about $25; the train all the way costs about $10 each way.

Citybus Express Coach offers bus service to Shenzen, Guangzhou, and so on. There is transfer service at the border. In Hong Kong, call ☎ 852/2736-3888 for more information.

Because you are crossing the border into mainland China, it's not a breeze to walk right in and sit yourself down. You must get off the train in the New Territories, exit the SAR by going through formalities and then walk into another building and officially enter China. Then you walk across a bridge and are in China. Going back, it's the same thing.

Needless to say, at each stop in this ritual, there's paperwork, lines, and plenty of bureaucracy. Wear comfortable shoes. During holidays, the wait in line can be 3 or 4 hours. Under normal conditions, expect the passage to take from an hour to an hour and a half. The Luohu border station is one of the largest in China, with over 40 million people coming through each year. And they all want to go shopping.

If you didn't get a visa before arrival, you can get one at the border station. This will take additional time.

Getting into China

Shenzen is so modern that it has a new airport and plenty of flights to other Chinese cities. The carriers are all Chinese, of course. Once you have the right kind of visa, you can make hay while the sun shines and even fly to Shanghai directly from Shenzen.

Canton is now called **Guangzhou** and it, too, is a special economic zone with excellent shopping. although it is farther from Hong Kong than Shenzen and is a hard day trip, or requires an overnight.

You can take a fast train from Shenzen to Guangzhou—written as FT on a schedule. The fast train will take about 2 hours. You don't even want to know about the slow train. You can also take a train to other Chinese destinations.

Getting Around

Shenzen is quite large and has many neighborhoods. Even assuming you are on a day trip and are just interested in shopping, you may want to hail a taxi in order to get an overview or see downtown. The main shopping district is not in downtown but in a commercial strip right near the crossing. If this is all you are interested in, you can walk.

Note that streets and buildings are not usually marked in English. Once you get oriented, so to speak, you will not need to read much—but you may find that my inability to give you more specific addresses is annoying until you get used to the lay of the land.

The Lay of the Land

While Shenzen has a lot more sprawl to it than you are expecting, to oversimplify things you can consider the main districts as an upside down L, branching from the train station at the border, or even a T.

The main drag, an enormous, wide highway with low-slung modern commercial centers in long strips is called "Sino-British Street," which is technically in Shatoujiao, the part of town to the east of downtown—and leading right from the Shenzen river and the Customs House. This street may be written as "Jia Dian" or "Jian She" in pinyin. Most streets have a directional assignation after the name, i.e., Shennan Road East or Shennan Road Central; Renmin Road South or Renmin Road North.

This highway is lined with commercial centers and malls, some have individual shops inside, many just have stalls or tables or tiny selling areas. These malls have names like Shenzen Commercial Center or Lo Wu Commercial Center and are hard to tell apart. They all offer four or five floors of selling space, with floors joined by escalators. Lo Wu specializes in imitation goods.

Fakes & Freedom

It is illegal to import fake goods into Hong Kong; your goods are subject to seizure and you can even be arrested. However, if you did not know about the law and the goods are not for resale (meaning there are limited amounts, which you claim as souvenirs), you can get off the hook.

Likewise, when returning to the United States, while it is illegal to bring in frauds and fakes, if you only have one of each item (and are caught), you won't be harassed too much.

While Hong Kong is very tough on the sale of fakes (which is why they are so hard to find in Honkers), China has not been able to enforce the law effectively, and is now concentrating on fighting illegal CDs rather than illegal Fendi baguette bags. Word in Hong Kong is that the fakes are even better in Guangzhou than Shenzen.

Money Matters

You can pay in Hong Kong dollars in Shenzen, or sometimes in U.S. dollars or in Chinese yuan. A few places take credit cards, but not American Express. It's best to have cash, because you can bargain best.

There are some 15 offices of major international banks in Shenzen; there are scads of ATMs.

Bargaining

Some bargaining is expected. As everywhere, the more you buy, the better the prices.

Sleeping in Shenzen or Guangzhou

Shenzen is a great day trip, but if you want to spend the night or go on to Guangzhou (Canton), there are plenty of fancy hotels where you'll be quite comfortable, especially for an overnight or weekend trip away.

In Shenzen I simply rely on Shangri-La, partly because I always rely on Shangri-La when I travel in the Far East and partly because the hotel is at the end of the main shopping drag, so it's very convenient.

In Guangzhou, the White Swan is considered the best hotel in town.

SHANGRI-LA HOTEL SHENZEN
East side, railway station
Jianshe Road, Shenzen
Local phone: ☎ 755/233-0888; fax: 755/233-9878

WHITE SWAN HOTEL
1 Shamien Nanjie (on Shamien Island), Guangzhou
Local phone: ☎ 020/8818-6968; fax: 020/8186-1188

WELCOME TO MACAU

Oy! Macau! A pain, I get a pain right here in my heart when I see what's going on here. How I hate progress. And Joyce, my icon, my heroine, my favorite retailer in Hong Kong, what have you wrought? An Armani boutique in Macau . . . aiiiiiii!

I welcome you to Macau with enthusiasm but reserve, with pleasure and terror, pathos and delight. I had Macau in my hands, and I saw it slip between my fingers.

The new Macau is almost as new as the new Hong Kong, and the old, good, funky stuff is being destroyed as you read. Don't bury my heart at Wounded Knee—Macau will do. The Chinese took possession in 1999, but the building and modernization started way before. So did the crime.

In fact, there are people in Hong Kong who will tell you that Macau isn't what it used to be, meaning not the addition of highrises, but that crime in the recent past has been so frightening that day trips and weekends away have significantly dropped off. Let the visitor beware.

Macau is a simple day trip from Hong Kong, or a weekend away, or can even be a hub city for visits to Hong Kong and other Pearl River Delta cities in China. Macau has opened a brand-new spiffy airport, and you can actually come here as a main destination and spend a day in Hong Kong!

Macau Traditions

Macau has existed in the Hong Kong reality as a series of specific local traditional options:

- You go to Macau to have an affair with someone else's spouse.
- You go to Macau to gamble.
- You go to Macau to save money on antiques.

I'm up for at least one of those options (the antiques), and am beginning to understand the other possibilities. I'd rather spend my money on antiques than gambling. Local tradition says that gambling and affairs are conducted on weekends, so it's better for tourists to avoid Macau at these times whenever possible. Hong Kong crowds consider a trip to Macau in the same vein that westerners consider a weekend in the country. They go to Macau to slow down, to take it easy, to relax. The notion is surely that Macau operates at a different pace from Hong Kong.

But if you think you're headed to a sleepy little island, think twice. Macau is beginning to boom; the skyline may soon look like Hong Kong's. Besides, Macau is not an island. It's a peninsula.

A Short History of Macau

The Portuguese got permission to use Macau as their window on the East in 1556. Their black ships departed from the harbor here, laden with the exotic trade goods that made continental Europe stand up and take note of all things Chinese, Japanese, and Asian.

In 1974 there was a coup in Portugal; the new government decided to dump colonies and territories. They tried to give Macau to the Chinese. The Chinese balked. In 1985 they all finally got it together and agreed that Macau would become a special territory of China (a Special Administrative Region, like Hong Kong) for 50 years. The 50 years began on December 21,

1999 (about 2½ years after the Chinese began their special relationship with Hong Kong).

Meanwhile, Macau has always generated its cash flow through gambling—the antiques and forbidden treasures of China slipped quietly across the border when no one was looking. And the husbands and wives slipped between the sheets while everyone was looking, but pretended not to be.

Growth in Macau is staggering; each time I visit I am amazed. More changes are planned constantly. Landfills continue to close in the harbor; more hotels are opening, and of course, roads and railroads into China are being built as we speak.

Phoning Macau

If you're in Hong Kong and want to telephone or fax Macau for luncheon reservations, or whatever, the area code is 853. The area code for Hong Kong is 852; don't get confused.

The Lay of the Land

Macau is connected to Hong Kong via a 40-mile sea lane; it's actually 64 kilometers and a million miles away. Macau itself is not an island, but the tip of a peninsula that is directly attached to mainland China. You can walk to the gate. You cannot walk through the gate without a visa.

If you want to understand where Macau and Hong Kong are in relationship to each other, picture an upside-down letter V. Hong Kong is the lower right point; Macau the lower left. Where they come together, you are firmly in China. If you drew a straight line between Hong Kong and Macau and made a triangle, you'd be drawing across the South China Sea.

Aside from modern downtown Macau, there are two islands: Taipa (where the new airport is located) and Coloane, which has the beaches and several new hotels that are going for the resort business. There are bridges to the islands and bridges that loop back toward the main gate and China.

The ferry terminal is not near much of anything, except the Mandarin Oriental and a lot of landfill. It may be closer to something else by tomorrow at the rate they're building.

You'll need a bus or taxi to get into town (you can also take a pedicab, if you are game); you will also need a taxi to get to various destinations. You can easily explore the core downtown area by foot, but you'll need wheels to get to downtown from the ferry pier if you arrive from Hong Kong via the sea and Shun Tak, or the international airport.

Since we're talking about day tripping, let's forget about the airport for now.

Getting There

Your choices are simple: one if by air and two if by sea.

Assuming you're not flying to Macau via the new airport, or crossing the hills from China, you are most likely coming from Hong Kong and most likely from **Shun Tak Centre.** Shun Tak Centre is the name of the quite modern, two-tower ferry terminal located in the Western District of Hong Kong. The MTR stop is Sheung Wan, which is the end of the line. The building and terminals are located several floors up in the never-ending lobby space; ride several escalators and read a lot of signs. Don't be in a hurry the first time you do this.

Lots of high rollers think it's terribly neat to come to Macau via helicopter. Since I am terrified of the things in the first place, and since I have survived number 8 typhoon seas between Hong Kong and Macau and wouldn't like to have been in a chopper at such a time, I can only say *bonne chance,* and have fun. The fare for the chopper is just slightly over $100 on weekdays; it runs more frequently on weekends and holidays, as these are peak travel times. The journey takes 20 minutes. There are several flights a day; eight people fit into the craft. You get tickets at the ferry terminal in Shun Tak Centre (MTR: Sheung Wan); you may also book the ride via any tour organization.

I've always come and gone to Macau via jetfoil. Although there are numerous seafaring vehicles and locals know the

Macau

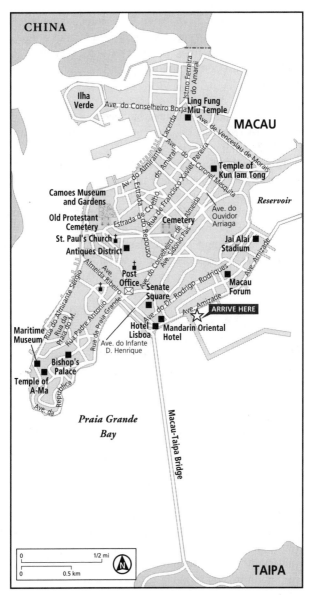

CHINA

Ilha Verde

Ave. do Conselheiro Borja

Ling Fung Miu Temple

Istmo Ferreira do Amaral

MACAU

Ave. de Venceslau de Morais

Temple of Kun Iam Tong

Ave. do Almirante

Av. do Amaral

Av. do Amaral

Lacerda

Ave. do Coelho

Estrada do Repouso

Rua de Francisco Xavier Coronel Mesquita

Rua de Francisco Xavier Pereira

Camoes Museum and Gardens

Old Protestant Cemetery

St. Paul's Church

Antiques District

Cemetery

Ave. do Ouvidor Arriaga

Reservoir

Ave. do Conselheira F. de Almeida

Ave. Vidónio Pais

Jai Alai Stadium

Ave. Amizade

Ave.

Almeida Ribeiro

Post Office

Senate Square

Ave. do Dr. Rodrigo Rodriques

Macau Forum

Ave. Amizade

Ave. Amizade

ARRIVE HERE

Rua do Almirante Sergio

Rua da Praia do M.

Rua Padre Antonio

Rua da Praia Grande

Hotel Lisboa

Mandarin Oriental Hotel

Maritime Museum

Bishop's Palace

Temple of A-Ma

Ave. do Infante D. Henrique

Ave. da República

Praia Grande Bay

Macau-Taipa Bridge

0   1/2 mi
0   0.5 km

N

TAIPA

difference between a catamaran, a hydrofoil, and a jetfoil, I can only tell you that speed is my choice here, and so I go via jetfoil. I've tried to sample the other methods, but fate was not with me. And I don't plan to be caught dead in a helicopter. So there.

- **Hydrofoils** take 75 minutes, but have an open deck.
- **Hover-ferries** take slightly more than an hour and depart via China Hong Kong City.
- **High-speed ferries** take almost 2 hours, so they are misnamed.
- **Jetcats** take 70 minutes and are similar to Jumbocats; they, too, depart China Hong Kong City.
- **Jetfoils** are made by Boeing, which will bring you great comfort when you begin to panic. The crossing takes an hour. They leave from Shun Tak; they have first-class service in an enclosed upper deck with a no-smoking area and beverage service. This is the most common way to get to Macau.

The fares do change, but the variables include the day of the week, the time of day (night costs more), and the class of service (first costs more). First-class service on a weekday is HK\$126 each way for an adult; departure tax adds another HK\$25 or so. Weekends and holidays are about 10% cheaper on the fare; they do not discount the departure tax. Sorry.

An off point: Weekends on jetfoils are cheaper than weekdays; weekends on hydrofoil (Jetcats) are more expensive than weekdays. Inscrutable all right.

While I don't normally travel first class on European trains, may I now explain to any and all that the ferry to Macau is not a European train. Economy seats are slightly less expensive. Don't do it. Trust me on this.

You may get your tickets up to 28 days in advance, which is nice, so you won't have too much pressure on you once you get to the Shun Tak Centre; this building is a tad confusing and may be all you can handle. **Ticketmate** outlets offer tickets; your hotel concierge can get them for you as well.

The price of your ticket includes exit taxes for both Hong Kong and Macau. You will have to fill in immigration papers on both sides of Hong Kong, and yes indeedy, you need that passport. Allow 20 minutes for the paperwork on the Hong Kong side; it's quicker leaving Macau, but you must still exit the country and go through security.

Once you have your tickets, report to the departure area (after clearing immigration, of course). There you'll see people milling around and standing in line, and you won't know what to do. Get in the line, dummy, you need a seat. Then you can mill around. There are kiosks selling food, drinks, magazines, and so on.

If you arrive early—as you may well do because you are so nervous about everything that has to get done—you may board an earlier boat. No matter what your ticket says, as long as they have seats, you can get on.

Arriving in Macau

You'll walk along a little gangway, enter a building, follow a walkway, and go through security. You are now in Portuguese Macau, and Portuguese is an official language. I spoke Portuguese to our taxi driver, who thought I was nuts. Better luck to you and yours.

Once you're outside the terminal, you'll note that there are bus stops and a hut for waiting for taxis. It's a little confusing, partly because so much construction is going on, and if you are used to the way it used to be, well, you'll find that everything is different.

Getting Around Macau

There are a million taxi drivers at the ferry pier who want to be your driver-cum-guide for a day and who will make a deal with you. It's harder to find a taxi to just take you someplace. **The Mandarin Oriental** is essentially across the street—it's a busy street and not easy to cross, but you can walk there if you don't have too much stuff. This is only one of many reasons to book the Mandarin Oriental for your stay.

If this is a day trip, you want to go to see *Igresia São Paolo* (see p. 138). I'll guide you beyond that in a few minutes. If you're staying a while, you obviously want to go to your hotel. Make sure you know where it is on a map. Just in case.

Money

Macau has its own unit of currency, called a *pataca*. It is traded on parity with the Hong Kong dollar, which is also accepted interchangeably, although change may be given in local coins.

Sleeping in Macau

THE MANDARIN ORIENTAL MACAU
Ave. da Amizade, Macau.

If you want to be part of it all, the Mandarin Oriental is the logical choice, if not the romantic one. This highrise poured-concrete hotel sits right at the harbor, a sneeze from the ferry terminal. It's got about 400 rooms, including several Mandarin suites; most rooms have views of the South China Sea. It's the only large five-star property in the heart of things, and it's where you want to be, if you need big and fancy.

Along with the usual Mandarin luxuries, the hotel has several famous restaurants, a beauty shop, business services, swimming pool, health club and spa, and all the features you come to expect from a Mandarin property. It is the best in town in terms of luxury, location, and complete facilities.

You can also get a promotional deal that will knock your socks off. Various weekday packages include Midweek Interlude and Macau Affair packages. (You know what I told you about Macau.) Packages include double accommodations, welcome fruit basket, jetfoil transfers, discounts on moke rental or tours, and either a dining credit or perhaps a meal on the property, depending on which promotion you luck into. Weekday promotional rates can be as low as $115!

Call ☎ 800/526-6566 for reservations in the United States, or Leading Hotels of the World, ☎ 800/223-6800. Local phone: ☎ 853/567-888; fax: 853/594-589.

WESTIN RESORT MACAU
Estrada de Hac Sá, Coloane, Macau.

Way out on the island of Coloane, which is developing as the beach-bunny resort area of Macau, this hotel is a destination unto itself and is marketed as such. There are plenty of places to eat and numerous recreational activities (including golf). There's a complimentary shuttle to and from the ferry pier, some 20 minutes away.

For reservations in the United States, ☎ 800/228-3000. Local phone: ☎ 853/871-111; fax: 853/871-122.

Shopping Macau

The main reason people come to Macau to shop is simple: The prices are lower than in Hong Kong, and the specialty is antiques and "antiques." Yes, friends, it is possible to see antiques being made in front of your very eyes. These copies are so good that you will never buy another antique again for fear that it just came out of the back room of a shop in Macau.

Quite frankly, if you could see what I have seen in Macau, you might be rattled to the very fiber of your being. The fakes were so good that I would never trust myself again. But I digress.

Every local from Hong Kong has his or her own private sources in Macau. Indeed, Macau is the kind of place where you need an inside track. There's no doubt that the really good stuff is hidden. And may be illegal.

The shopping must be considered fun shopping, unless you have brought with you a curator from a museum or Sotheby's and really know your faux from your foo. If you give it the light touch, you're going to have a ball.

The Best of Macau

Since addresses are hard to find in Macau, and many places don't even have their names clearly marked, the way for me to show you the best of central Macau's shopping area is to take you on my walking tour.

If you are visiting Macau on a day trip, take an early jet-foil from Hong Kong so that you hit St. Paul's by 10am. You can wander happily for a few hours, and then taxi to the Bela Vista for a 1pm lunch. Book the 4pm jetfoil back to Hong Kong.

- Tell your taxi *Igresia São Paolo* (St. Paul's Church), or be able to point to it on a map. A *Macau Mapa Turistica* is handed out free in Shun Tak Centre. This particular map has a picture of the church, but no number or letter beside it, so it may take you some time to study the map and learn the basics of the town. If you have other tourist materials with a picture of the facade of the church, you may show that to your driver as well.

- This church was built in the early 1600s; it burned to the ground in 1835, leaving only the facade, which is in more or less perfect condition. (It was recently restored.) Not only is this quite a sight to see, but it's the leading tourist haunt in town and signals the beginning of the shopping district. Exit the taxi at the church.

- The church is up a small hill, with two levels of stairs leading to a small square. If you go down both levels of the stairs, you will be at the major tourist-trap area and flea market heaven where dealers sell mostly new antiques . . . although you always hear stories of so-and-so, who just bought a valuable teapot at one of these stalls.

- Before you go lickety-split down all the stairs to the stalls, note that if you descend only one staircase, there is a small alley on the right side of the stairs—an alley that runs alongside the church. It's only a block long and ends just past the rear of the church, where you will find a tiny shrine.

- Not that it's well marked, but the name of this alley is **Rua da Ressureciao.** It's lined with tourist traps, porcelain shops, antiques stores, and even a ginseng parlor. You've got **Keng Ngai Antiquano** (no. 5) and **Tung Ngai Antiquarios E Artisanato** (no. 3), and so on. Don't expect any bargains in these shops and by all means know your stuff, but begin your shopping spree here. I must say that most of these stores are rather fetching: plates in the windows, red lanterns flapping in the breeze, maybe even a few carved dragons over the doorway. They all take credit cards, and you may have a ball here. I'm suspicious of any place that's too clean and too close to a major tourist haunt such as the church, but you could spend half a day happily enjoying these stores.

- After you've done this alley, work your way around the vendors at the main "square" in front of the church steps. Film, soft drinks, and souvenirs are sold here; there are no particular bargains. I once bought a very good Chairman Mao button here (ceramic), which has become valuable in the intervening years, but there isn't much that's particularly inexpensive. Be prepared to bargain; be prepared to walk away and possibly return later.

- Now then, normal people head into town by walking down the hill to the market and shopping as they go. The way to do this is to head down the Rua de São Paolo to the Rua da Palha, passing shops as you go. This walkway leads directly to the marketplace and the Senate Square, which is the heart of downtown. There are a few cute shops this way, and I have even bought from some of them.

- But I'm sending you down the hill the sneaky, nontouristy way. If you have the time, you may want to go down my way and then walk back up the main way, so you can see the whole hill (and shop it, of course). Also note that if you're with people and decide to split up, you can always meet back at the church stairway flea market area at an appointed time; this is a good place to get a taxi later on.

- The big red stall is not a toilet; it's a postal box. You can mail postcards here.
- If you do head down Rua de São Paolo, be sure to look in at **Cheong Weng Trading Co.** (no. 26A), which sells hand-crafted wooden items—toys for kids, nutcrackers, picture frames, and non-touristy items. Next door (no. 28) is **Chan Pou Maniek Hong,** where you can buy newly made porcelains for tourists. I bought a tea mug (with lid) for HK$10. I bought the exact same mug in a street market in Hong Kong for HK$18, so you can see where Macau got its reputation for lower prices.
- If you are standing with the church to your back, a major tourist trap called **Nam Kwong Arts & Crafts** should be to your right, with the red postal box in front of it. Shop here if you are so inclined, then make a hard right (under the laundry from the balcony above) onto a small unmarked street. (There are other branches of Nam Kwong in town.) Once you have turned right, look to the left for an alley called **Calcada do Amparo.** Enter here and begin to walk downhill.
- It's not going to be charming for a block or so, and you'll wonder where the hell you are and why all the tourists went the other direction. Trust me, you're headed into the back alleys of the furniture and antiques area, as you will soon discover. You are wearing good walking shoes, I hope. This is called the Tercena neighborhood, by the way.
- The reason I haven't given you shop names and addresses should now be abundantly clear—there's no way of really even knowing where you are when you walk down this hill. In about 2 blocks your alley will dead-end into a small street called **Rua Nossa Senhora do Amparo,** which may or may not be marked. These little alleys are called walkways or *travessas* and may have names (look for **Travessa do Fagao**).
- In terms of getting your bearings, you're now halfway to the main downtown square of Macau and on a small street that branches off from Rua do Mercadores, the main small

shopping street that connects the main big shopping street to the area above at the top of the hill.

- This will make sense when you're standing there in the street, or if you look at a map. But don't do a map too carefully because part of the fun of the whole experience is wandering around, getting lost and found, and feeling like what you have discovered is yours alone.

- When you are back on the Rua Nossa Senhora do Amparo, you'll find a ton of little dusty antiques shops (they start opening around 11am; don't come too early)—some have names and some don't. As a starting-off point, I send you to **Cheong Kei Curios Shop** (no. 10)—it's written **Ferros Velhos Cheong Kei** in black letters over the door on a big sign—this is the musty dusty antiques shop of your dreams and is in the core of what I call "Antiques Heaven." Segue onto **Rua das Estalagens,** which has more antiques shops as well as some fabric shops and jobbers.

- I wouldn't begin to vouch for the integrity of any of the shops here. I can only assure you that you'll have the time of your life.

- When you have finished shopping the antiques trade, work your way laterally across Rua das Estalagens to Rua do Mercadores. If you turn right, you will connect in a couple of short blocks to Avenida de Almeida Ribeiro, the main drag. I suggest instead that you keep moving laterally, so that you run smack into the market.

- The market is called **Mercado de São Domingos;** it has an outdoor fruit and veggie portion tucked into various alleys, an indoor livestock portion, and a dry goods portion. Wander through as much as you can take, and find yourself at the main fountain and a square (Senate Square), which instinct will tell you is the main square.

- If instinct isn't enough, look for the restored colonial buildings, the tourist office, a large neon sign featuring a picture of a cow (I call this the Ma-Cow sign; Ian does not think this is funny), the main big post office, the deliciously dilapidated Apollo Theatre, and the Leal Senado, which is the Senate building. You have arrived in the heart of town. After you've spotted the spotted cow (I love that cow, sorry), you'll note that there are several pedicabs—rickshaws drawn by bicycle—clustered here. You may book a ride or take a snapshot. It costs about $5 to ride to the waterfront.

- There are a few shops clustered here; some are liquor stores, which specialize in old port wines from Portugal, among others. After you poke around, and drop into the excellent tourist office (for postcards, no stamps), cross the street and head into the white stucco Leal Senado building just to stare—it is beautifully restored with tons of old Portuguese blue-and-white tiles, a garden, a library, and some magnificent colonial touches.

- The address of the tourist office (in case you need help, a place to meet up with the people you came with, or someone who speaks English and can teach you how to use the phone or write something for you in Chinese) is: 9 Largo do Senado.

- The huge post office across the square is where you buy stamps; but beware, there can be long lines.

- Once finished at the Leal Senado, walk to the right—this is toward the water if the Senate building is to your back. You are now on Avenida de Almeida Ribeiro, the main drag. Here you can stare at the contrasts in architecture and note the old and the new, the shabby and the luxe. The stores here include the gourmet market I was telling you about, a branch of the local Chinese arts and crafts store **Nam Kwong** (no. 1), and an antiques shop or two.

- You can walk just about to the waterfront here, certainly to the **Hotel Lisboa,** where you may want to gamble at the Atlantic City–looking casino or look at the Bank of China building across the street. Or taxi back to the ferry to head for home.

Chapter Seven

....

SHANGHAI

WELCOME TO SHANGHAI

....

Shanghai has been simmering in my blood for decades: tales of a world gone wrong from my Chinese Auntie An Lin, fox-trot scenes from 1930s movies about glamour and decadence, opium and sin; visions of tailors with giant scissors sluicing through bolts of silk spinning in my dreams.

Madonna may have made silk brocade dresses and capris a hot fashion statement a few years ago; Suzy Wong may have made the cheong sam (*quipo*) an international icon, but I always knew that when I got to Shanghai I would be the original material girl. I planned to scarf up bargains right and left. I planned to enjoy the funky flavor of mixed cultures and the wicked world. I was ready to do the cha-cha at the Peace Hotel: one-two cha-cha-cha; one-two, shop-shop-shop.

As it turned out, I had the good luck—or the bad luck— since this is China and everything is a matter of perspective— to be part of the enormous consumer changes in Shanghai. I'm not talking about the differences between 1965 and 1995, oh no! I saw, and felt, a city change beneath my sensible shoes in the span of a year and a half on the very cusp of the century and the 50th anniversary of Communist China.

The first time I visited Shanghai, she was not yet ready for prime time; many shopping sprees were downright disheartening. Shanghai had no soul; she was depressed and depressing. Yes, there was fancy architecture, and Dickson Poon had already brought big brands to China, and there were plenty of fancy hotels and restaurants. But the city was over-built; business was bad; she didn't come together and she just didn't click. All the magazine articles about the boom in Shanghai seemed a bad joke to me.

The New Shanghai that everyone was raving about did not dazzle me; she broke my heart—I saw skeletons of buildings turning to rust as bankrupt builders gave up on the over-building; I saw stores that sold glitter than no one bought; I saw people who did not know how to smile. I felt that either I had been duped by the press or the press had been duped by Shanghai. As recently as 1998, Shanghai was *not* one of my favorite cities.

When I returned a year and a half later, Shanghai had been transformed into Oz, a miracle that outshines Hong Kong. Toto, we're not in China anymore. I quickly discovered that the ruby slippers were not just made for bound feet.

If you want to know about the communist years, or even the years that led up to 2000, you must now go to history books. Shanghai has found itself, its heart, and even its soul. *Vive la différence* and welcome to Shanghai.

Nihau indeed, and welcome to Shanghai, a city that touches my soul and stirs in my heart; a city I wouldn't mind moving to. I welcome you to the new Shanghai, a communist plot to brainwash you into the delicious state of euphoria gleamed only from luxury hotels, fine restaurants, clean streets, and fabulous shopping. I am dreaming of my new letterhead. It says:

SUZY GERSHMAN

BOSTON   PARIS   SHANGHAI

If you're not quite as eager to move here as I am, don't fret. No matter how many times you've already been here, Shanghai is a changed city. If you've never been, you are in for the shock of your life. Pack an empty suitcase. Bring cash.

A SHORT HISTORY OF SHOPPING IN SHANGHAI

Shanghai has always been different from the rest of China. A divided city with foreign concessions—parts of town won as booty in war and "owned" by the French, the English, the Americans, who developed them in western ways and created the largest trade market and financial center of the Far East on the shores of the Huangpu River. In fact, Shanghai was a city with her own constitution—almost a country within a country.

She was acquired—like Hong Kong—during the first of the Opium Wars, and at first divided into three concessions; later two merged to create an international zone. The concessions ran east-west across the span of the city, so that each one had direct access to the river, the lifeblood not only of Shanghai, but the main port for commerce to the interior and therefore the wealth of China.

As China moved into the 20th century, she was not in great shape—there were peasant rebellions, attempts to overthrow the Manchus, warlords who fought for territory—many of these wars and revolutions coincided with the labor unrest in Europe and Russia and culminated with World War I. The Manchus fell in 1911; there was no organized formal government from then until 1932, when the Japanese took over. In 1949, right after World War II, the Communist Party took Shanghai and all of China, sending refugees to Hong Kong, Taiwan, or immigration points.

For decades, workers from all over China had flocked to Shanghai to work in her factories, her shipping, and the textile world. The mix of population was 50% Chinese and 50% foreign. During the chaos that followed World War II, Shanghai, which was not under Chinese law or rule, temporarily became a haven for this population.

After the communist took Shanghai, they shut down the window on the world. If China turned gray, Shanghai became invisible.

A shopper's stroll through Shanghai, even in the 1990s, could prove that the reason that communism doesn't work is simple: Communists know nothing about shopping.

While that may be obvious to you from a theoretical position, it hits you right in the jet lag if you begin your shopping spree in Shanghai at its most famous store—Number One Department Store. Thankfully Number One does not represent the New Shanghai and will now only tickle your funny bone. Underneath, there's not much to laugh about—without the creation of the New Shanghai, Communist Shanghai was not a shopping paradise, nor were the people here entitled to double happiness.

The city remained a shadow in film noir until the People's Republic of China (PRC) decided to counter the glory and glitter of Hong Kong with its own version of Shangri-La. Most of the current leadership of China comes from Shanghai; they knew the city's geographic and historic position were unique. They were also dreading the Hong Kong takeover and the problems that it could bring; they needed a very big stick with which to tame Hong Kong. Shanghai became the stick.

Now Shanghai shimmers in the luster of marble highrise towers, oddly shaped skyscrapers by internationally famous architects, and a whole new sister city called Pudong, located just across the river. There's even a version of the Star Ferry that shuttles across the river, connecting Pudong to the Bund, the most famous waterfront promenade in China. Cruise ships carrying decadent western tourists with deep pockets arrive right in town and planeloads of business travelers and sightseers are now visiting China's number-two city.

A new airport and a western-style arrival await all. The city's main shopping street, which I first walked as the only westerner for miles, is now paved over in marble and filled with people—all races—day and night. In fact, night is the most fun.

The architecture, which for many years left the city disjointed with thousands of building cranes poking into the air, has mostly been completed so that visitors stare in awe at the creativity of the architects and the money lavished on the projects that make Shanghai so stunning that it hardly even feels like China. Architecture in Shanghai almost rivals Hong Kong and will probably eclipse it.

As the leading port city of China, Shanghai is indeed the window on the new world. You can shop for everything from designer clothing from all the global big names to street fashions, big brand fakes, and Chinese antiques. The best buys are furniture and antiques. While there is some overlap with availability of merchandise in Beijing; there is little overlap with Hong Kong.

And they have ATMs.

HONG KONG VERSUS SHANGHAI

Since locals delight in drawing parallels between Shanghai and Hong Kong, partly because of the series of internationally famous and dramatic-looking buildings that dot each venue, it's also easy to describe the geography of the two cities in the same manner. (See below.)

The comparisons are, of course deeper, and often related to politics. Many people find Shanghai is cleaner than Hong Kong; the streets better cared for. Shanghai is cheaper than Hong Kong and has a lower cost of living. Shanghai is the favored smile on the face of the PRC; Hong Kong is not out of favor but it is a special region—a mole on the face of China.

Shanghai is getting more and more luxury hotels, but is nowhere near the glam spot that is Hong Kong. There are far more language problems in Shanghai, understandable since it was not a British Colony for 100 years. There are some excellent restaurants, but not nearly as many as in Hong Kong. In short, Hong Kong has arrived and can never be replaced. But Shanghai is on its way and is so impressive you will be knocked right off your sampan.

Electronically Yours: Shanghai

- Shanghai Tourist Information & Service Center:
  www.tourinfo.sh.cn
- Shanghai on the Internet:
  www.sh.com
- The Shanghai Guide:
  www.shanghaiguide.com

GETTING THERE

Please note that there is a section on air carriers and tours in chapter 2 and in chapter 5. The information here is more city specific.

You can get to Shanghai via transatlantic or transpacific corridors; it just depends on your own methods for dealing with this long-haul flight, jet lag, and where you actually live. As explained previously, I regularly do this trip on SwissAir via Zurich, but most European carriers have nonstop flights to Shanghai from their hub cities.

This includes: British Air and Virgin—both from London; KLM from Amsterdam; Lufthansa from Frankfurt; Austrian Airlines from Vienna (Austrian Airlines also does a code share with SwissAir). Air France has begun a new promotional project to make Paris an international hub city and is featuring its Shanghai service as well as its overnight service to Hong Kong, with more than 100 connections through France. Note that Air France also partners with Delta.

Flying transpacific, you can fly into China via connections in Japan, Korea, Canada, or even nonstop from a few U.S. cities. Because Shanghai is so "hot," there will be more and more gateways opening, and more and more routes that avoid layovers or connections in Narita.

For specific and immediate flight information for world travel from Shanghai, look in the English-language newspaper the

Shanghai Star, which posts the complete schedule list for 17 carriers that fly from either or both of the Shanghai airports.

Round-the-World Tricks

As you already know, about the least expensive way to get to the Far East is with an around-the-world ticket; these especially offer value in business and first class. (See p. 68.) Around-the-world tickets differ with the carriers and the connections, but one trick is to buy a ticket that offers Hong Kong and then add on a round-trip to Shanghai on your own. Dragonair flies nonstop from Hong Kong to Shanghai; the flights lasts about 2½ hours. Dragonair is a division of Cathay Pacific. Note that the official designation for Dragonair is KA; Cathay Pacific is CX.

If you use a web site and a consolidator to get a round-the-world fare, you can end up paying about $1,200 for a ticket that takes you New York–Paris-Delhi-Malaysia–Hong Kong. For approximately another $300 you can add on round-trip airfare to Shanghai.

ARRIVING

Arrival by Air

Shanghai has two international airports. On your outbound flight, if you are departing from Shanghai by plane, it would be a good idea to look at the ticket and know which airport you need to get to.

If you arrive in Shanghai from an international destination (this includes Hong Kong), you will be asked to fill in a landing card and will, of course, already have a visa. There may also be a health card to fill in. The lines move quickly and you will be through immigration in no time, waiting at carousels for your luggage. Luggage carts are readily available.

Now then, about that visa. Don't panic. Under some circumstances you don't need a visa—if you are in the country less than 48 hours with a group (possibly on a cruise) or you hold a passport from one of the 17 countries that have recently relaxed their relationships with China so that visas are no longer needed. For more on how to obtain a visa as an American citizen, see p. 12.

Since I've only been to one of the two airports, I can report on Hongqiao (say "Hong-Chow") International Airport—it's not plush, but it has clean western-style toilets (you must tip the attendant or pay to use them). Once you're through the formalities you either make your way outside to the taxi stand or go to the hotel desk where your hotel rep is waiting to assign you to a car that you (or your travel agent) preordered.

All this works pretty much the same as in Hong Kong; however, the hotel limo transfer costs $35 to $55—far, far less than Hong Kong. Also note that Hongqiao is in the middle of a very chic expat residential area (this is possibly where you will want to live when you move here) and it is also the furniture district, so you will be returning to this area with a moving van, one way or the other.

The Pudong Airport is one of the new architectural highlights of town, with art objects hanging front the ceiling and lots of glass and light, reflecting the latest trend in airports that resemble museums. Among its numerous architectural feats is a series of support systems that allow the floor space to be free of pillars.

Again, after clearing formalities, you go to the hotel desk for your transfer—or outside for a taxi. Driving time from the Pudong International Airport to the Pudong Shangri-La is about 40 minutes, so figure 50 minutes to a hotel on the Bund and 1 hour to a hotel on the other side of the Bund, deeper into Shanghai. A metro line is being completed (Line 2) for those who prefer to connect to either airport by train. A hotel car for the transfer costs about $55; a normal taxi is less than $20.

A short story about the Pudong International Airport will tell you everything you need to know about the New China. This airport was scheduled to be completed in the year 2005. It opened in 2000, a full 5 years ahead of schedule. When the

Chinese government wants something done, it gets done. As you travel, especially through Shanghai and Beijing, you will see more examples of this.

The Pudong International Airport has been designed to handle up to 20 million passengers per year. In its first year it is expected to handle 8 million, with 10 million flying into Hongqiao.

Arrival by Cruise Ship

Shanghai's importance to China has always been her port; today many cruise ships come to port here at a wide number of berths on the Huangpu River; the fancier ships usually get berths near the Bund or right near the Pudong Shangri-La Hotel. Shanghai has long been a port of enormous popularity; in the days of the World Tour it was the must stop that everyone dreamed about.

There is boat service from both Hong Kong and Japan; it takes days. Since this is not a touristic journey, I am waiting for Paul Theroux to try it first.

Train Travel

I seem to be a creature of habit and therefore depart from Shanghai by train, but have never arrived by train. Whether you are coming or going, your biggest problem will be your luggage.

Porters are not plentiful and are normally banned from taking you directly to the platform or from actually loading the luggage onto the train for you. This can be overcome with some pleading and some tea money, but may cause heartburn until you are safely arrived or departed. Those who can manage their own luggage were not born to shop.

If you are departing from Shanghai by train, there is no need to rush to the station "to be safe," as you will not be allowed out of the lounge area until 30 minutes before the train leaves. The lounge area is quite nice (for China), but you are a long way from done with the journey—you may have to go up an escalator, down a hall, down sets of stairs, and walk a mile along

Riding the Not-So-Red Rooster

I first chose to travel between Shanghai and Beijing by train for only one reason: fear of flying. After that, I thought this could be one of those once-in-a-lifetime adventures, a tale I would dine out on for years to come; a way of satisfying my yen to ride the Trans Siberian Express.

Naturally I raced off to the bookstore and bought Paul Theroux's *Riding the Red Rooster,* his book about traveling all over China by train. Although my route was mentioned, it was given only a few pages and was not at all informative. I did learn that the food on Chinese trains wasn't up to Michelin star standards and that everyone travels with his or her own tin cup—two good tips.

Although I already had a tin travel cup, I found a larger one at Old Navy for $5 and splurged on it. I also packed Cup-o-Soup, Slim Jims, and some Ramen Noodle soups.

Now then, here comes an important confession. The first time I traveled to China I went on an official trip as a journalist, and many details were taken care of by CITS, the official travel agency run by the government. They got my train ticket, and they actually put me onto the train. I mention this because the second time I did it, nothing was the same.

The first trip was more fun, of course, because I was alone and frightened. If there was a western-style toilet, I never found it and cursed myself for wearing trousers. As the 14-hour trip progressed, the stand-up toilet did not hold up well, nor did the hems of my trousers.

The train I was booked on, which I thought was the only train each day, left Shanghai at 4pm and arrived in Beijing at 8am the next day. I was booked in soft-seat class and frankly, it was no different from any European train—except for the stand-up toilet.

On the second trip, I discovered that the train has both western- and eastern-style toilets, and that there are two trains per day (or there are at some times of the season). This time we departed Shanghai at 8pm and arrived in Beijing at 10am. This made sleeping easier, but meant we lost more time in Beijing on arrival.

First time out, everyone in my car was friendly and tried to communicate—the 3-year-old girl was the icebreaker since she could not stop staring at me and was fascinated by the food treats I gave her. I let her listen to Johnny Hallyday on my Walkman and taught her to wave her arms in the air and shout, "Johnny, Johnny." I am certain I have corrupted one more Chinese person. At least, I hope so.

The Chinese family claimed the free meal provided on the train was not good; the Danish woman and I both had brought supplies. The Chinese family shared their three pears with us. The little girl slept in my bunk with me, which was adorable and fine with me since I didn't sleep too well despite my flask of Benedictine and a Xanax. I think this was because everyone ate dinner at 6pm and settled in to sleep by 7pm with lights out.

Second trip, I slept great. We had enough food for the Chinese Army with us, but we never even ate our picnics on the later train—Peter went to the dining car (who knew there was a dining car???) and Maggie and I had pigged out at Planet Hollywood right before we left Shanghai. The bathroom was fine on the second trip, and we did not need the sheets we had bought at the market or any of the extras we had bought for rough travel. In fact, the trip was so simple that there was nothing to write about. For Beijing arrival details, see chapter 8.

the platform before you find your car. Should your nerves be strung anything like mine, or your luggage pile be half the size of mine, you will find this a rather tense adventure.

On my last visit, I was traveling with two friends, so we bought all four bunks in the "soft seat" cabin. This allowed us a lower bunk for the luggage, since the luggage was far too cumbersome to get it to an upper berth. In fact, I didn't think I could get into the upper berth—but somehow I managed.

I've read articles about two women traveling together who bought all four bunks just for privacy. This is completely legal, but the Chinese think it's hilarious that anyone could be so decadent.

The first time I made this trip, I was alone and had only one bunk. I had enormous mountains of luggage (what else is new), which was taken from me and stored and for which I paid an overweight charge. Or that's what they said it was. My roommates were a Danish woman of about 70 and a Chinese family with their 3-year-old daughter. For more on train travel, see the box on p. 152.

LAY OF THE LAND

If you're familiar with Hong Kong, you'll quickly adjust to my Hong Kong parallels here. Pudong is Kowloon—the boomtown on the far side of the river. Today it has an impressive array of towers and tenants (including the luxury Shangri-La Pudong)—they all have a breathtaking view of the Bund. In 10 years, Pudong could rival "downtown." (Maybe in 10 minutes.)

Before we go any further, a quick Chinese lesson will serve you well. The word *pu* means river, as in the name of the river in Shanghai, the Huangpu. *Dong* is west and *xi* is east—so the two sides of the river are called "Pudong" and "Pu Xi" (say "Pooh She"). You'd be surprised just how useful this is going to be; obviously these directionals are also used on streets.

If you've never been to Hong Kong, don't fret. You can still find your way around simply by realizing that a river separates the two parts of town and that the giant Pearl Tower is in Pudong, on the far side of the river.

The rest of Shanghai lies on the eastern bank of the river (you remember that lesson: Pu Xi) , laid out in neighborhoods somewhat according to where the foreign concessions once stood (the French concession is still the nicest) and where the original Chinese city was placed (the walls are long gone).

Despite its size, there actually is a system, especially to the streets in "downtown"—north-south streets are named after

Chinese provinces; the east-west streets are named after Chinese cities. Of course you need to learn your provinces from your elbow in order to use this information.

The main shopping drag, known as the number-one shopping street in China, is Nanjing Road, which stretches from the river for some 6 miles. It's not a casual stroll through the park; it is an east-west street (therefore named after a city). The worthiness of the stores is very uneven.

The Bund is perhaps the most famous part of Shanghai and is one of the world's most distinctive identifying parcels of geography. It was the main drag along the river where the western business and financial firms had their offices in the old days; it more or less faces the river and is perpendicular to Nanjing Road. Ships loaded and unloaded their booty in this harbor; the Bund was once filled with banks and warehouses. western-style colonial buildings were created during the colonial years—many of been torn down with total disregard to history, although the Bund itself is more or less intact. The Bund skyline forms one of the visual landmarks Shanghai is famous for. (You can get it imprinted on a mouse pad—great souvenir!)

Shopper's note: There's not much shopping on the Bund.

The city's other iconic landmark lies directly across the river from the Bund in Pudong—the space station–esque Pearl TV Tower, ugly from an architectural standpoint (think of a pregnant Eiffel Tower with the Seattle Space Needle as blood relative), but quite beautiful when you are lost, see no street signs in English, and can only find your way by using the Pearl Tower as a homing beacon. At night, or when cloud coverage is low, it also has an eerie otherworldliness to it that can give satisfaction.

While Pudong is still being built up, "downtown" Shanghai is an enormous sprawl of modern architecture and multi-lane freeways, cantilevered above the streets and laid with flower beds and neon lights that glow in fashion colors at night. There is rumor that more and more colonial buildings are being torn down; there is an effort, mostly by westerners, to preserve

Shanghai Orientation

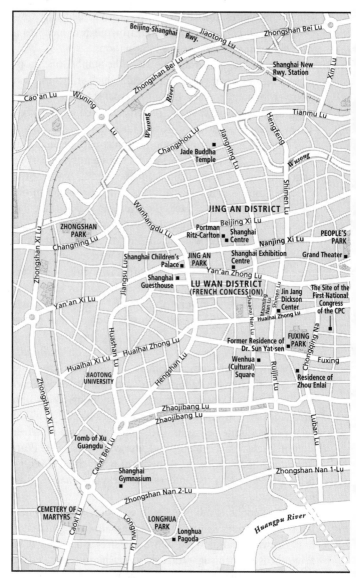

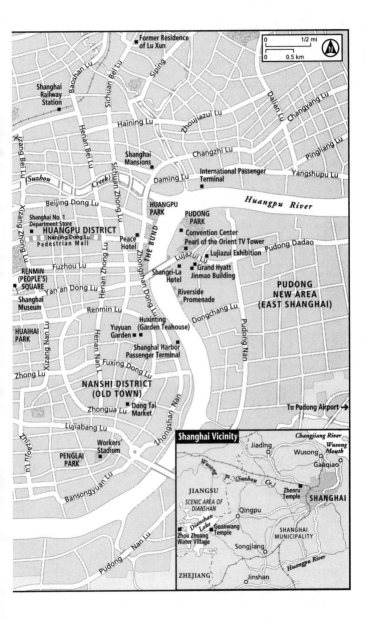

Former Residence of Lu Xun

Shanghai Railway Station

Baoshan Lu
Sichuan Bei Lu
Siping
Dalian Lu
Changyang Lu

Henan Bei Lu
Haining Lu
Zhoujiazui Lu
Pingliang Lu

Xizang Bei Lu
(Suzhou
Creek)
Sichuan Zhong Lu
Changzhi Lu
Yangshupu Lu

Shanghai Mansions
Daming Lu
International Passenger Terminal

Beijing Dong Lu
Huangpu River

Shanghai No. 1 Department Store
HUANGPU PARK

Xizang Zhong Lu
HUANGPU DISTRICT
Nanjing Dong Lu Pedestrian Mall
Peace Hotel
PUDONG PARK
Convention Center
Pearl of the Orient TV Tower
Lujiazui Exhibition
Pudong Dadao

Henan Zhong Lu
Fuzhou Lu
Lujiazui Lu

RENMIN (PEOPLE'S) SQUARE
Shangri-La Hotel
Grand Hyatt
Jinmao Building

Yan'an Dong Lu
Zhongshan Dong Lu
THE BUND

Shanghai Museum
Renmin Lu
Riverside Promenade
Dongchang Lu

PUDONG NEW AREA (EAST SHANGHAI)

HUAIHAI PARK
Huxinting (Garden Teahouse)
Yuyuan Garden

Henan Nan Lu
Xizang Nan Lu

Zhong Lu
Shanghai Harbor Passenger Terminal
Pudong Nan

Fuxing Dong Lu
Zhongshan Nan

NANSHI DISTRICT (OLD TOWN)

Zhonghua Lu
Dong Tai Market
To Pudong Airport →

Lujiabang Lu

Zhizhaoju Lu
Workers' Stadium

PENGLAI PARK
Bansongyuan Lu

Pudong Nan Lu

Shanghai Vicinity

Changjiang River
Jiading
Wusong
Wusong Mouth
Wusong R. (Suzhou Cr.)
Gaoqiao

JIANGSU
SCENIC AREA OF DIANSHAN
Zhenru Temple
SHANGHAI

Qingpu
Dianshan Lake
Guanwang Temple
Zhou Zhuang Water Village
SHANGHAI MUNICIPALITY

Songjiang
Huangpu River

ZHEJIANG
Jinshan

1/2 mi
0.5 km

those that haven't yet fallen. As much as we mourn the loss of the old buildings, the new ones are so dramatic that you can only be awestruck. The Chinese did not tear down paradise to put up a parking lot.

The Old City is located in a nugget not far from the Bund, but hidden behind new buildings; it is either disappearing quickly or being rebuilt with Disney-esque proportions. Those who expect to find the Shanghai of 1930s-style movies will be sorely disappointed. Those who understand that the crane is the symbol of everlasting life will delight in knowing that 40% of the entire world's building cranes brought you today's booming Shanghai. More than 1,000 highrises were built between 1990 and now.

GETTING AROUND

Traffic is not nearly as bad as in Beijing or Bangkok, but it takes a while to get to outer reaches of the city, like the Number One Silk Printing & Dyeing Factory, which one of my official CIT guides took me to when I expressed interest in a silk factory (most are closed). Taxis are inexpensive, but distances even on the Shanghai side of the river can be significant. You will find that whatever area your hotel is located in will seem like home to you and everything else will seem far away. Still, taxis are cheap.

Walking

Shanghai is a very, very large city, so you will enjoy walking hunks of it, but you cannot walk everywhere. If you think you'll just stroll Nanjing Road and get a sense of the city, think twice: It's 6 miles long.

The first time I was in Shanghai, all signs were in Chinese characters only. Now signs in the tourist parts of town are in Chinese and pinyin. Some even have their old and new names or the old and new numbering system marked. Love those progressive Communists. If you are the kind of visitor who likes to walk from your hotel and have your hotel be somewhere, pick it with care. I'm not sure if this counts as a walk, but the adventurous might want to try the pedestrian tunnel under the Huangpu River, which connects the Bund to the Pearl TV Tower.

Taxis

Taxis are plentiful, especially at hotels. There are new, clean cars and fleets that can be identified by their livery colors, such as metallic soft green or Bordeaux lacquer. Drivers don't expect to be tipped; surprise them! Teach them capitalism! You can hail a taxi in the street, just as in New York. If this method doesn't work for you, find one at a hotel

Private Cars

Most luxury hotels do a good business in private cars; this pays if you have lots of stops to make or need to be very dressed up for appointments. Fees are based on the type of car you want and the length of time needed; there are also flat fees for airport transfers and for day trips. Half day in a Lexus is about $125; a car to Suzhou for the day (and back) is about $300.

Taxis are so inexpensive and easy to find that I have never felt the need for a car and driver. On the day that I wanted to do a lot of antiques and furniture shops that were spaced around town, I simply made a deal with a taxi driver. Waiting time was $1.50 an hour. If you do not have a native speaker (a guide) with you, have everything written in Chinese on a piece of paper by your hotel concierge before you depart. You can make a multistop deal with mime and a fistful of yuan—I've done it.

Metro

There is a great metro system, but it's not very extensive (see map on p.161). Still, it's fun to do and stops are announced in English. It's often called a subway in Shanghai in U.S. fashion, but the official names are Metro Line 1 and Metro Line 2.

Important Announcement

No matter where you go or how you get around town, make sure you have one of the hotel cards on you that says "My hotel is . . . " These are given out by the zillion. Most hotels also have short charts of addresses in English and Chinese and often also in pinyin, so you can point to where you want to go and show it to the driver. Take it from me, no Chinese person will understand your pinyin pronunciation on anything more extravagant than hello: *nihau* ("knee-how").

Note that all station names are written in pinyin and that Renmin Square Station is also called "People's Square Station." Line No. 2 serves Pudong and actually connects the two international airports; in so doing it connects the two sides of the city. Line No. 3 is in the works and is almost finished.

Trams

Yes, those are trams in the old-timey postcards you bought or in photos you saw when you did research before the trip. Yes, there was once a shopper's tram that ran from the Bund to Jing An Temple, about a mile past the Portman Ritz-Carlton. The trams were dismantled in the 1960s and 1970s. However, there is a shopper's miniature train-tram that travels the paved marble pedestrian mall on Nanjing Road; it costs $1.

Boats

The ferry runs from the Shangri-La on the Pudong side to the Bund on the Shanghai side. You only pay for service one way; the other way is free. The toll is about 85¢. After I buy and renovate the Peace Hotel, I will buy the ferry and turn it into a cutie-pie version of the Star Ferry and make a killing. I will be the Ferry Queen in the *Wall Street Journal*, I just know it. There are also boat tours on the river and excursions through some of the canals, but most of the canals are gone now.

Shanghai Metro

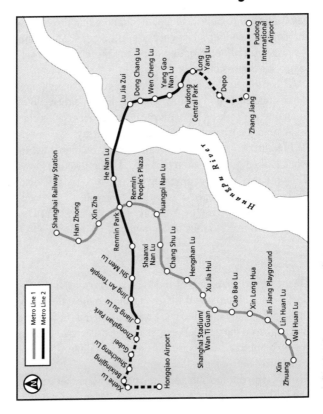

About Addresses & Guidebooks

A guidebook to China is a good starting point, but no guide-book—especially a printed and bound one from a bookstore, library, or on-line book seller—can keep up with the changes in China, especially in Shanghai. Buildings and stores are being torn down in Shanghai so fast that they can disappear overnight. Add to that the long lead time in rewriting and publishing books and there's no telling how accurate any guide will be.

Even "new" editions of the previous years' guides may not have accurate information. A store that I know is long gone has continued to appear in a name-brand guide through two revisions—the guide's fact-checkers still don't seem to know it's missing. I'm not claiming to be any more accurate— I'm saying it's impossible to be 100%.

This problem doesn't exist just with guides; many (maybe most) concierges don't know what's going on either. No one in Shanghai can keep up with the changes. Hearsay is cheap and cannot be trusted—even concierge hearsay.

I fell in love with an American expat in Shanghai because when I asked her a question she said, "I honestly don't know." The only way to know anything for sure is to try it yourself. And even then, it might not work out for you.

Let me tell you my Fu Yu story. And you can soon know what Fu Yu really stands for in my book . . . hmmm.

THE FU YU STORY

On my first trip to Shanghai and to Beijing, I arranged my travel days because I had heard there was an incredible flea market in Shanghai only on Sundays, known as the Fu Yu Market. I had to give up the flea market in Beijing in order to be in Shanghai on a Sunday, but I was told this was a fabulous market.

My wonderful guide, Su, from CITS took me in hand that Sunday, with our first intended stop being this market, although she told me she thought it was closed. We agreed we would check it out anyway. We got there—no market. Su talked to several vendors and then reported to me that the market had closed because a subway station was being built there. It would reopen in a year. Su took me to other nearby places, and we had a great time—so it goes in the world of Born to Shop.

One and a half years later, I returned to Shanghai for a weekend in order to catch this flea market. In the intervening years I have read reports that it has reopened, closed, never closed and still exists, moved, disappeared, and so on. I have five reputable guidebooks with five different stories. I have three concierges from three top hotels with different stories. I have official government tourist people with yet other stories.

I decide that I must go and see for myself. I go with my Chinese guide, Albert, and we are dropped exactly where Su had taken me on the previous visit. No market. No new subway station either. Albert makes inquiries and we wander into alleys and speak to possibly five or six different people. No stories match. We walk on Fu Yu Road and soon find a fabulously funky little antiques store, the dirty kind that is crammed with God only knows what. I tell Albert that since the competition always knows what the competition is doing, to ask here about the flea market. Lo mein and behold, we are sent a block away to one of the best flea markets I have ever been to in my life.

Now here's where we get inscrutable. Did the market always exist and Su took me to the wrong place? Had the market changed venue? Did any guidebook writer ever walk the streets to investigate the whole thing? And most important, in Shanghai, does anyone know anything?

Thankfully, none of these questions can be answered. Let the shopper beware.

SLEEPING IN SHANGHAI

The new Shanghai has had enough business travelers visiting over the last decade to assure that there are plenty of suitable hotels with western-style amenities. Just about every big, four-star chain already has a hotel here, maybe more than one. Luxury hotels—drop-dead, Hong Kong–style, serious luxury hotels— are still coming on board. Because Shanghai is so spread out, where you stay can be important to how you feel about Shanghai; on the other hand, where you stay doesn't matter that much because little in Shanghai is within walking distance.

Do note that hotels always have promotional rates, depending on their occupancy rate or the phases of the moon. Ask. When the Shangri-La opened in Pudong, rooms began at $138 each! Ritz Carlton had a summer special for Visa cardholders with their Shanghai hotel at $130 per night on the weekend and $150 per room on a weekday.

Be sure to ask about upgrades and don't grab the least expensive room. Because of business travel to the better hotels, they all have executive floors with many perks that often make paying more money a bargain.

Shanghai Center (Pu Xi)

PORTMAN RITZ CARLTON
Shanghai Centre, 1376 Nanjing Xi Lu

As we go to press, the Portman is the fanciest and possibly best hotel in Shanghai and one of the best located hotels in town—although location is pretty meaningless in this town. But there are places you can walk to from the hotel, and there's a cluster of other luxury and business hotels in the neighborhood, so you are well situated. Also the hotel has plenty of different kinds of restaurants either within the hotel itself, attached to the hotel in the Shanghai Centre (an office and apartment tower), or across the street at the exhibition center.

Furthermore, there are executive floors with lounge privileges that really make a difference in the comfort of your stay and more than pay for the price of the upgrade with the perks you gain. There is also an excellent business center (I had no trouble getting onto America Online) and what many expats say is the best hairdresser in town.

The hotel is large, and I think the concierge staff downstairs is overworked, which is one reason why it pays to upgrade to a room that has use of the lounge with its private concierge service—which is fabulous. In fact, I tried to hire away one of their executives from this floor. The lounge is also a nice place to meet people and chat about Chinese travels and share experiences.

For me, the Portman is the center of the world in Shanghai. That could be because it has a branch of Watson's, the pharmacist, attached to the hotel, and an American coffee bar, but for those who don't want to suffer the slings and arrows of the real world—this is a great choice.

U.S. reservations: ☎ 800/241-3333. Local phone: ☎ 86-21/6279-8888; fax: 86-21/6279-8887; on-line: www.portman.com; rates normally are about $250 per room, but there are specials.

GARDEN HOTEL
58 Maoming Nan Lu

In terms of shopping, this hotel has a super location—right in the heart of the shopping district in the part of town that was once the French Concession. The building itself is built into or over the former French Club and is stunning. The hotel actually opens onto a garden, hence the name. You feel quite elegant, civilized, and contented to arrive here.

There are also a lot of hip restaurants nearby; the hotel itself has several stores within the lobby; there's a metro stop within walking distance. The hotel's library is so gorgeous you might want to go there just to stare; they have a shipping desk right inside the library (ground floor), so that you can send home your excess baggage or extra purchases. That's the good news.

The bad news is that several of the people I interviewed who have stayed here—westerners all—found the hotel, which is owned and managed by the Okura Group—to be too Japanese in management style. Still, the hotel is a member of Leading Hotels of the World.

U.S. reservations: ☎ 800/223-6800. Local phone: ☎ 86-21/6415-1111; fax: 86-21/6415-8866; on-line: www.gardenhotelshanghai.com; rooms begin around $250.

FOUR SEASONS HOTEL SHANGHAI
Civic Centre, Weihai/Shimen Roads

As we go to press, the Four Seasons is far from open (scheduled for late 2001), but you all know I am a big fan of Four Seasons properties and the French general manager of this hotel is a friend of mine, so you might want to consider seeing if it's open and available for your stay. The site is close to the Portman and JC Mandarin.

PEACE HOTEL
20 Nanjing Dong Lu

Someday someone is going to ask me what I want for my birthday and I will request ownership of the Peace Hotel, right on the Bund and the most famous hotel in Shanghai. Ownership of the hotel, however, will not be enough; then I want about $50 million to renovate the hotel. After that, it should pretty much be perfect.

As it is now, it's worth visiting for the historical perspective; the stories about spending an evening listening to the jazz band are romantic gibberish (I did it; yawn) and even though the location is divine—right there on the Bund—you aren't that near too much, except The Friendship Store, which isn't a good Friendship Store. But you wanted to know, so I told you.

U.S. reservations through Utell: ☎ 800/207-6900. Local phone: ☎ 86-21/6321-6888; fax: 86-21/6329-0300; on-line: www.shanghaipeacehotel.com. Rates begin at $125 for a single; executive superior suites have a rack rate of $350.

SHANGHAI MANSIONS
20 Bei Suzhou Lu

OK, we all know that I like luxury hotels, and for me, even the Peace Hotel is not fancy enough. However, if you want the real thing, and want to save some money as well, this hotel was once called "Broadway Mansions" and was *the* place to live when it opened in 1933. It's a bit north for my taste, and not quite funny enough, but rooms are about $100 a night and you can't beat the nostalgia. Local phone: ☎ 86-21/6324-6260; fax: 86-21/6306-5147.

Sleeping in Pudong

PUDONG SHANGRI-LA
33 Fu Cheng Lu, Pudong

The first time I visited Shanghai, I stayed in Pudong at the Pudong Shangri-La, which was inspirational. First of all, as an old China hand—or old Hong Kong hand—I can appreciate what Pudong will become. As a regular at the Regent in Hong Kong, I can appreciate the location of the Shangri-La in terms of the ferry and the view. As a newcomer to the city, I loved being where all the action is, of understanding that it was Deng Xiaoping himself who looked across the river, pointed to the rice paddies of Pudong, and said "Build." I have seen the future of Shanghai and I have been part of it, and that feels great.

As a guest, I also have to say that the Shangri-La works. It is not the fanciest hotel in town, or even in Pudong. But it's one of the best hotels in Shanghai because it works and because it well serves both the tourist and the businessperson. It also has some fabulous gift shops. And let me tell you about those brown noodles (see p. 168).

If you haven't read the part of this guide about hotels throughout China, then I will quickly remind you that Shangri-La has some unusual extras that can be included in your rate and are very much worth getting—such as airport transfers and many other amenities. The ferry is located at the base of the property; there is also a brand-new metro stop—or you can take a taxi, which will give you a quick ride through the tunnel. And did I mention the brown noodles?

U.S. reservations: ☎ 800/942-5050. Local phone: ☎ 86-21/6882-8888; fax: 86-21/6882-6688; on-line: www.Shangri-La; promotional rates for under $200 per room, but Bund view rooms have a rack rate of about $300 per night.

GRAND HYATT PUDONG
JinMao Tower, 2 Century Blvd., Pudong

I haven't stayed at this hotel, nor do I intend to, as I am desperately afraid of heights and this hotel's lobby doesn't even begin until the 30-some floor of one of the tallest buildings in the world, the 88-story JinMao Tower (the restaurant, Cloud Nine, is on the 87th floor). Still, I know you want to know all about the hotel and I do suggest that if you don't stay here, you at least come for a cup of coffee or a meal or a jaw-dropping stare. The hotel has some shopping in the lobby, but is actually more in the business district of Pudong and is closer to the tunnel than the ferry or metro station.

U.S. reservations: Local phone: ☎ 86-21/5049-1234; fax: 86-21/5049-1111; on-line: www.hyatt.com.

DINING IN SHANGHAI

Shanghai is famous for its own style of cuisine (rather bland, actually), its crabs (in season in November), and its panfried brown noodles. I have not only become addicted to these noodles, but have now tasted them in enough places around town that I know where the best ones are. They are also one of those things that you can hardly ever go wrong with—while they do taste different at each place that makes them, they are still just noodles—good for kids, picky eaters, and those who are travel weary. Brown noodles are made on the street; I don't normally eat street food when I travel, but sometimes you may be tempted by the noodles.

If you are the kind of person who is not only terrified of street food, but afraid of unknown eateries, remember that all the hotels have a selection of dining rooms, coffee shops, and in some cases, brand-name franchises, like Hard Rock. There are McDonald's restaurants with pictures so you can point to what you want.

For those who are looking for more than a few McNuggets, there are dining possibilities in all neighborhoods, in all price ranges, and in all styles of cooking, from the variety of Chinese provinces to international cuisines. A friend told me you can't get a great pizza in Shanghai, but you can easily eat western or Chinese food.

M ON THE BUND
No. 5 The Bund/ 20 Guangdong Rd., Floor F

If you are only picking one dress-up western-style restaurant, I beg you to include this—to me, it offers one of the most romantic and exciting evenings in the world. What makes it so fabulous is the combination of great food and location, location, location. M on the Bund is indeed on the Bund and you can go out on the terrace with your cocktails or coffee and feel as if you are actually flying over the Bund. You see the lights of the Bund and Pudong, the buildings on both shores, the river, and the boats. It's magic.

About the address. The building is on the Bund, but the door is on Guangdong Rd. Take the elevator to the 7th floor. There's a sign with directions.

The food is New Age cosmopolitan style, created by Australian chef Michelle Garnaut, who first came to fame in Hong Kong where she has another restaurant (M at the Fringe). Her ingredients come from Australia, Europe, and the United States; all fresh veggies are from the local organic market. The restaurant is open 7 days a week for lunch and dinner and serves brunch on weekends. Reservations are essential, especially for dinner: ☎ 86-21/6350-9988; fax: 86-21/6322-0099.

PARK 97
2 Gaolan Rd., Fuxing Park

Our schedule got a bit shifted around, so we never got here—but it is the talk of the expat world and considered one of the best restaurants in town. Reservations: ☎ 86-21/6318-0785.

1221
1221 Yan An Rd. West

This is another of the eateries famously "in" with the expats; you can tell who knows what by how they pronounce the name. Say Twelve TwentyOne in order to pass. Reservations: ☎ 86-21/6213-6585.

GAP SALON
127 Maoming Nan Lu

This is a bit of a shaggy dinner story, but it's very, very important. I chose the Gap for dinner because I wanted to test it for readers; I had read a lot about it, knew it was at one time the "in" restaurant with Shanghai yuppies, and so I asked the concierge at the executive level to make me a reservation. I also knew that the Gap had several branches and that I wanted the main Gap, often called Gap Salon—its official name. I thought it was in the French concession, but I wasn't going to swear to that. (It is.)

In getting the directions written by the downstairs concierge, he said the Gap was 2 blocks away and we could walk. I thought I was a genius for choosing a nearby restaurant. To make a long story short, he sent us to a branch of the Gap and not the right one. We eventually got it straightened out (since we were meeting people), but it was frightening. We had address problems on almost all our adventures in Shanghai, so make sure you meet your friends at the right places.

You want the main Gap because it's the one with the crowd and the scene. It is noisy, people dine early (make a 6:30pm reservation), and the food is not what you go there for—although I thought the food was perfectly good. Also the style of Chinese cooking is the local Shanghai cuisine. The idea is to merge western decor with home-style Shanghai cooking and sit back and laugh.

You go for the decor and the crowd; some people go for the band. I had four guests for dinner (we were five) and we each had a drink and more than we could eat, and the entire bill, with an extra cash tip, was about $100. I thought that was rather incredible. The restaurant is across the street from The Garden Hotel. Reservations: ☎ 86-21/6433-9028.

GARDEN VIEW RESTAURANT
Shangri-La Pudong

This is the hotel's casual restaurant where you can eat three meals a day, either from a huge buffet or from the menu. They have the brown noodles that I adore here; I make dinner here a first night in town stop—it's also a fun orientation place for first timers, as you can cross the river by ferry and then look back at the Bund and see the view at night. The Shangri-La also has fancy restaurants, but they don't serve brown noodles. Reservations are not needed. Before or after dinner you can walk around Pudong; you can get there by metro, taxi, pedestrian tunnel, or ferry.

Snack & Shop

If you're out sightseeing or shopping and want to know where to go for a simple lunch or quick bite, here's a few of my regular choices. I also eat at McDonald's.

SHANGHAI MUSEUM CAFÉ
Shanghai Museum

This modern cafe has a limited menu but serves western-style snacks and is clean and convenient.

LAKE PAVILION TEAHOUSE
Yuyuan Gardens

When you go to Yuyuan Gardens and see the teahouse in the center, you will invariably want to dine there. I can't tell you the whole deal because we went on a Sunday and were trying to beat crowds, so we were there at an odd hour and most everything was odd. However, here goes: The type of tea you are served and the price are related to your location in the teahouse. Upstairs is better. There are set tea menus, but you get no cucumber sandwiches, just tiny eggs and bits of local nibbles. While we saw people eating dim sum downstairs, they seem to have brought in their dim sum from a nearby take-out place. We were not amused.

OLD CHINA HAND READING ROOM
27 Shaoxing Rd.

This will probably require a taxi ride and will not fall into your lap, so to speak, but is really fun and possibly worth doing, especially for the ladies as the place is right out of a novel or a movie—a true English tearoom with chinoiserie edges for those wearing whalebone and toting stiff upper lips. Britannia rules the waves.

SHOPPING SHANGHAI

Stores in Shanghai are an incredible jumble of styles; few were what I was expecting. I mean, I did not come to Shanghai to buy Lalique! Or Ralph Lauren, for that matter—real or fake.

The stores in Shanghai suffered very much from the attitudes of the past decades, with Number One Department Store as the lowest of the low in terms of style and class—although it did gross $250 million last year and many Chinese people come from the provinces to see this shopping wonder.

The Friendship Store is better than Number One, but not nearly as good as the Friendship Store in Beijing and not anything to consider a must-do. The stores in and around Yu Yuan Gardens are fabulous and should probably be the highlight of your first day in town.

Beyond that, most retail is western to some degree—from Watson's (the pharmacist-cum-variety-store brand from Hong Kong) to the Dickson Centre, the five-star luxury mall owned by Dickson Poon, who owns Harvey Nicks in London. In case you were wondering what you were doing here, you came for the flea markets, antiques shops, and junk.

Shanghai Shopping Style

Shanghai may have lost its bid to get the next Disneyland (Hong Kong got it), but this just reinforces the understanding that there is nothing Mickey Mouse about Shanghai style. Architecture is the most prominent issue—each new building has tried to outdo the neighbors and create a memorable landmark at the same time.

Aside from the Bund and the Pearl Tower, few of the buildings are actually memorable to anyone except students. Yet the Stock Exchange—located in Pudong—looks like a cross between the Arc de Triomphe and the Arc de la Défense. The nearby Jin Mao Tower is one of the tallest buildings in the world.

While there was romance in 1930s Shanghai style, few in Shanghai have looked backward for inspiration. Only David Tang has used this format in his Shanghai Tang stores and his China Clubs (private clubs). Designers seem rather to look to Hong Kong and then figure out what they can do to top it.

With these glamorous surroundings, and the influx of business travelers and tourists to Shanghai, the local population has style fever. It's just within the last 5 years that Chinese workers were granted a 2-day weekend, so shopping has become a national pastime. Locals, of course, want western style. Tailors Lane, where tailors used to sit outside at their sewing machines and where locals came to have their clothes made, has all but disappeared. Shanghai's best tailors fled to Hong Kong in the 1940s.

Duties on foreign-made merchandise are incredibly high, so that name-brand goods have never offered any value when bought in China. Although all brands are now available, even Hong Kong is cheaper on such items. In Shanghai, the luxury brands are either in hotels or in the Jin Jang Dickson Centre, Dickson Poon's beautiful (and empty) American-style mall near Huai Hai Road.

Because these duties are so high, there are more interesting marketing schemes in China. Many European brands go into business with a local partner and bring their design and manufacturing expertise into a local factory; Chiara Boni is an example of this type of business—this well-known Italian men's suit maker (a division of GFT, which used to make the Armani clothes) now has stores in Beijing, Shanghai, and Tianjin.

Once there were 400 department stores in Shanghai. Now there are more than 50 major department stores, so you can understand why there could be a glut of retail space. Another totally different concept being used in many of the big buildings that were department stores: Some have become what in European retail lingo is a *galerie*—a store where departments are leased to manufacturers and wholesalers directly. This means that just about each counter or selling area you go to within any one department store has its own cashier because it's a separate business. Yoahan in Pudong is an example that locals are talking about. (Trust me, it's not worth your time—maybe because one of the owners is Shanghai Number One Department Store!) Several other stores—these in Pu Xi—have also converted to this form of selling. Oy, as my grandmother used to say in French.

We all know that China is expected to be the world's largest consumer market. With Shanghai considered a more fashion motivated city than Beijing, most brands have tried to break into the Shanghai market, although the brands already established in both cities often say they have better customers in Beijing, and that Shanghai shoppers are too picky.

Shanghai shoppers are getting more and more local brands to choose from; some come from Hong Kong, others are truly local. It's all not without a political edge—Giordano, a huge Hong Kong chain (sort of like the Gap), was closed by the government after the company head in Hong Kong insulted Chinese premier Li Peng.

There have also been many retail ventures that simply guessed wrong. One of the most famous families in American retail was among the first to open in China, selling American casual sportswear that they expected to be devoured. Instead, the clothes were ignored (too casual) and the firm eventually closed.

Yet with a huge population of 20- to 30-year-olds, and all of them on a shopping frenzy each weekend, you know that Shanghai style will find its own place on the global front.

Money Matters

There is a complete section on money in chapter 2. Note, however, that money changing via ATM is much easier in Shanghai than in Beijing—at least, as we go to press. There are ATMs everywhere in Shanghai and it is very easy to get cash from a machine, just like at "home." You'll pay a higher exchange rate if you change money at a hotel, but you do need to know what kind of a fee your bank charges for use of an ATM. Fees can be $5 per hit.

Bargaining

Bargaining in Shanghai is done in markets, not fixed-price stores. My experiences bargaining at Dong Tai Antiques Market on my second day of the first trip to Shanghai marked a changing point in my shopping adventures in China. I became confident and ruthless. I started to bargain fiercely, paying about 25% of the asking price in each negotiation—I may have a Big Nose (Chinese call westerners Big Noses), but I am also an old China hand. As Confucius undoubtedly once said: The true price of any item offered to a foreigner is a fraction of the asking price, not half price.

I had a dreadful experience with a colleague who overpaid dearly for an item while I was looking on. Stupidly, I rushed in and told her what the right price was, some $15 less than what she had agreed to pay. She was upset and, of course, the vendor was furious. She did not bargain any further, overpaid for the item, and did not speak to me for several days. As Confucius also says: Some people like to pay their price, good or bad.

Tipping Tips

As you all remember from Communism 101, which we were taught in high school near our bomb shelters, communists do not believe in tipping. As I've already made clear at the beginning of this chapter, they didn't used to believe too much in shopping either, but that's another discussion.

At one point tipping was almost illegal; then it was merely frowned on. Now it seems to be frowned on by westerners and expats who don't want you to ruin the system, since they have been getting by without tipping.

Alas, the best way to teach capitalism is to prove that it works; that is not done with a lecture—but with a tip. I tip everyone, and I tip big time for work well done (which is hard to find) or total generosity of the spirit—not hard to find.

The only time I had trouble with tipping (in my own mind) was with the concierge desk at one of my luxury hotels. Without naming names or pointing fingers, this desk not only screwed up everything they did, but cost me a lot of time and a fair amount of money because of their errors. I didn't want to tip; I wanted to report them to their general manager.

In the end I gave a very modest tip and wrote this note, "I understand how overworked the concierge desk is and appreciate your help." Then I signed my name and room number. I expect to return to that hotel some day and I don't want any thousand-year-old eggs in my bed. On the other hand, I would have tipped generously if they had gotten anything right.

You can indeed tip in U.S. dollars.

Hotel Gift Shops

After shopping in Shanghai's markets, I found it hard to adjust to regular retail. And then again, regular retail in China is not regular by western standards. As a result, most of the best shops for western shoppers with good taste are in hotels.

The gift shop at the Pudong Shangri-La turned out to have wonderful products from a local firm called **Creachine**—most of the items were tabletop designs made from raw silk, including napkin rings made of silk knots; $16 for four. I didn't buy them because I was used to street prices, but later regretted it when I found the same items for $25 at the gift shop in the Portman Ritz Carlton.

The Portman Ritz Carlton has several gift shops, one on the ground floor and two upstairs on the mezzanine. I was shocked (don't ask me why) when I heard a solo man say to the salesclerk, "Just pick out what you think my wife wants."

Museum Shopping

There are many museums in town and all of them have gift shops. The Shanghai Art Museum is a new, modern structure, part of the pride of the new Shanghai, and a must-do even for those who hate museums. Although the style of the building from the outside is a bit fanciful for my taste (it looks like a basketball stadium with a lid), it is a stunning museum inside, with four floors of exhibits including a gallery devoted to ethnic clothes made in silk.

The museum is a sanctuary of art and style, with a large gift shop patterned after the shops in the Metropolitan Museum of Art in New York and the Victoria and Albert in London. Aside from the two-part gift shop on the street floor, each floor of the museum itself has a gift kiosk selling goods related to that floor's exhibition.

Although prices on silks were a little higher than in regular stores, the atmosphere was so seductive that I simply didn't care. I bought everything from silk ties ($55) to silk dévoré scarves (cut velvet) for $50 each. I would have saved 10% if I had the Visa promotional coupon provided by many hotels.

The dévoré silk scarves became my barometer of good taste in town. While I found silk yard goods to be of no exceptional value in Shanghai, these silk cut-velvet scarves were selling in the United States for four times their Chinese price. I began to hunt them out in every shop I went to and found a variable in price, silk, and sophistication.

There is a totally separate antiques store inside the museum, upstairs.

Postcard Shopping

Don't laugh, but Shanghai has about the best postcards in the world—this due mostly to the city's reputation made in the 1930s and the large number of available photos of cigarette girls, and so on, from that time period. You'll find reproductions of these photos, or old photos of buildings and streets sold in sets of cards. Naturally there are modern cards, too, but the hand-tinted old-fashioned kind are fabulous

Guided Shopping

I spent my first day of my first visit to Shanghai on my own; it was not pretty. It was a different Shanghai than the one that exists now, and it totally defeated me. I found myself attracted to the lobby of the Sofitel Hotel just to hear people speak French so I could listen to a language I knew how to cope with. I was also sick and tired of people staring at me. At the end of the first day I limped back to my hotel for a massage, aromatherapy, and room service. I think I considered hiding under the bed.

Although my very first day in Shanghai had been frightening, my second day out, with JJ, a professional guide, was sensational. I realized I had been a fool to attempt to explore Shanghai on my own without a guide. JJ was a guide hired for me by CITS (Xu Jing Jing; ☎ 86-21/6289-3010). I suspect he probably specializes in working with journalists. His English was perfect and he was very, very slick.

For day three of that trip, I asked the hotel to get me a guide. I don't know where or how they found her. She met me the next day at 9am in the lobby, saying her English name was Ginger. Hmmm, as in "jar," I thought. I asked Ginger to call me Suzy, but the concierge said this was bad manners, so we settled on Mrs. Suzy, and off we went.

I was to pay Ginger 300 yuan ($37.50) for the half day, 400 yuan ($50) for the full day, and all her expenses. Although the prices were fair enough, I hesitated while still in the hotel lobby—I had a bad feeling about Ginger. She was wearing white shoes after Labor Day, and I didn't think she'd understand my needs. But to refuse her services would cause her to lose face and perhaps trigger an international incident.

With a native speaker on hand, I wanted another view of the real China, so I whipped out my guidebook to Shanghai and insisted that Ginger take me to a store written up as the best silk store in Shanghai.

Ginger struggled with my directions, studying the page of the book as if it were the Holy Grail. First she tried to tell me that she knew other stores that were better than this one. Then she told me that we could, if I insisted, wander around this part of the French Concession, a nice area for shopping (which was also on my to-do list for the day).

The more she opposed me, the more unreasonable I became. Suddenly, I wanted that special store, then and now, and no other. Like most of my guides, Ginger had the habit of trying to tell me what to do and how to do it. I finally screamed at her, "I'm the one who's giving the orders and we will do what I say; and from now on call me Mr. Suzy!"

Only when we got into the taxi did I realize the serious nature of the problem, the fact Ginger could not explain: The name of the store in the guidebook was in English, with no Chinese translation, and there was no way in the world to communicate, even in Chinese, with the taxi driver. We just had to go to the street address. On the way there, I fumed while Ginger whipped a mobile phone from her handbag and began to telephone the number listed in the guidebook. I realized that Napoléon was right. When China wakes, the world will tremble.

We might have reached détente had Ginger been able to get a cell; alas, she couldn't, and we struggled on—arriving at the street address to find the most basic of local ironies: The store had been torn down and was now a construction site, like most of Shanghai. Indeed, most guidebooks are useless, as all of Shanghai is being torn down and rebuilt at a frightening pace. I fired Ginger an hour later. I don't care how much face she lost; she got 400 yuan.

On my last day in town, a guide from CITS teamed me up with Su, the best guide I had in my week in Shanghai (Su Hui Juan; home phone: ☎ 86-21/6404-1477). We returned to the area around Yu Yuan to more cutie-pie lanes of stores and more bargains. She explained that a flea market I had stayed in town to enjoy (Fuyou Lu) was temporarily closed because of construction, but took me to another, a market for toys and paper goods, that was sensational. At the end of the day, she put me—and my five pieces of luggage plus three carry-on shopping bags—on the train at Shanghai Number One Train Station, settled me into my "soft seat" compartment, and pumped my hand as a good-bye gesture. When I hugged her, she seemed shocked at my western decadence and lack of good manners.

On my next trip to Shanghai I did not use a local guide. I was traveling with Albert, my translator, and felt very much that I knew my way around—partly due to my having used guides, and partly because I had spent a lot of time out on the streets wandering around and getting lost. All the horrors and humiliations of the first research trip paid off on the second trip, which was heaven. There is nothing that can replace coming back to a place or a situation you already know.

Every now and then you can luck into a taxi driver who is really plugged in and can work as a guide, although again, you will most likely have a language barrier. Albert was invaluable in this situation, and possibly the single best store I went to in Shanghai was one that a taxi driver took me to: Hu & Hu (see below).

Shanghai Shopping Neighborhoods

PUDONG

Pudong isn't really a neighborhood; it's a city. It's a different city from Shanghai, a bit like Minneapolis and St. Paul or Buda and Pest. It is written "Putong" in the old fashion, so don't get confused. To further confuse you, the business district of Pudong is called Lujiazui; this is where the Stock Exchange is located as well as many main offices of the big banks, the Jin Mao Tower, the Shangri-La Hotel and, of course, the Pearl TV Tower. In short, tourists call it Pudong and some business guys call it Lujiazui, but they are the same destination.

Pudong has changed so much that there's not much I can tell you that will remain accurate. Whether you choose to stay in this part of town or not, you must, must, must come over here and get a view of the Bund at night. And don't forget the brown noodles.

THE BUND

Located on a bend in the Huangpu River, the Bund is enhanced by the river's natural curve. It is called *Waitan* in Chinese (go figure). There are buildings on one side of the waterfront, then comes the part for cars (some call this a street) and then, right alongside the quayside, there's a large boardwalk so that one can promenade along the river. Yes, there are guys with cameras who will take your picture for a small fee; it's just like Atlantic City!

NANJING ROAD

Perhaps the most famous street in Shanghai after the Bund, Nanjing Road (see map on p. 183) is also the city's main shopping drag, despite its enormous length (over 6 miles). Remembering our little directions lesson in Chinese will help you to find your way on Nanjing Road (and also Huai Hai Road, below)—that means there's Nanjing Dong (east) and Nanjing Xi (west). The infamous Number One Department Store is on Nanjing Dong; the Portman Ritz Carlton is on Nanjing Xi. Aren't you glad you speak Chinese now? To find the most famous part of Nanjing Road, go to Number One Department Store, especially at night where one mile of shopping street has been paved with marble and is a pedestrian mall.

HUAI HAI ROAD

This can also be written as Weihai Road. If you care about your sanity, avoid Huai Hai Road (formerly avenue Joffre to the French) on a Saturday. This is the main drag of the fashionable French Concession and the high street for local fashionistas, aged 20 to 30. Most of the stores are either big-name global brands or Chinese inspirations, copies of European trends selling at low Chinese prices, with equally low quality.

In the crowd, I began to experience strange psychological reactions to my immediate world—I sank into Chinese philosophy, suddenly feeling very small, very insignificant, very stupid for having thought I mattered. Instead, I realized that the huge buildings around me would last and become China's new legacy. I was a mere speck of unimportant sand in the wind, as I was pushed along the crowded streets and shoved into masses of moving humanity that certainly never heard of Miss Manners. Like I said, avoid Saturday shopping here.

Otherwise this street is fun, even if you do a drive-by in a taxi first, to find the parts you want to explore on foot. Not only is the street very long, but it also has an east and west portion.

JING AN

This is the part of town where the Portman, the Four Seasons, the JC Mandarin, and many, many other hotels—and a few shopping malls—are located. It includes West Nanjing Road and the Shanghai Exhibition Centre, which is across the street from the Portman. The Shanghai Hotel and the Shanghai Hilton are at the far end of this district.

OLD CITY

This is the name most often given to the oldest part of town, which was the Chinese city in the days of the foreign concessions. It was walled years and years and years ago. It is also called Nanshi in Chinese. It is quickly being torn down and replaced with the New China, but there are some quaint winding roads and alleys and tin shanties left to fill you with glee. There are also the Yuyuan Gardens, a Disney-meets-Chinatown parcel of land with buildings and gardens, a tea house, a temple, a market, and antiques stores. It's the city's number-one tourist attraction—and for good reason. The Dong Tai Antiques Market is also in this district, but not in walking distance from Yuyuan.

DOWNTOWN

This makes me nuts because it's all downtown, but many hotels advertise that they are downtown and most consider the district surrounding Renmin Park (also called People's Park) to be "downtown." This is not walking distance from The

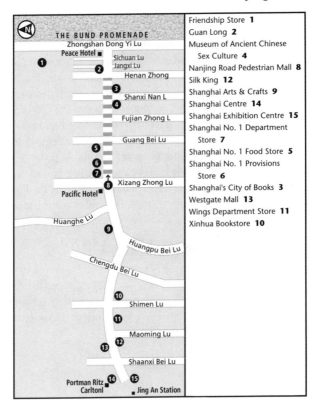

Portman or the Bund. Hmmm, well, actually I have walked from there to the Bund, but it was a big walk.

HONGQIAO

This is the area that includes the Hongqiao International Airport, many furniture and antiques warehouses, a mall or two, and huge gated communities where wealthy expats live in either modern highrises or townhouses organized as village developments.

HONGKOU

The famed Jewish Ghetto where the "Shanghai Jews" lived during World War II. Jews who tried to escape Hitler but could not get out of Germany through continental Europe or go to the United States, Canada, or South America often fled to the east, traveling across Russia or Mongolia. From 1937 to 1939, 30,000 Eastern European Jews arrived in Shanghai, because here they needed no passports, no visas, and no documentation of any kind. Those ending up in Shanghai hoped to find ships to the Americas, but all they found was a ghetto. The Jewish community has dwindled (and now meets at the Portman Ritz Carlton). But the ghetto is a popular visiting spot.

SHANGHAI RESOURCES A TO Z

Note: If you don't find listings here that are mentioned in other guidebooks, there could be a good reason. Maybe they are gone, or maybe I didn't think them worth your time, or maybe something else inscrutable happened. . . .

Antiques

KANG YUAN GU WAN
43 Liu He Rd.

Is this the real name of the shop? Beats me. I took that off the line that isn't the one that says the manager's name. But you won't need a name to find the store because your feet and eyes will lead you here while you are exploring the Dong Tai market. This is one of the freestanding shops, and it is a wonderful shop, filled with pottery and ceramics and ivory and wood and pipes and papers and the most magnificent blue-and-white ceramic water cooler I have ever seen in my life. It cost only about $75, but was almost 3 feet tall, and I couldn't quite fit it in my handbag, or luggage, so I left it behind—but my heavens, what a day.

MINGYUAN ANTIQUES STORE
Cui Xiu Hall at Big Rockery, Shanghai Yu, Yuyuan Garden

Maggie the Marvel found this one. She said it was expensive but that they had excellent stuff. Note that it is inside the actual garden part of Yuyuan gardens, so requires a paid admission to the gardens.

SHANGHAI MUSEUM ANTIQUES SHOP
Shanghai Museum, 16 Henan Lu

Not to be confused with the downstairs gift shop, this is an upstairs shop, maybe 800 square feet, of expensive but government-approved antiques. Everything is behind glass and it looks much like an exhibition; lots of little teapots. Lots of high prices.

Antiques Markets

If you only go to Shanghai for one shopping experience, it has to be for buying antiques, both smalls and furniture. The antiques markets are heaven and the prices are so low you will want to weep. There are also good markets in Beijing, so don't blow your wad.

DONG TAI MARKET
Dong Tai Lu

This is one of my favorite addresses in Shanghai where, on my first visit, I could have bought out all of the stalls. My second visit, I had already found a new Number One Favorite, so I wasn't as madly head over heels in love with this venue—but I still enjoyed it and rank it as the number-two best antiques market.

An outdoorsy type of thing, the market is not particularly large and just takes place on two streets which cross each other to form a T. The vendors sell from wagons or little trailers; there are a few shops. Not too many dealers speak English, but I didn't find that to be a problem. In fact, when I did the shopping with my guide JJ, I felt I was being treated as a rich western lady with guide and money in tow. When I did it alone, and we wrote numbers on papers and swapped calculators and laughed and traded, I was much more comfortable.

HOABAO BUILDING
Yuyuan Garden

Yuyuan Garden is the number-one most visited tourist spot in Shanghai, with good reason. It's also the perfect place for the first day in town. And the antiques shopping is downright fabulous. Of course, many people don't even know there is an antiques mart within the "village" of the gardens, or another one a few blocks away.

Yuyuan looks like EPCOT Center in its old-fashioned Chinese perfection, fully qualifying for as many rolls of film as you can afford. You almost hate to leave its splendor by going downstairs into the neon-lit basement of the Haobao Building where the antiques market (250 stalls) is held daily. But baby, it's fun down here.

The prices on antique silk garments and other items here are so low that I became giddy on my first trip; I touched and tried everything from padded silk jackets in dusty mauve to small embroidered pockets, popular because Chinese clothes do not come with pockets, so that they must be attached to the garments. Subsequent visits were just as much fun, although the second time around my eye was more used to spotting fakes.

Bargain like mad. Many dealers do speak English.

FU YU MARKET/SHANGHAI OLD STREET
Henan Nan Lu and Fuxing Zhong Lu/
Fang Bang Zhong Lu

This is the infamous missing flea market that was so hard to track down, possibly because it's on its way to becoming Disney-ized and may be nothing more than a tourist trap by the time you get here. It is a few blocks from Yuyuan on Fuxing

Street. Do both at the same time, but I would start here and then head over to Yuyuan for one helluva day.

Now then, there's a very commercial section that almost looks like a festival marketplace from a bad American mall, with carts set up in the street and vendors selling baskets and kites. Slowly, the closer to Henan Lu you get (and therefore the farther away from Yuyuan), the more it turns into antiques and something that feels authentic.

On weekends there are antiques in the street and more dealers sitting on the curbs with tote bags crammed with hot or fake (or both) Ming vases that they will try to entice you to buy. Right off the street is a five-story warehouse, which is the antiques market itself, although there's plenty outside on the street. Yummy yum yum.

Now then, this market is held every day. *But* it's not very good on weekdays, when only about 30% of the vendors show up. On weekends, especially Sunday, it is crammed and quite the scene. This is Maggie's and my favorite flea in Shanghai.

If you approach from the Henan Lu side (and after 11am on a weekday; 9am on weekends), you see rather touristy torri gates and a pedestrian shopping street that almost looks like a photo op. Before your eye can figure out which part is real and which part is stagecraft, you see the dealers and spy the heaps of delicious junk, on the curbs and falling out of stalls and tiny shops—these are to your left if your back is to the torri gate and Henan Road.

After you pass this sort of courtyard of delight, you see there is a bunker or warehouse or old house. Enter and go for the five floors of delight. Note, the building seems to have two different kinds of markets. The ground floor and the mezzanine are more upscale. Then you go up the side stairs (only slightly frightening) and walk into empty warehouse space that is crammed with dealers who set up on tables, on blankets, on the floor, on old newspapers. There's another three floors of these guys on Sundays. Hmmm, hmmm, goood.

Arts & Crafts

SHANGHAI ARTS & CRAFTS CENTER
190–208 Nanjing Rd.

This is the kind of store that I wanted Number One Department Store to be; it's what I call a "Chinese Department store"—it's most like department stores in Hong Kong, but does not feature a food department nor snake wine.

Anyway, the store is four floors of fun—every type of craft product you can imagine is sold here, including silk by the bolt and all sorts of silk products. I bought printed silk scarves and also cut-velvet silk scarves. The pajamas were rather expensive and no one at home would ever believe you paid that much for them ($85 to $100).

Books

I actually did more book shopping and buying in Beijing; however, most big bookstores have a section of books in English. These are usually nonfiction titles and possibly art books. I bought several art books in Chinese because, uh, a picture is worth 1,000 words and who wants to read all that stuff anyway? Chinese-language books for kids are great gifts (at least, I think so). Finally, believe it or not, all of the international airports I traveled through in Hong Kong and China had an amazing selection of local-interest books, including tomes I thought would be banned in China.

Booze

Many years ago I did an article on a health food restaurant in Hong Kong. At the street level was a doctor at a desk. You went to the doctor for an examination, then he wrote you a prescription of what to eat for dinner that would cure your ills. You went upstairs to the restaurant and ordered that dish. No, I am not making this up. The man I went with (Ian Cook, Born to Shop photographer) had a bad back and was told to drink three-penis wine. Therefore I knew that such products existed.

Look in the foodstuffs listings below for large food empo-
riums; the ones that have liquor departments usually sell specialty wines that include dead mice, snakes, and so on, in
them, or are made with parts of animal bodies. I bought
superchef Alain Ducasse the seal-penis wine for his birthday.

You will pay top yuan for international brands of booze
but local brands are inexpensive. Ones with snakes in them
do cost more.

Department Stores

SHANGHAI NUMBER ONE DEPARTMENT STORE
*830 Nanjing Rd. (corner Nanjing Dong Lu and Xizang
Zhong Lu); on the mall*

I was expecting Number One Department Store to be a funky
emporium of silken treasures and cashmere sweaters offered up
by indifferent or even surly sales help, a type well known in Chinese stores in Hong Kong. Instead, I entered the Hall of Shame—
the Soviets should be punished for what they did to retail—and
almost burst into tears. Was it the jet lag or merely the lag?

Number One Department Store is a freak show of blond,
western-style mannequins dressed in the ugliest silk clothes (western style, copied perhaps from the 1952 edition of the JC Pen-
ney catalog) you have ever seen. There are hundreds of these
mannequins lined up to form the ""walls" of the boutique areas.

Salesgirls (Chinese) wear the same outfits as the mannequins—although it takes a while to figure this out since
they look nothing like the models—and line up next to the mannequins, assuming the same pose, mime style, until a likely shopper happens by. Since 150,000 people shop here each day, there's
a lot of action. When shoppers wander by, the girls jump out
of their frozen state, wave their arms aggressively around your
body, and shout "silk," possibly the only word they know
in English.

It's enough to send you out into the streets screaming, wondering what happened to the old-world charm you were

expecting; or where there's a version of the Hong Kong brand of Chinese department store.

Drugstores

WATSON'S
Shanghai Centre (Portman Ritz Carlton Hotel)

Watson's is one of my favorite stores in Hong Kong, so it's no surprise that I love it in Shanghai. The Watson's attached to the Portman Ritz Carlton is not large, but I can still spend a few minutes there each day, loading up on candy bars and soft drinks, health and beauty products, medicines and gadgets. Avoid U.S.- and European-brand makeup and fragrance, which are stunningly expensive. I've bought many marvelous (read cheap) gifts here for my $3 friends. The gifts look like they are worth at least $5, maybe more.

FRIENDSHIP STORE
40 Beijing Dong Lu

Hmmm, another bust as far as I am concerned. The Friendship Store is in "downtown" on Beijing Road, right off the Bund and 1 block from Nanjing Road and The Peace Hotel. It was boring, filled with cheap silk pajamas ($45) and traditional items as well as souvenirs and tchotchke —not the quality goods I was dreaming of. It's a large store; it did have a grocery store out back that was fun. The store carries a little of everything and you may indeed find things to buy, but it's all so dull that you could simply waste away from the ennui. Wait for the Friendship Store in Beijing, which is super-duper.

MAISON MODE
1312 Huai Hai Rd.

One of the upscale department stores that carries fancy western brands such as Ferragamo. Possibly the classiest department store in town.

PRINTEMPS
939–47 Huai Hai Zhong Lu

Oui, this is the same Printemps as in Paris. Oui, the similarity ends there. I don't mean to be rude, but I laughed myself silly here. The Sèvres vases, taken in context, are especially rich.

ISETAN
1038 Nanjing Xi Lu (Westgate Mall)

This branch of Isetan is about 1 block from the Portman Ritz Carlton and in a very nice, modern, western-style mall filled with big-name stores. Isetan is a Japanese department store, known for younger brands, kickier fashions, and lower prices than some of the other Japanese department stores. There's not only an international lineup of brands, but many names do specialty lines (such as Michel Klein) and there are many super brands you just haven't ever seen before. Large sizes need not apply. The other Isetan is in the French Concession: 527 Huai Hai Zhong Rd.

YAOHAN DEPARTMENT STORE
501 Zhangyang Lu, Pudong

The good news if you are on the Pudong side of the river and you don't feel like the 10-minute taxi to the Pu Xi side, you can take a 5-minute cab ride past the financial district to a shopping mall and the Yaohan Department Store, which is nothing like any Yaohan I have ever seen. In short, this one is nothing to write home about. The mall was nearly frightening. A visit to the Pearl TV Tower in the same area might be more fun.

YUYUAN DEPARTMENT STORE
Yuyuan Gardens

I discovered this department store by accident, while shopping the downstairs flea market. This is sort of a smaller and classier version of Number One, but they not only have a good fabric department but actually bargained with me while the sales girls fought each other for my business. I paid $12 per meter for silk dévoré (cut velvet).

Fakes

HUA TING MARKET
Huai Hai Rd. & Changsu Rd

Because China is, shall we say, soft on copyright enforcement, all sorts of fakes abound in the markets. However, Shanghai is not the best city for fakes, especially fashion fakes.

This could be a little awkward, but here goes. I don't get it at this market. According to guidebooks, magazine articles, and even taxi drivers, tourists love this market. I don't think those people are Born to Shop readers. I have now been to this market three different times; I hated it each time. Maggie hated it on her first time and would never go back.

But now that I've warned you, here goes. The market is held in an alley (Changshu Road), so that it's outdoors and if it's raining, you'll get wet. It's almost always crowded, so it's hard to move, and of course, I worry about pickpockets in conditions like that. The market is about 2 big blocks long, with storefronts on each side of the road; they sell from the street and from inside their stores.

Most of the merchandise is, shall we say, *inspired* by European designers; that means, fake. Prices are much higher than Hong Kong for fakes, and quality is not as good as Shenzen; also the vendors are not as eager to bargain and won't go toe-to-toe with a westerner. Merchandise obviously changes with whatever is in style, but last time I was there you could pick from Fendi baquette bags, Ralph Lauren polo shirts, and Louis Vuitton pastel patent leather. Also CDs and DVDs and some computer programs.

Foodstuffs

No. 1 Food Provision Store
720 Nanjing Rd. East

This just might be my favorite store in Shanghai. It is located on the pedestrian mall part of Nanjing Road and is open into the evening, so you can go here on a nighttime stroll. The store is large, in the colonial European architectural style, but only two stories high.

The ground floor sells fresh produce, dried fruits, liquor, and gift baskets made of food items. It's Harrods Food Hall come to Shanghai. All signs are in Chinese (no pinyin even). Albert, my guide, read the signs to me—they give the province where the fruit was grown. (I had the worst mango of my life and should have known better, explained Albert, who knew it would be bad because of the province where it was grown.)

Upstairs there is a full supermarket and a cafeteria. Yes, I ate here once. Hard to swallow because everyone stared at me so much, but otherwise just fine.

No. 2 Food Provision Store
887 Huai Hai Rd. West

This store is smaller than No. 1; not nearly as much fun and somewhat ruined by the enormous KFC sign out front, but is otherwise worth the visit if you are strolling this part of Huai Hai Road and haven't been spoiled by No. 1. Excellent mangoes.

Häagen-Dazs
777 Nanjing Lu

If you are terrified to eat Shanghai street food, but into the strolling festival one evening, this branch of the famous American (despite it's name) ice-cream brand should put you at ease.

STARBUCKS
Lippo Plaza, upstairs
816 Huai Hai Lu

While there will probably be 1,000 Starbucks by the time you arrive in Shanghai, this is the first one, and it opened while I was in town. It's upstairs and kinda hard to find. I went in Beijing; see the report on p. 255.

Furniture

Growing up, I was never that enamored of Chinese furniture—and my Chinese Auntie An Lin had a house full of it. Middle age got me interested in the sleek lines, but my true interest is really in the more rustic and funky pieces, especially the hand-painted ones. You'll find it all in Shanghai, which is the city to shop for furniture because the climate is suitably humid and the shipping facilities are plentiful.

There are so many furniture warehouses in Shanghai that you will go nuts with greed and desire (at least, I did). It's easiest to give all your business to one dealer in terms of bargaining on final price and making shipping arrangements.

You'll pass many of the furniture warehouses as you drive into town if you arrive in the Hong Qiao Airport—Hong Qiao is the main district for antique furniture warehouses, but not the only district.

Note that many an expat has taken the furniture back to a different climate in the United States only to have it crack during the first winter.

Also as an editorial point: In the end, I bought a piece of rustic-style chinoiserie at Galeries Lafayette in Paris (for my Paris apartment) for $600, delivery and taxes included. This turned out to be a better deal than shipping from Shanghai, although the actual piece that I bought would have cost only $200 to $250 in China.

And speaking of price: While I found prices in Shanghai laughably inexpensive—dealers say that outside of town there are warehouses that are even cheaper, such as Nineteen Town

(19 Jin Xin Lu) in Jiu Ting. Needless to say, the farther off the beaten path you wander, the more you need a translator.

G-E TANG ANTIQUES
7 Hu Qing Ping Hwy.

This source is extremely tourist oriented; they have a Web site (www.getang.com), they advertise in the city's freebie tourist map, and they have a reputation among visitors and expats; they even have a most impressive English-language brochure.

The shop is very chic and sleek; the young men who work here are dressed in black T-shirts and black trousers and could have stepped out of an Armani showroom. Many speak English. The goods are gorgeous.

Too gorgeous (and too expensive) for my taste. I found the whole setup very touristy and bordering on offensive. I cannot find anyone who agrees with me. I asked them to show me the junk and was led to a warehouse in the rear where the nonrestored furniture was kept. This was much more fun. I was quoted various prices for the same piece—as is, cleaned up, or restored.

Shipping usually doubles the cost so that a painted blanket chest (maybe it was a tea chest?) or a set of drawers would end up being $700 to $1,000 landed in the United States. Having seen the quality of the pieces before they were restored, I simply didn't think they were worth it.

But the place is very seductive and also a good place to start to learn what you want and what you want to spend.

HU & HU ANTIQUES
1685 Wuzhong Lu

This store is not far from the Hong Qiao warehouse district, but is not really in it. It is the rage of town and everyone's favorite shop; certainly it was one of my most fantastic shopping experiences in all my years of doing Born to Shop—and I didn't buy a thing.

First off, one of the Hu is a young woman named Marybelle Hu who is American-born Chinese (ABC) and who attended Smith College and has since come back to China. I hope she gets into politics and becomes president, or whatever they have—emperor? Needless to say her English is flawless, her organizational skills are amazing, the store functions like a professional New York showroom. I haven't seen anything like this in China before or since.

The warehouse is a low-slung affair, modern, not crammed or dirty and dusty, although they also have that (I love that, personally). There's a concrete courtyard for cars and taxis, there was a old wagon filled with flowers as a decorative touch that was stunning when I was there last. The main showroom has restored antiques and had many of the Tibetan painted pieces I adore. Unfortunately, they were all sold and I couldn't buy the piece I wanted.

Have you ever loved an item so much that you didn't care what it cost? That's how I felt about a specific blue chest, painted with flowers. It would have cost about $1,000 to have it landed in the United States or in France, and I would have happily paid that price. Alas.

For information or even photos on-line, contact hu-hu@ online.sh.cn

Malls

JING JANG DICKSON CENTRE
400 Changle Rd.

The fanciest and most upscale western mall in Shanghai is owned by the same businessman who owns Harvey Nichols in London and who bid for Barneys in New York. The mall is so chic it doesn't open until 11am (but stays open until 9pm). Most of the really big-name shops, including Ralph Lauren, Lalique, and so on, are located in this mall, which is the kingpin of the Huai Hai Road shopping district. The building is new, but done up like redbrick-goes-art-deco. If you haven't already guessed, there are no bargains on designer goods in China as the import taxes are outrageously high. The stores are mostly empty and the help is very cool, probably terrified you will require them to speak English.

GUBEI
268 Shuicheng Nan Lu

It's a mall, it's a suburban neighborhood, it's a Yuppie way of life. There's even a branch of the French hypermarché (superstore) **Carrefour** here; you'll pass it from the Hongqiao airport on the way into town.

WESTGATE SHOPPING MALL
Nanjing Rd.

I like this mall because it's 1 block from the Portman Ritz Carlton, across the street from the JC Mandarin and near the new Four Seasons Hotel—and it's brand new and very, very western with a branch of Isetan, the Japanese department store, and a branch of everything else, too.

Photography

FUJI PROFESSIONAL LAB
459 Wulumuqi Lu

Ever since I began to travel with a professional photographer, I began to use a professional lab—even for my amateur pics. This is the lab most pros use in Shanghai; you can call ahead at ☎ 86-21/6249-0359.

GUAN LONG
180 Nanjing Dong Lu

This is the premier photography shop in town, with two floors of stuff, although I always use a professional lab for E-6 (slides)—these guys will print your snaps, and the price is good. They sell professional film, but not too many people here speak English so you better know what you want or what you are doing.

Silk & Textiles

NUMBER ONE SILK FACTORY (TULIP SILK FACTORY)
2839 Changning Rd.

The store at Number One Silk Factory is not silk heaven, but it's so much better than Number One Department Store that I mention it, in case you really hanker to see a real silk factory. But before you go, call ☎ 86-21/259-8098 as a precaution, because you might want to make sure this venue is still open before you schlepp out there.

The ride there took about a half hour —we drive mostly on freeway, but then through a real-people part of town. Looking at the low-slung buildings, the brightly colored plastic wares at markets, the fruit stands, and the people on bicycles, I sigh to JJ, "Ah, this is the real China I love."

"No," he says sharply, "this is China post 1949."

Like everything post-1949, the factory is run by the government; it has fixed prices and a quality guarantee. I am the only western shopper, but have gotten used to being stared at by locals—my day at Number One Department Store and subsequently strolling Nanjing Road have prepared me for the fact that if a Martian landed in Shanghai, it would get no more attention than my arrival.

Every item I express interest in causes a curious buzz, and sometimes, giggling. The silks by the yard are not dirt cheap, but I have fallen for the quality sales pitch and pay $10 to $15 per meter (39 inches) for silk, with jacquarded silk—silk that is created on a loom that weaves the pattern right into the fabric—being more expensive.

I spent about $200 at the factory (credit card, yes!), which bought me 4 meters of dreamy, creamy water-blue silk, 1½ meters of black jacquard silk, a pair of copper silk charmeuse pajamas guaranteed not to shrink, and a willow-green Chinese dress, size 6, with hand embroidery in the traditional style, for my 6-year-old niece. I am also given instructions, in English and Chinese, on how to wash silk. I have spent a lot of money and not seen everything the town has to offer, but I take the gamble, mostly because during the factory tour, I was very impressed by the technology.

The factory part of the operation is large and modernized with the most advanced printing machinery, imported from Japan. Japan and Italy set the industry standards for silk printing, going back to experience gleaned since the time of Marco Polo. In fact, the Chinese have been famous for their mulberry (what silk worms eat), but it's European craftsmen and engineers who have created the finesse that is associated with quality silk products.

Yet I am impressed with Number One Silk because I was able to watch their manufacturing process and see the way the fabrics are printed and rinsed. The trick in silk quality is not only in the silk screens themselves, but in the way the silk is rinsed and treated with hot water and steam in the early stages so that it does not shrink later.

It is this process that convinces me to blow $125 on the silk pajamas. They come in a size "large"; I ask for an extra-large, since Chinese sizes tend to run very small, but was told A) there was no extra-large, and B) these pajamas were guaranteed to fit. To prove this, a flock of salesgirls moved in on me with a tape measure in one hand and the pajamas in another and through clucking Chinese, hand motions, and assorted measurements proved that I was wrong and they were right.

That night, in the privacy of my room overlooking the Bund, it turned out that while the pajamas fit onto me, they did not fit properly and are for someone about 4 inches shorter and 10 pounds lighter. It was an expensive lesson in Chinese sizes and Chinese friendly persuasion. However, my friend Suzy Stark loved them. She's 6 inches shorter than I am.

I had hoped to load up on silk jammies as gifts, but was dismayed at not only the high prices throughout Shanghai, but also the American perception that silk pajamas are a cheap commodity. Even the touristy ones for children cost $20 to $25 a pair; adult sizes begin at about $45 a pair and escalate with the quality. The good ones are almost always over $100 per pair, while your gift recipient is used to TJ Maxx prices.

SILK KING
819 Nanjing Xi Lu

There are three branches of Silk King, a store so popular that heads of state are brought here (and photographed, of course). I just chose the one that was walking distance from the Portman Hotel and enjoyed it a lot, although I would not use their tailoring services and did not actually buy anything. Still, they had bolts and bolts of all kinds of silks; most were priced in the $6 to $10 per meter area, making them a good enough price. Some were washable, others not. Some of the help spoke a little English; they were most anxious to please and did not stare too hard.

ZHANG YAN JUAN
Wife Ding Cloth Store
438 Fang Bang Zhong Lu
(Old Shanghai St.)

This store is part of the development called "Old Shanghai Street" that I adore. The store features only fabrics and items made of the fabric in the homespun blue cloth of a special region of China. For blue-and-white freaks, this is really a find.

Supermarkets

NO. 1 FOOD PROVISION STORE
720 Nanjing Rd.

There's a supermarket upstairs. See p. 193.

WELLCOME
Shanghai Centre, Portman Ritz Carlton Hotel
Nanjing Rd.

I'm not certain if you would make a special trip here just for the Watson's and the adjacent Wellcome, but boy was I excited to find them. Their Hong Kong–style luxury was a welcome after too many dog days on the streets, and I was also happy to load up on snacks and my favorite fiber cereal for breakfast.

PARK N SHOP
Westgate Mall (and others)

Another Hong Kong supermarket chain; there is a branch in the Westgate Shopping Mall right near the Portman Ritz Carlton.

Wedding Photos

Although there are also wedding-photo salons in Beijing, the ones in Shanghai are better and much more fun. I will not name any specific addresses, but point you in the right direction so you can stare, or dare.

Now then, with China evolving into a western consumer market, nothing is more valuable than a western-style wedding or even, the wedding photo. Since few can afford the real thing, there are zillions of salons where bride and groom go for the day to be made over and photographed. Hair, makeup, and clothes are provided, you just say cheese.

I was tempted to do this many times but figured that no wedding dress would ever fit me . . . and I didn't want to have to be the groom!

TOUR: ONE PERFECT DAY IN SHANGHAI

Depending on your time, travel method, and cultural needs, you will have to juggle a little bit—but I'd say start at Old Shanghai Street, do the Fu Yu Market, walk from there on Fang Bang to Yu Yuan Gardens and explore the entire site, plus the antiques building. Lunch there or at the Shanghai Museum of Art, which has a wonderful collection and a great gift shop. Finish up the evening with a stroll on Nanjing Lu.

DAY TRIPS & OVERNIGHT EXCURSIONS

....

Suzhou

I don't know how to put this diplomatically, or even politely, but I feel strongly that my duty has never been more clear. Forget Suzhou.

If that's not enough for you to trust me, I'll just say a little more.

First off, I have dreamed of Suzhou; she has been part of my Shanghai fantasies. The Venice of China, a city of canals, home of the old silk factories, shopper's pearl-bargain heaven. What's not to like?

Suzhou, now. Maybe Suzhou was great. I don't know when—100 years ago? Fifty years ago? Not last year, trust me. Yet no guidebook writer has been here recently or will run the risk of butting up against myth and magic.

The silk factories are a joke; the main shopping street has nothing attractive about it and is only amusing in that A) you're a long way from Shanghai architecturally and B) it looks like news footage of Hanoi in 1969. Sure, the pearls are cheap; they're cheap everywhere and you're gonna have more fun buying pearls in Beijing; I promise.

Getting There: Most people take tours to Suzhou, enjoy its delights as part of the package to China they bought, or they take a hotel car and driver. You can get there by train—and back in a day; it's about an hour train ride. My hotel concierge quoted a price of $300 for a Mercedes with driver for the day trip (flat fee).

Shopping Suzhou: Puh-lease.

The Magic City of Zhouzhang

I am a little loathe to tell you about this because it is so fabulous that you will rush there immediately and then it will be overrun with tourists and ruined. But since you've just read my rip on Suzhou, and you're thinking I'm as bad as any theater or restaurant critic, and mumbling that it's easy to find what's wrong without finding what's right, well, I have found the real Shangri-La.

First, some history to put this in context, so you know from whence I come. Maggie the Marvel had the name of someone's daughter who was living in Shanghai; she met with the young woman, Carol, and immediately liked her and accepted her opinions. All Maggie could talk about was that Carol said to forget Suzhou and go to Zhouzhang (say "Ju-Jong"). I told Maggie that while I appreciated Carol's opinion, since no one could tell me word one about Zhouzhang and Suzhou had an international reputation, well, I had to see Suzhou for myself.

I saw Suzhou for myself and ran out of there screaming. My faith in mankind, and good old Carol, were reinforced when we got to Zhouzhang—the absolute movie-set medieval Chinese city, with tons of shopping (of course). It, too, is a canal city, but is totally closed to auto traffic and is virtually the Chinese version of an ancient Italian city—the Marco Polo thing is unmistakable. Carol, you have done a service for all mankind.

Sooo, here goes. Zhouzhang is truly an ancient city, south east of Suzhou and about 2 hours from Shanghai. The city actually has two parts—modern town and old city, located across a series of bridges and closed to vehicular traffic. You can walk or take a pedicab from the new city to the old city and then stroll the landmark as your leisure. Since it's so scenic, it might be the most romantic place on earth at night, but would entail an overnight in a hotel that does not compete with Four Seasons or Shangri-La.

Located in what is called the "Water Country," Zhouzhang is everything that I wanted Suzhou to be.

Hangzhou

Although I have not been to Hangzhou myself, another travel writer that I know and trust went, so herewith a few words from her. This is not a day trip, it's at least an overnight, and

people go for the tea and the tea gardens, not the shopping—
although there is a lot of silk and the usual things to buy; prices
are fair since there are few western tourists. However, it is a
Chinese resort city and has been for eons. The best hotel in
town is Shangri-La, which was just totally renovated. The
hotel is close to West Lake, which is what tourists have been
coming to see for centuries and the scenery really does look
like a virtual calligraphy. You can get there by train: about a
3-hour ride. The hotel will meet you at the train station.

Chapter Eight

....

BEIJING

WELCOME TO BEIJING

....

My many years of travel and my constant wonder at the way some of the icon cities of the world fail to meet my expectations has led me to create this little maxim: There are Nantucket people and there are Martha's Vineyard people; there are Athens people, and there are Istanbul people. It's not the city, it's just what touches you. So after my first visit to Beijing, I decided that there are Shanghai people and there are Beijing people. I was not comfortable in Shanghai (this was the old Shanghai) and I loved Beijing sooo much that I began looking for a job there.

Today that makes me sigh, as Shanghai has come a long way and Beijing no longer has the "gansta" edge to it that first appealed to me. Maybe I wanted to be a shopping outlaw. Don't ask me, I'm just a primitive soul. A soul who historically had little interest in Beijing, who had always dreamed of Shanghai. Yet on that first trip to China, I found that Shanghai left me cold, while Beijing was more than the temple of heaven— it was heaven on earth.

Beijing, at least, still feels like China; Beijing still has a few raw edges and slices of reality. So welcome to Beijing, a city without the highrises and modernity of Shanghai but with just as much architectural pleasure, albeit through buildings that are 1,000 years old. Welcome to Beijing where you can still see the contrast between old and new; old communist China and the new not-so-communist China. Welcome to Beijing, which is no longer the Forbidden City. And the food's great.

A Short History of Shopping in Beijing

Because it is not a port city, Beijing does not have as rich a historical connection to trade or shopping. On the other hand, this is Marco Polo country, so many western ideas (and shopping concepts) originated here and traveled, usually via the Silk Route to the sea and from there into Europe. You might say that medievally speaking, Beijing is the mother of all malls . . . and all smalls.

Originally called Ji, Beijing was founded as a frontier trading town in the second millennium B.C. It later became Jiching; and in the 7th century B.C. became the capital of the Yan Kingdom, known as both Jiching and Yanjing (see, even then there were different names for this city). In 1153, the capital of China was moved southwest of Beijing; Kublai Khan built a new capital back in the area, now part of Beijing, called *Dadu* and this was indeed where Marco Polo came to call and trade.

You remember in the history of both style and shopping that by the 18th century continental Europe was over the moon for Chinese products, imports, and style—tea, porcelain, and silk were the very foundations of chic. Yet during that time, the Chinese had no interest in European goods or products. In fact, the British were so desperate for trade to go both ways that they began bringing in opium from Turkey, to the great detriment of China (thus, the famed Opium Wars).

So Beijing has always been a city of trade as well as a diplomatic city with foreign visitors. Other than those few foreigners, it has also always been a closed community—with a walled and ancient city (the Forbidden City) in the center—and a very distinct diplomatic quarter. Beijing was where foreigners were terrorized during the 2-month siege of the Boxer Rebellion in 1900. Under old-style communist rule, Beijing was just as closed.

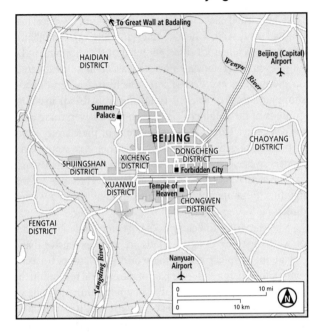

But right now, Beijing is more open than ever with better shopping ops than ever. When Beijing finally allowed international retailers to open their doors—as long as they were in partnership with a local Chinese firm—the results on the bottom line were far from spectacular. Many stores and brands rushed to get a foothold, only to end up closing their doors. Even those foreign brands that are still in business in China often admit that they are not making money; they are just hanging on to establish brand recognition. Yet the beat goes on.

And some brands *are* making money, especially luxe brands, which are in high demand by the suddenly wealthy nouveau riche who come to Beijing from the provinces to spend their money. Beijing has a more tightly organized core of luxury shopping than Shanghai, where stores sprawl all over. In Beijing, the luxury districts are all together and near each other.

Beijing still has a number of real-people neighborhoods and many shopping districts, whether for locals or for tourists, that feel Chinese and excite the senses. These parts of town feel more original and, well, Chinese, than anything in Shanghai. In fact, there is a historical feel to much of the shopping in Beijing—even the Friendship Store, the last communist statement on shopping, is excellent. There's the historical reproduction shopping street of ancient times (Suzhou Road) inside the grounds of the Summer Palace; then there's everything else in the city center, from old-fashioned turn-of-the-century venues in the antiques district to communist big box stores, on to modern, western-style malls. Galeries Lafayette (in Chinese partnership format) has already come and gone. The sands are shifting, but the shopping tide has already changed in a westerly direction.

Still, the visitor to Beijing does not come for designer brands or western stores; designer goods are more expensive than in just about anyplace else in the world. One comes to see the remarkable energy and to be part of the cultural revolution that, in this case, means bringing the shopping culture to Beijing.

Tourists will find the best buys are traditional Chinese goods, be they arts and crafts, silks or antiques. While there is a fair amount of antique furniture to choose from, smart shoppers buy (and ship) furniture from Shanghai because the climate there is less drying for wood and the shipping port is readily available.

Now that the powers that be are softer on communism and strong on consumerism, note that history is rewriting itself, and shoppers are being encouraged to spend big bucks. "Beijing Welcomes Visa (Tips for Prosperity)" is one of my favorite new promotions—it's a coupon book sponsored by Visa and the Beijing Tourist Administration. (The booklet includes stores and hotels.) Go figure. There are ATM machines, credit card promotions, and deals for dollars. Never has shopping in Beijing been more exciting.

Architecturally Yours

Just because Beijing is not awash in wall-to-wall highrises like Shanghai and Hong Kong does not mean there are no highrises

Electronically Yours: Beijing

Please note that these sites are specific to Beijing; see chapter 2 for more options.

- www.beijing-olympics.org.cn is the official Web site for year 2008 bid for Olympics, which China is expected to get. There's also much about Beijing in English, along with a vocabulary lesson.
- www.beijing-cityedition.com is a city magazine in English, even has want ads and personals.
- www.beijingnow.com— in English, *bien sur*.

or fancy or memorable new buildings, or that modern architecture does not interest the ruling class. Several world-class architects have, or are in the midst of, new projects in Beijing, many of which are highly controversial. So we're not talking wall-to-wall; ha-ha, we're talking downtown to Wall. Wall Street to Great Wall? Well, you get the drift. The only bad news is that the old parts of Beijing will probably vanish, just as they have from Hong Kong and Shanghai, so get there while you can and enjoy the contrasts.

The rebuilt capital is new and exciting visually; Paul Andreu—a French designer—is building that new national theater complex, which looks something like a cross between a macaroon cookie and a sea urchin. It will sit in a lake and be entered through an underwater tunnel. Confucius says no fortune needed in this cookie: This is the New China. It's to open in 2003.

Historically, Beijing has the Forbidden City, the Summer Palace, the Temple of Heaven, and even Tiananmen Square as architectural landmarks. There will be many more new ones to come.

Phonetically Yours

Note that the place name Beijing is made of two different calligraphy symbols, *bei* and *jing*, meaning "northern capital." Many stores print their addresses in English using the divided distinction: Bei Jing. Also there are several ways of transliterating many words, so don't get confused between Tiananmen and Qianmen—they are the same place, more or less. You may also see Tiananmen written as "Tian Anmen."

GETTING THERE

There is a section on air carriers for travel into all parts of China, including Beijing, in chapter 2. The information below pertains specifically to Beijing. Note that because of its diplomatic position, Beijing has more international air traffic than any other city in mainland China; there are 98 international connections and more than 700 domestic routes. More than 40 foreign airlines have offices in Beijing.

SwissAir was the first international carrier to serve Beijing, beginning more than 50 years ago; the carrier has enjoyed such a special relationship with the city that on the 50th anniversary of the airline and the regime's coexistence, a special exhibit of the famed Cow Parade, which originated in Zurich, was brought to Beijing. SwissAir has nonstop service 6 days a week.

Austrian Airlines, which also has a code share with SwissAir, has been pushing into China recently, and is increasing service continually, partly based on the advantage of Vienna's being the closest European city to Beijing and Shanghai with major and regular air service. Austrian Airlines now has nonstop service to Vienna 3 days a week, and from Shanghai, twice a week.

Finnair also has service to Beijing; they launched with wonderful promotional prices and have a sound safety record. Virgin has been so successful that they just added on a fifth day of service from London.

For round-the-world options, see "Round-the-World Tricks" in chapter 7.

ARRIVING & DEPARTING

....

Arrival & Departure by Air

Actually, I have never arrived in Beijing by air, because I have always journeyed from Shanghai by train. I have departed, however, and can report that the airport has been renovated and is modern and easy to use. For departures, there are VIP lounges with free soft drinks and tea; the duty-free store is large and well equipped.

Warning: If your departure is to a destination in Europe—mine always has been to Zurich because I fly SwissAir and lay over there—you are asked to comply with European luggage regulations and, if you have been on the shopping spree I expect of you, may be asked to pay overweight charges. This may be reason enough to book a round-the-world ticket, arriving transatlantically but departing transpacifically so you can get the benefit of better luggage regulations. For more information on this option, see chapter 7.

Also note: As the main airport for China, not only is the airport busy but flights book up quickly and it may be hard to make changes on tickets for availability reasons. If you are a member of Marco Polo Club (Cathay) or any other priority airline clubs, you may need to use pull to change your tickets.

Taxi service to or from Capital Airport and central Beijing is about $12. All major hotels have transfer packages that cost about $50. Most arrivals arrange a hotel pickup, so go directly to the hotel desk of choice on arrival.

On departure from Beijing's Capital Airport, note that there is a rather peculiar system in place—your driver will drop you and your luggage off at the curb and possibly even get you loaded onto a cart. However, you aren't allowed to take the cart into the airport terminal for security purposes. You must transfer to another cart, piloted by a bellboy (flat fee), who will take you to the airline check-in desk. For a little extra, he may even take you right through immigration and get you to the lounge. All I had was a $20 bill on me (had already spent all yuan on Louis Vuitton and tips with the hotel driver), which I happily gave the young man who helped me with my mounds of baggage and got me right to the lounge. Money talks, even in China.

I had to tip in U.S. dollars because I didn't know this system existed and unloaded all my Chinese money on the guy who got me to the airport and into the cart, never knowing he would hand me off to yet another person. Urrrrrgh!

Duty-Free Shopping

There is an excellent duty-free store in the Beijing airport; they even have cute plastic shopping bags with pandas on them. Prices aren't dirt cheap, but aside from the usual perfumes and bottles of booze, there's a section of traditional Chinese medicine, Chinese arts and crafts, and even foodstuffs. I had not bought some panda cookies in town, which I later regretted; I found them at the duty free for more than the in-town price, but who cared? No Hermès scarves.

Arrival by Train

The main train station in Beijing has also been renovated and looks much like a Christmas ornament at night or like the train station at Disneyland in Anaheim. On arrival, if you are at an outer platform, it can be a bit stark, but the cute comes when you hit the marble pavement and then the station house. There are not too many porters, but if you have a lot of luggage or cannot manage on your own, it pays to have arranged a hotel transfer and asked to be met at the tracks. Last trip there were three of us, with heaps of suitcases and packages, so I also ordered a van from the hotel.

For details on the Shanghai-Beijing train (or the Beijing-Shanghai train, depending on your perspective), see "Riding the Not So Red Rooster," p. 152 in chapter 7.

Arrival by Cruise Ship

As already noted, Beijing is landlocked; however, it is not terribly far from the sea and many cruise ships use Beijing as a "turnaround city" and then transfer passengers by bus to either Tianjin or directly to the port itself in Tianjin. Some ships have only a day in town which is handled with a motor coach tour—first timers wouldn't want to go into "town" for a day on their own anyway.

LAY OF THE LAND

While Beijing is, of course, enormous, it doesn't feel quite as big as Shanghai because it has a definite system to it that makes sense. Beijing has purposefully been built in a series of circles—starting with the Forbidden City as the core—and has added consecutive ring roads so that you can define where you are by the ring—sort of like the age of a tree. One refers to them as "First Ring Road," and so on.

Three ring roads are now in place, rings four and five are in planning and building stages. For all I know, while you read this, they are already finished. When the Chinese government sets its mind (and work crews) to do something, it's done quickly and it's done well. The road to and from the airport is as modern as any new U.S. highway. (Are there any *new* U.S. highways?)

One of the reasons the ring-thing works so well is that the core of the city, what you might call city center, is still medieval and Confucian (which is not confusing) so that it all makes sense—there is a clear north-south axis as well as a new, modern east-west main drag. Most of the city walls (except to the Forbidden City) are gone now, the last of them torn down in the 1960s. But with the Forbidden City as the center of the universe, it is easy to divide central Beijing into four quadrants for directional purposes. With quadrants and ring roads, the lay of the land is pretty easy to understand.

Beijing

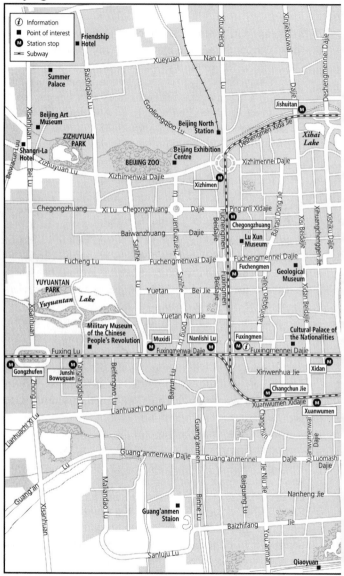

Legend:
- (i) Information
- ■ Point of interest
- Ⓜ Station stop
- ▪▪▪ Subway

Friendship Hotel
Summer Palace
Xueyuan Nan Lu
Xtucheng Lu
Xinjiekouwai Dajie
Deshengmennei Dajie

Beijing Art Museum
ZIZHUYUAN PARK
Baishiqiao Lu
Goujlongqiao Lu
Beijing North Station
Jishuitan
Xihai Lake

Xisanhuan Beilu
Shangri-La Hotel
Zizhuyuan Lu
BEIJING ZOO
Beijing Exhibition Centre
Deshengmen Xida Jie
Xizhimennei Dajie

Bei Lu
Xizhimenwai Dajie
Xizhimen Ⓜ
Ping'anli Xidajie
Bai'asi Dong Jie
Xisi Beidajie
Xihuangchenggen Jie
Xishiku Dajie

Chegongzhuang Xi Lu
Chegongzhuang Dajie
Chegongzhuang Ⓜ
Fuchengmen Beidajie
Lu Xun Museum

Baiwanzhuang Dajie
Sanlihe
Fuxingmen Beidajie
Fuchengmennei Dajie
Fuchengmen Ⓜ
Geological Museum
Xidan Beidajie

Fucheng Lu
Fuchengmenwai Dajie
Sanlihe
Yuetan
Bei Jie
Zhanlanguan Lu

YUYUANTAN PARK
Yuyuantan Lake
Yuetan Nan Jie
Dong Lu

Military Museum of the Chinese People's Revolution
Muxidi Ⓜ
Nanlishi Lu Ⓜ
Fuxingmen Ⓜ(i)
Fuxingmennei Dajie
Cultural Palace of the Nationalities

Xisanhuan
Fuxing Lu
Fuxingmenwai Dajie
Xinwenhua Jie
Xidan Ⓜ

Gongzhufen Ⓜ
Junshi Bowuguan ■
Zhong Lu
Yangfangdian Lu
Beifengwo Lu
Bajiao Lu
Changchun Jie Ⓜ
Xuanwumen Xidajie
Xuanwumen Ⓜ

Lianhuachi Xi Lu
Lianhuachi Donglu
Guang'anmen
Guang'annei Dajie
Changchun
Xuanwumenwai Dajie
Luomashi Dajie

Guang'an
Xisanhuan
Guang'anmenwai Dajie
Maliandao Lu
Binhe Lu
Guang'anmennei Dajie
Baiguang Lu
Jie Niu Jie
Nanheng Jie

Guang'anmen Staion ■
Baizhifang Jie
You'anmen

Santuju Lu
Qiaoyuan

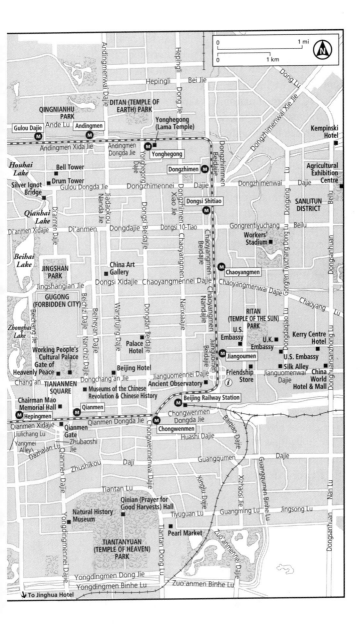

There's more about shopping districts below, but suffice it to say that Beijing is a city of neighborhoods and cliques. Beijing has more than 10 million inhabitants (and most of them smoke) as well as a large expat population. There are more than 50 different nationalities in the population mix. Because the traffic is so terrible, people rarely venture too far from their regular neighborhoods. It's even more rare to go out to dinner in a way-out area, unless the venue is known to be exceptional. Locals give you directions by ring road, but the truth is that the city is so well organized that you can use the clock system of telling time for giving directions. Everything radiates from the Imperial City.

The city is the transportation hub for all of China, with five different train stations. And, no, you will not be overwhelmed by the number of people on bikes; it's the car traffic that's a killer. Where you stay almost doesn't matter, especially if you travel by motor coach or touring van—it can easily take an hour to get any where.

GETTING AROUND

Taxis

Visitors who haven't been to Beijing in a decade remember it as a city of bikes without taxis. No more: There are plenty of cars and almost 100,000 taxis. There are three different sizes of taxi cabs in Beijing with three different flag drops that I found; the flag drop is posted in the side window. Fares are either 1.20 yuan, 1.60 yuan, or 2 yuan per kilometer—the more money, the greater the size and the luxury. Few 1.20-yuan taxis have air-conditioning, which you will care about in spring and summer. The government says there are eight classifications of taxi.

Taxis are fairly easy to hail in busy shopping districts; not so in out-of-the-way districts or at some tourists sights. If you taxi to the Summer Palace, have your cab wait for you.

As in most cities with a tourist business, each hotel hands out a taxi checklist in English and Chinese, with a long list of possibilities. I must tell you that the final choice on the Palace Hotel check list is "Please take me home," which seems to be a very literal translation. When I pointed to this line in one taxi, the driver blushed and then shook his head "no." Maybe his mother wouldn't approve of me.

I don't think I had four honest taxi drivers in my whole stay in Beijing. The first trip to Beijing, I didn't know my way around well enough to judge, but on the second trip, while there was no outright cheating, I noticed an unrelenting talent for taking either the long way or for choosing the most trafficked route in order to run up the meter. As I got into a regular pattern, I would tell the bellboy at the hotel who fed people into taxis the directions that I wanted followed, and he would repeat them in Chinese. (Don't tread on me.) If I knew for a fact that a driver had gone the long way, I cut back on the tip or did not tip him.

Note, though that you shouldn't be quick to find fault—there are a lot of one-way streets in Beijing, so sometimes a direct route is not possible. There are also a fair number of alleys; I reward those smart enough to use them.

My favorite guy is the driver who kept a washcloth over the meter. Make sure the meter is on; if it isn't, get the driver's attention, point to the meter, and make a fuss. If he says it's broken (sure it is), take down the number or take the taxi company card from his car and make motions like you are going to report him.

Learning some basic directions in Chinese is good also.

There are night rates from 11pm to 5am. Receipts are provided on request and are pretty hard to get. Taxis rarely have change for big bills and, yes, they think 100 yuan is a big bill. Normal drivers do not expect tips but those savvy ones who work the hotels regularly known that westerners often tip; you can sometimes feel the question in the air.

Pedicabs

I am a little embarrassed to say this, as it must be quite socially incorrect, but I love the pedicabs in Beijing and I will be sorry when they disappear, as invariably they must. For those dancing in the dark, a pedicab is a rickshaw attached to a bicycle. A few are enclosed, but most only have sides and a back and some sort of upholstery. The drivers range in age, which I always take into account, depending on how difficult the journey. A few speak some words of English, but don't count on it. Your taxi cheat-sheet will work well as will a little bit of mime and the use of fingers or paper/pen to determine price. Always determine price before you get in. A tip is not expected, but I tip if extra effort has been made; I may even tip extravagantly. I love capitalism.

My most common pedicab run is from the Pearl Market to the Palace Hotel, which costs about 50 yuan. This is the same price as a taxi actually. (An honest taxi.)

Although I am not a risk-taker by nature, and I hate scary rides at theme parks, a pedicab ride in Beijing can be the equal of an E-ticket ride at Disneyland, and is either thrilling or terrifying; it can be dangerous too. Also remember to negotiate the fare upfront because afterward the driver can always quote you a different price or say the price he gave you was per person. Nonsense.

Buses

There's a great system of buses and they only cost 1 yuan a ride, but traffic being what it is, and taxis being affordable, I don't suggest you bus it.

The Metro

The metro (also called "the subway") is marked in English; the straight line trips are a breeze. Note that there aren't any direct connections between the two lines right now, so you don't need to worry about making a complicated transfer.. You can easily connect from the China World Hotel or the Beijing Friendship Store to "downtown" (Tiananmen) on your own.

The subway begins around 5:30am and runs until 10:30 or 11:30pm, depending on the line. The fare is about 25¢. The

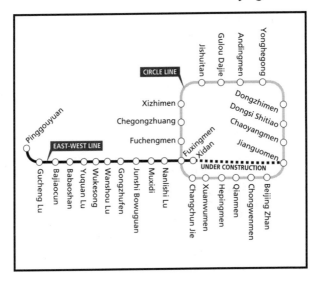

symbol for the subway is a little square inside an incomplete circle, sort of like the letter G.

SLEEPING IN BEIJING

Because Beijing is a city of neighborhoods and because the traffic is so terrible, your trip is very much defined by where you stay. This is a city where location and luxury are both important—luxury if you are used to western-style hotels and you want the electronics to function. There is no such thing as "the best" hotel in town; it's all a matter of what is convenient for your needs—obviously business people have different needs from tourists; tourists in groups or on tours have different needs from independent travelers.

Beijing is a town where weather somewhat influences hotel rates, except at the very top venues. It is very hot in the summer and very cold in the winter—both conditions discourage mass tourism during large stretches of time, so that hotels may have promotional rates. However, luxury hotel competition is very stiff and not that flexible since there is a constant flow of business people into the city. Almost all major hotel chains are represented in Beijing. Some airlines have associations with hotels so that you can check in your luggage at the hotel.

PALACE HOTEL
8 Goldfish Lane (Wangfujing)

For me, this is the best location in Beijing and therefore the best hotel. It is one of the fanciest and most western (member of Leading Hotels of the World); it also has the largest luxury shopping in town with freestanding branches of everything from Hermès to Chanel and much, much more. And my girlfriend Flavia works here. Who could ask for much more?

From the outside, the hotel doesn't look like much: The lobby is in a neoglitz style, while the outside is rather bland in the highrise-with-Chinese-ornaments style. But wait—the hotel is managed by Peninsula Group from Hong Kong and they know a lot about running a hotel. There is an executive floor with extra privileges; standard deluxe rooms are traditional, with great bathroom amenities, including a new toothbrush every day (these make great gifts). Because of its reputation for quality, this hotel sells out faster than any other in town, so it pays to book in advance. Also there's an English-speaking doctor in house!

When you ask the concierge to make a dinner reservation for you, you are presented with a formal card in English and in Chinese with your reservation information on it, both as a reminder to you, and to use to give directions to your taxi. All you need do is not lose the card, show it to your taxi driver, and show it again at the restaurant.

One of the best things about this luxury hotel is the location, which to me is the best in Beijing—it's 1 block from the famed Wangfujing, or pedestrian walking (and shopping) street; it's right near Food Street (not that we eat too much street food in China, but it's fun to dream) and you can walk to Tiananmen Square and the Forbidden City (a big walk, but doable).

They too offer a discount with the Visa promotion.

U.S. reservations through Leading Hotels of the World, ☎ 800/223-6800. Local phone: ☎ 8610/6512-8899; fax: 8610/6512-9050; on-line: www.lhw.com.

CHINA WORLD HOTEL
1 Jianguomenwai Dajie, China World Trade Center

Because this was the first hotel I stayed in while visiting Beijing, it is a sort of "home" to me and I feel comfortable the minute I walk into the lobby. The lobby is very glitzy, so it may take you a few seconds to adjust; the hotel itself is located inside an enormous highrise/trade center complex of many buildings. The basement includes the second best luxury shopping in town, as well as a connection to the metro (and there's a supermarket!).

Among other benefits of the hotel: A cybercafe is in the mall downstairs on street level (go out hotel front door, look to your right); there is a Mongolian cashmere store across the freeway (which I discovered by looking out my hotel window; talk about a good view) and you are walking distance from both the Silk Market and the Friendship Store. There are many restaurants in the hotel, including one of my favorites in town, Aria. I have been known to taxi here from another hotel just for dinner (and the chef is adorable).

Meanwhile, back at the highrise, this hotel is part of a virtual city—behind it is Traders Hotel, a business and residential hotel that is worth knowing about. A block away (big block) is the Kerry Centre Hotel.

U.S. reservations through Shangri-La, ☎ 800/942-5050. Local phone: ☎ 8610/6505-2266; fax: 8610/6505-0828; on-line: cwh@shangri-la.com

KEMPINSKI HOTEL BEIJING LUFTHANSA CENTER
50 Liangmaqiao Rd. (Chaoyang)

This hotel is on the Third Ring Road in the popular Chaoyang district; it is in the first part of Beijing to open up to foreigners and is near several other hotels, including Sheraton Great Wall and Beijing Hilton. It is also attached to a mall (Lufthansa Centre) and has many airline ticket offices. Wait! There's more—there's a small (but nice) antiques center across the street. The hotel is modern, a member of Leading Hotels of the World and one of the old faithfuls around town. Frankly, I don't like this location as a regular hangout, but if you need to be in this part of town, it's a great choice.

Because so many business people book this hotel, they have special weekend rates and package, including Weekend Rendez-Vous, with rooms at 50% off or about $225 per room per night. There's a minimum 2-night stay and a Saturday night must be included; you also get a full breakfast for each day of your stay. Also available through the Visa promotion.

Reservations through Kempinski, ☎ 800/426-3135. Local phone: ☎ 8610/6466-3388; fax: 8610/6465-3366; on-line: www.kempinski.com.

St. Regis Hotel
21 Jianguomenwai Dajie

Managed by Sheraton, and located in the diplomatic section of town, this hotel is in walking distance of the Friendship Store, Silk Alley, and China World Hotel, which has its own shops as well as a mall and supermarket. I mention all this up front because there is little shopping in the St. Regis Hotel and not much of anything else except luxury. In terms of decoration and price, this is the fanciest hotel in Beijing—and it gets the kind of clients who step from limo to limo and don't know (or perhaps care) too much about the real world. Yes it's clean and it's fancy, but its also sterile and cold. I get the feeling that the people who stay here are not going to the Great Wall or on a shopping spree; they're probably in town on business and must get in, get out, and possibly pick up a Mao alarm clock for the wife back home—conveniently these are sold (at thrice the price) in the store's arts and crafts concession.

U.S. reservations through Sheraton, ☎ 800/325-3535. Local phone: ☎ 8610/6160-6688; fax: 8610/6160-3299; on-line: stregis.com/beijing

BEIJING HOTEL
33 Dongchangan Jie

I have not stayed in this hotel, but it has a fabulous location and part of it is an icon in Beijing in terms of the foreign delegations who called it l'Hotel Beijing when it was built in 1900. It has been added to and renovated since the Boxer Revolt (also in 1900); in fact, since the 50th anniversary of the arrival of the communist regime (1949–99). The hotel is quite large, is more of a fancy four-star than a complete five-star hotel, but may serve you well.

Note that the Beijing Hotel and the Grand Hotel Beijing are virtually connected—both are worth checking out; both have discount programs with Visa, which are not applied to walk-in clients—you must book ahead and ask for the Visa promotional rate.

The Grand Hotel is a member of Leading Hotels of the World.

U.S. reservations through Leading Hotels of the World, ☎ 800/223-6800. Local phone: Beijing Hotel ☎ 8610/ 6513-7766, Grand Hotel Beijing ☎ 8610/6513-7788; on-line: www.lhw.com.

KERRY CENTRE HOTEL
1 Guang Hua Rd.

This is more of a four-star hotel, and the location is off by a block, but by saving a lot of money on a room, you can spend it on taxis. The hotel is brand new and is part of the Shangri-La Group (so everything works). It has the best sports center in Beijing (I saw Arnold Schwarzenegger there) and is a block from the mall at China World Hotel. The hotel also has Horizon Club rooms with extra perks and is very child-friendly.

U.S. reservations: ☎ 800/942-5050. Local phone: ☎8610/6561-8833; fax: 8610/6561-2626; on-line: www.shangri-la.com

SHANGRI-LA
29 Zizhuyuan Lu

Because this particular Shangri-La is such an unusual property, I want to tell you about it—it's also the official hotel of many cruise lines, and you may be wondering where the hell it is or what you've gotten into. Rest assured, this is a terrific hotel and while its location is a bit unusual, this actually works for you—especially if you're doing a lot of tours.

This hotel is in the northwestern part of Beijing; there are few other famous western hotels out here; you are very close to the Summer Palace. The hotel has a garden and teahouse and some good shopping within the lobby and because it is on a ring road, you can get to "downtown" rather easily. It's not in a walking-around, central district, but it's a fine choice.

Rates depend on promotions but are about $200 per night; U.S. reservations: ☎ 800/942-5050. Local phone: ☎ 8610/6841-2211; fax: 8610/6841-8002; on-line: www. shangri-la.com

DINING IN BEIJING

....

If one more person tells me the food isn't good in China, I may poke at him with my chopsticks. Most luxury hotels have several restaurants, with at least one regional Chinese restaurant. That's not to say you should stick to hotel meals! There are good places to enjoy in shopping districts and in some out-of-the-way places, which are so much a part of local legend that they should be included in your stay.

Your hotel will make reservations for you and give you a reminder card; you may find it frustrating to try to make reservations yourself.

QIANMEN QUANJUDE ROAST DUCK
32 Qianmen St.

This famous eatery is on the far side of Tiananmen Square and is across the street from one of my favorite "real people" shopping districts—the stalls across the street from the restaurant are actually open into the night, so you can shop and sup. Please note that you enter the restaurant through the courtyard, which resembles a driveway. We entered through the front and after waiting over a half hour for a table found out we were in the take-out department!

The restaurant does not take reservations, gets every tourist in the world, and is a schtick (yes, they sell their own products in a gift shop)—all that understood, it is much fun and the duck was good. The duck is priced according to quality; it helps to have a native speaker with you.

LI FAMILY (LI JIA CAI)
11 Yangfang Hutong (Xicheng)

If you go to only one restaurant out in Beijing, please pick this one—but reserve ahead. I have heard it's as difficult to get into as Restaurant Alain Ducasse in Paris. On the other hand, with only 3 days notice last May, I was able to book in. I have been several times; each time is the same or better—it's the kind of place that's better with a group of 6 to 10 people as there is so much to try.

Now then, to start at the beginning. This is the Li family home (honest) and they have room for maybe 40 diners; dinner is served in two different salons or outdoors, weather permitting. You pick the menu not by what you want to eat but how much per person you want to spend. The food just keeps coming; it is excellent. There is no table linen (they use oilcloth) and the toilet is the stand-up kind. There is a western wine list.

Dr. Li, who speaks English, makes the rounds and tells you his life history, which is interesting the first time, but expect to hear it every time you visit. He is a mathematics or physics professor who taught in the United States.

They don't take credit cards. I took four of us to dinner for about $200. You may want to have your taxi driver wait for you, as getting a taxi home may be iffy. For that matter, finding the place is iffy—it's in the Houtong and, especially in the dark, difficult to spot. Have your hotel make the reservations. Local phone: ☎ 8610/6618-0107.

FANGSHAN
Beihai Gongyuan, Xicheng

I include this because it's so famous you may well feel the need to visit, and it certainly is beautiful to look at; arrival through the park is fabulous, especially if you hit it at sunset. It's also good practice for fascist-style restaurant situations, of which there are still many in Beijing—you sit, you decide how much to pay, you wait for the bad food to come. They don't know from cocktails, wine, or service. They do have clean bathrooms and a gift shop. Not far from Li Family Home; have taxi wait.

CHINA CLUB BEIJING
51 Xi Rong Zian Hutong (Xicheng)

This is an icon of another color. It has two parts—the private club, which seems to have no reciprocity with any other private clubs in the world, even its own, and the to-the-public part—which has absolutely depressing decor, good enough food, and fabulous details.

All will be revealed. You see, China Club is the baby of David Tang from Hong Kong who is the father of Shanghai Tang, and an international stylemonger. It was he who created Mao-chic: He used images of Mao and other Chinese communist symbols in hot bright colors, blended them with nostalgic decor from 1930s Shanghai and Beijing, and added a few touches of genius that make the clubs the "in" invitation in Hong Kong or Beijing.

I happened to think the private club was gorgeous; Maggie sniffed that it was the Chinese version of The Groucho Club

(London). I think Groucho has less style and is shabbier, but Maggie was not as impressed with Tang and his style.

The Beijing club has a few private rooms upstairs that are to die for, chic and gorgeous (members only and their guests); the cafeteria where we ate could be fabulous if he would just let me to a little decorating. The location is in the middle of nowhere—on the other hand, the club and restaurant take up a full house, once an imperial palace and loving restored, and just to see it all is a trip to the other side of the moon. I thought it was worth doing; Maggie says thumbs down. Your hotel can make the reservation for you or you can become a member for $25,000. Local phone: ☎ 8610/6605-1188.

Snack & Shop

MCDONALD'S
Wangfujing

This was once the largest McDonald's in the world, but since renovations, is rather ordinary in all aspects. Still, they will give you a chart with photos, and you just point to what you want.

Big Duck Takeout

QIANMEN QUANJUDE ROAST DUCK
32 Qianmen St.

Absolute must-do, for the duck, the take-out place (which actually has tables, chairs, and normal service), and for the Qianmen shopping district, one of the oldest in Beijing. Plan your day around it; no reservations.

SHOPPING BEIJING

Barbra Streisand was just beginning her rise to stardom when I was finishing high school; I used to play her first album over and over again and try to learn the words to the song "Come to the Supermarket in Old Beijing." All I remember now (alas) is "Noodle soup? Poodle soup?"

That pretty much sums up the shopping scene, even today.

Beijing is one big circus to me, all the more fun because everything can be reached rather easily—I am a child with hands out, grabbing for everything. On my second trip to Beijing, I don't think a day went by when I didn't finish off at the Hong Qiao Market (Pearl Market). There's a range of everything you might want to take home from Beijing—antiques are the best buys, but I found great needlepoint carpets, the "pearls" were among my best buys, the lamps were incredible (any plug possible, no problem), and the visual pleasures of all the shopping were often stunning.

There's no question that the shopping scene is funkier than Shanghai, and while there's a marvelous congregation of fancy stores and big name boutiques, prices on designer goods are about 15% higher than elsewhere. I really don't need a Kelly bag, let alone the opportunity to overpay for one. However, if you've been to Hong Kong lately, you've noticed that the factory business there has pretty much dried up and manufacturing has really moved into China. Therefore there is some shopping opportunity in Beijing for overstocks, items that fell off a truck, and so on.

Indeed, pashmina and cashmere are still selling briskly; there's a pretty good business in fakes and in assumed factory overruns. The quality and selection of these items is superior in Beijing to Shanghai. For the overall selection, Beijing is better than Shanghai.

For tips on bargaining, see chapter 7, p. 175.

Money Matters

While the Visa brochure says there are more than 70 ATMs in Beijing (and surely more by the time you read this), I had a heck of a time finding one and was told at my hotel that the nearest one was a taxi ride away. As it turned out, there were tons of ATMs right on Wangfujing—a 1-block walk from the hotel. You can always change money in hotels and in some cases, American dollars are welcomed.

Shopping Hours

Stores are open 7 days a week, usually from 9:30am until 8pm, but many malls stay open until 10pm, as do stores on the pedestrian street, Wangfujing. Note that it is a rather recent phenomenon that office workers have both Saturday and Sunday off; their leisure time is often spent shopping.

Shopping & Shipping

After I got carried away with myself at the flea market (Dirt Market, see below) and ended up buying two porte-mirrors (matched set, of course), I thought I better investigate shipping from the hotel. I could not imagine how I was going to get all my luggage and purchases into the hotel car, let alone on the plane.

I had seen a series of FedEx ads geared toward international travelers, saying they specialized in shipping home your shopping. I went to my hotel desk and asked about Federal Express shipping. I was told yes, indeedy, they did that—go to the Business Centre.

The Business Centre informed me that they did not have Federal Express, but they had either DHL or a Chinese freight firm. Each had a different way of calculating the cost of the shipment; the hotel did not have a scale to weigh my stuff, so I would have to guess on the weight (in metric system no less). To make a long story short, I spent 45 frustrating minutes there. No one knew anything, I had no way of knowing if my package would arrive, so I decided to hand-carry the mirrors.

From what I could tell, it costs between $300 and $500 to send a package of 20 pounds into the United States. Because my experience was so frustrating, I suggest you do some research before you leave the United States, then be prepared to take care of the phone calls yourself once in China. There are also a handful of FedEx offices in Beijing, but I'd call before jumping in a taxi. FedEx offices in Beijing: ☎ 8610/6466-5566.

For more serious freight, there's a shipping desk at Beijing Curio City, or you might want to contact Sinotrans, famous for their services: air cargo: ☎ 8610/6501-1014; sea cargo: ☎ 8610/6465-2354.

Hotel Gift Shops

Several hotels are attached to small or even medium-size malls; the Palace Hotel has a lock on all the luxury big names, but the China World Hotel mall, China World Center, is more like a mall, and it's attached by some tunnels to the Kerry Centre, another mall (with its own hotel). The Kempinski is also attached to a mall.

Aside from these more or less traditional malls, all the big western-style hotels have some sort of gift shops, even the St. Regis Hotel, which otherwise has very little shopping (there's a news kiosk at the other end of the lobby). The Shangri-La properties, of which there are several in Beijing, all have many rather good gift shops in their lobbies.

Prices in hotel gift shops are always higher than on the street. Maggie bought some linen shirts in the gift shop at the Palace, later to find the exact same shirts on the street a block away for half price. Usually hotel gift shop merchandise is classier than what you find on the street, and therefore worth the extra price, because they found it and you didn't.

Many hotels have antiques shops in their lobbies.

If you are looking for English-language paperbacks, you will often find them in hotel gift shops.

One of the items I have found only in hotel gift shops (for some reason I do not understand) is the collection of note-cards and stationery items in the Chinese Farmer style of painting. They cost about $2 a card, and sometimes you can find a boxed set. I think they're wonderful; I especially like the brand from Red Lantern Productions, which comes with a little logo sticker inside the cellophane pack.

Museum Shopping

Beijing is one giant museum and has plenty of shopping inside museums to go along with it, although nothing as sensational as the gift shop at the Shanghai Museum of Art. On the other hand (heh-heh), there's nothing like a little shopping at Mao's Mausoleum Museum.

Postcard Shopping

Both Shanghai and Beijing are big postcard cities, of course—and you can find anything if you look hard enough. However, aside from the photos of famous landmarks, the arty postcards in Beijing tend to be just that—arty while in Shanghai, they are reproductions of cigarette cards, adverts, or old photos from the turn of the century—the two styles are as different as San Francisco is from Los Angeles.

My favorite postcards from Beijing came in a packet named (in English) "Commemoration of Former Chairman Mao Zedong"—with an artistic rendering of Mao on the front of the package that would have made Andy Warhol proud. The paper packet came with a dozen different contemporary artists' renderings of the chairman plus a curriculum vitae of Mao, in English! Note Maggie was offended by my fascination with communist art, so others may be too.

The other postcards I got into were a collection called "Insect Paintings" by Qi Baishi and one of Chinese emperors. Am I artsy or what?

I found my artistic postcard packets at the international bookstore on Wangfujing, but they are available all over town and in many hotel gift shops and the Friendship Store.

Tour & Guided Shopping

All motor coach tours will make shopping stops whether you want them or not and yes, of course, the guides get kickbacks. Even if you take a taxi or a private driver, expect kickbacks to be involved in your shopping treats, especially when drivers or guides accompany you and translate.

Most hotels offer their own private tours so you need not travel via motor coach; these are often in a Mercedes-Benz with an English-speaking driver, and may even include a picnic lunch. Prices can be as high as $150 for a person alone or $90 for two people together in a private car. You can invariably do these "tours" on your own with a taxi and save a lot of money.

On my first trip to Beijing, I was treated to the Hutong Tour, a pedicab tour of an old Beijing residential neighborhood. It was one of the most fabulous and memorable things in my life, so I sent Maggie and my translator Albert to do it on another visit to Beijing—Maggie's first. Well she came back really pissed off at me and said it was a tourist rip-off of the highest order and that she was shocked that I had sent her on this obstruction of justice.

I was so surprised that we compared my memories to her experiences and decided that there were either two companies running the show or that it had gone too touristy. Let the visitor beware. (For a walking tour of your own doing through a hutong, see "Houhai," below.)

Maggie also took a tour by herself, arranged through a hotel, so she could go to the Great Wall and Ming Tombs. She did not want Badaling Great Wall, or anything touristy and specifically told this to the guide. Nonetheless she was still taken to a tourist restaurant where a set meal was ordered for her and she had to sit alone to eat it. She was not amused.

Communist Shopping

So I admit it, the term "communist shopping" is an oxymoron. I guess what I mean is shopping for communist souvenirs—of this there is much to behold. My very first trophy was a ceramic figurine about 14 inches tall. I paid about $35 for her and treasured her, certain she was a genuine piece of art. Later (years later), I discovered there is a huge business in communist souvenirs and these little babies are popped out of the molds and onto the streets by the thousands. OK, well. . . .

A big item seems to be the Mao cigarette lighters (many of which are musical). I bought about a dozen worker's posters—one real and the rest reproductions. I began my collection in Shanghai, but found a better selection (and better prices) in Beijing.

One of my best gift items—which I really stocked up on as best I could—was Mao alarm clocks and even Mao desk clocks—these are rather big and heavy, so not ideal for packing and schlepping. The alarm clocks have everything from Illushin airplanes on the second hand to workers who beat their fists on the tick-tock.

Communist souvenirs are sold in all antiques and flea markets and at Mao's Mausoleum. Many hotel gift shops sell some items, at high prices of course.

BEIJING NEIGHBORHOODS

Wangfujing

This is the main drag in Beijing. It has recently been paved and made a pedestrian-only street in the blocks between the Beijing Hotel and the Palace Hotel—the selling space is 1.5 million square meters, which is larger than any giant megamall in the United States. The street is more than 100 years old and is named after a Ming dynasty well. After 8 years of renovation, there are planters filled with flowers, a fountain or two, several wonderful Seward Johnston–type sculptures, some street actors (mimes, and so on), and the usual hordes of tourists, many of whom are lining up to have their photos snapped with the sculptures. All the big department stores are here, there's McDonald's, some local pharmacies (Chinese medicine–type stores), some discount stores, a silk shop, a few arts and crafts stores, banks, Popeye Fried Chicken, and so on. Even though it's clean and modern, it does not feel at all like Shanghai—this is the new Beijing. There is a lot of action in the evening in good weather.

Liulichang

Antiques heaven. Photo ops galore. Fun for days. *Note:* There are two parts to this street, which do not readily connect visually; they also sell two different types of antiques. On one end, it's more like a series of indoor flea markets selling fun junk; the other end is high-end stores that mostly sell the real thing, and I don't mean Coca-Cola. I call this "Lily Street," because I can't pronounce the name in Chinese. It is perhaps the best shopping district in Beijing and has been so for 500 years.

Qianmen/Tiananmen

If these sound suspiciously alike to you, it's because they are basically the same, and the Qianmen shopping district is a spoke off of Tiananmen Square. It is one of the oldest shopping districts in town, and while a little bit funky and junky, is enormous fun—especially at night. Many of the stores are hundreds of years old; there is a main drag of stalls that are open late at night. There is not a more perfect evening than to shop around here, have dinner at the Duck Restaurant and then take a pedicab to Tiananmen Square.

As for Tiananmen Square itself, there are many vendors who wander around the vast square, selling things like snacks, postcards, or kites. Inside the nearby museums (and mausoleum) there are souvenirs for sale. Tanks for the memories.

Forbidden City

The royal residence part of the old Imperial City, the Forbidden City is a living museum now—with several opportunities to shop, which begin immediately as you enter the front gate and pay your entrance fee. The best thing I saw to buy here, and never saw anywhere else in Beijing or China, is a silk scarf with a map of the Forbidden City printed on it—about $25.

Wangfujing

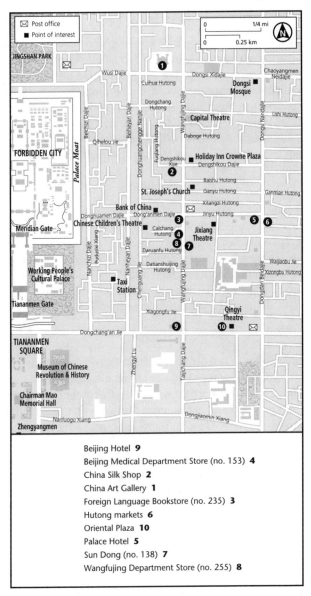

Beijing Hotel **9**

Beijing Medical Department Store (no. 153) **4**

China Silk Shop **2**

China Art Gallery **1**

Foreign Language Bookstore (no. 235) **3**

Hutong markets **6**

Oriental Plaza **10**

Palace Hotel **5**

Sun Dong (no. 138) **7**

Wangfujing Department Store (no. 255) **8**

Chang An Avenue

This isn't a neighborhood, it's a geographical marker since this main highwaylike street runs about 25 miles long, right through the heart of the new Beijing and is where the highrise hotels and business centers are located; there are some malls and some specialty shopping venues such as the Friendship Store and Silk Alley, which are a block from each other. It does change names many times along the way to the Friendship Store, but you won't notice that unless you are looking at a guidebook or a map.

Sanlitun

Rumor has it that the shopping portion of this area is being razed, as is possibly the whole area. At night, it is the swinging part of town, filled with clubs where expats mix and mingle. The shopping area is similar to Silk Alley, if it's still there, near the hotel district on the Third Ring Road. Last time we heard, The Club Vogue was the place to go. There is an officially designated Sanlitun Bar Street.

Houhai

If you want to wander in a real houtong, don't want the possibly touristy houtong tour (see above) and want to find a few 100-year-old eggs along the way, get yourself to the Drum Tower (also part of the official houtong tour) and start explorations on the west side of Houhai from Deshengmennei Lu. Skirt the lakes, pass the park, as you walk east. When you find a statue of a bearded man doing exercises, turn into the alleys and explore. Get lost to get found. Cross the Silver Ingot Bridge, then find Old Pipe Lane, filled with old- fashioned shops. You will end up at Di Anmenwai and back in the real world, where you can take a taxi.

Temple of Heaven

OK, so it's a cultural site to you—to me, it's a shopping neighborhood . . . and talk about heaven. This is where you'll find

Liulichang Antiques Area

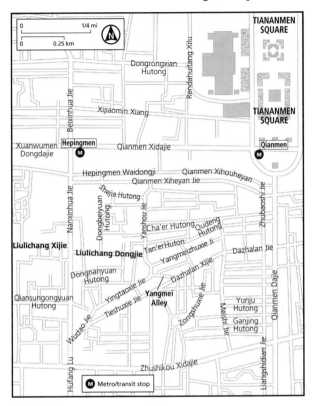

the Pearl Market (Hong Qiao) and its outdoor mall, across the street. But don't tell your taxi "temple of heaven," point him right to Honggiao, which is preprinted on every hotel taxi check list.

Punjiayuan

This is a district of Beijing and the location of the Saturday and Sunday flea market, which has become synonymous with the name of the destination. Expats often call it the "Dirt Market" because some of it is in a dirt yard.

Great Wall (Badaling)

The most commercial parts of the Wall (Badaling being the most commercial and closest to Beijing) has tons of shopping in terms of souvenirs stalls and even freestanding antiques shops.

Summer Palace

There isn't a lot of shopping at the Summer Palace, or a lot of good shopping, but there is certainly more opportunity to shop than I had expected. The most important thing you will buy, and it pays to get it from the vendors out front, is a map in English and Chinese. You might also want to splurge for a private guide—there are several out front hawking their services.

BEIJING RESOURCES A TO Z

A note about addresses: Although addresses are often listed below, most of the venues in this section are on the standard preprinted hotel taxi checklists, already written out for you in English and Chinese, which is far more useful than my listings. I've been to every venue on every major hotel checklist; if said venue is not mentioned in this section, there is a reason.

Antiques

Also see Flea Markets and Markets listings.

You may not know it, but you came to Beijing to buy antiques or so-called antiques. This is tchotchke heaven. You will find everything from fake to real, valuable to worthless and much that looks great and therefore means something to you, regardless of its true value.

While there are some nice furniture stores (see p. 250), remember the warning to buy furniture in Shanghai if you can. Therefore Beijing is the "smalls" capital of the world.

If you have time for only one antiques shopping stop, head immediately for Lily Street (Liulichang Lu) which is not far from Tiananmen Square. If you are in town over the weekend and like funky flea markets, get to the Dirt Market in Punji-ayuan. Do remember that a lot of the antiques were made last week.

A few favorite specific sources:

MENG QING HE
No. 9, North House, Liangma Market
Liangjiu Lu (across from Kempinski)

The best selection of ancestor paintings, the best quality (most on canvas, some on paper), and the best opening prices. Note that the ancestor paintings can also be called "forefather paintings" or "family tree pictures."

HOHOHANG ANTIQUE FURNITURE
43 Huawei Bei Li
Jinsongqiaonan Zhaojiachaowaishichang

I wish I was clever enough to find a resource like this on my own, but the truth is it came from Lourdes, executive house-keeping manager at the Palace Hotel, who is the hotel guru on antique furniture. This source sells furniture only, much of it restored; they have a huge building/warehouse. They actually have a showroom and a warehouse—one out toward the airport; the other is near the P Market.

GREAT WALL ANTIQUE STORE
Great Wall, Badaling

Sorry I have no more specifics on this store, but their card is totally in Chinese and all I could get in English is the official name and their phone number (☎ 010/6912-1432). However, don't fret, you will have no trouble finding this place—it is the big antiques store that looks real and does indeed have antiques with wax seals, showing they can be exported. There are many rooms of antiques, from many periods and in many formats. I bought a small rug after much bargaining, for about $100. In fact, they took an American Express traveler's check for $100.

When I say small, I mean small—less than a square meter (maybe half that), but very nice. I have no idea what I will do with it.

Arts & Crafts

There are a few stores on Wangfujing that sell arts and crafts to tourists; mostly, I hated them—way, way too touristy. There are some crafts in almost all markets; you will probably find what you want at the Hong Qiao Market (Pearl Market). There is a small selection of arts and crafts at the duty free store in the Beijing airport; almost all hotel gift shops also sell arts and crafts.

FRIENDSHIP STORE
17 Jianguomenwai Dajie

This is an excellent source for Chinese arts and crafts, although prices are a tad high. See listing under "Department Stores."

Big Names

Giorgio Armani: Palace Hotel

Aquascutum: China World Shopping Centre

Baccarat: Palace Hotel

Bally: Palace Hotel

Hugo Boss: Palace Hotel

Burberry: China World Shopping Centre

Cartier: Palace Hotel

Celine: Palace Hotel

Cerruti 1881: China World Shopping Centre; Palace Hotel

Chanel: Palace Hotel

Christian Dior: Palace Hotel

Dolce & Gabana: Palace Hotel

Dunhill: China World Shopping Centre

Escada: Palace Hotel

Fendi: Palace Hotel

Fogal: China World Shopping Centre

Gucci: Palace Hotel

Hermès: Palace Hotel

Lancel: China World Shopping Centre

Bruno Magli: Palace Hotel

Mont Blanc: China World Shopping Centre

Nina Ricci: China World Shopping Centre; Palace Hotel

Trussardi: Palace Hotel

Versace: Palace Hotel

Louis Vuitton: Palace Hotel, China World Shopping Centre

Zegna: China World Shopping Centre

Books

FOREIGN LANGUAGE BOOKSTORE
219 Wangfujing

This is toward the Palace Hotel end of Wangfujing, right across from McDonald's (one branch of McDonald's actually) and is a wonderful store; don't forget to go upstairs if only briefly. The store sells books but also videos, computer programs, and so on. On the street level there's a large selection of fabulous postcards (the artsy kind), many slides of tourist and artist sites and sights, books in foreign languages (here Chinese is not a foreign language), textbooks, medical books, newspapers, and kids' books—my favorite are the language books for children; I think they make good gifts.

FRIENDSHIP STORE
17 Jianguomenwai Dajie

The bookstore, near the supermarket end of the Friendship store, has a decadent number of foreign devil magazines and an OK selection of guides and books in an assortment of languages.

Nowhere near as comprehensive as the Foreign Language Bookstore, but worth visiting while you are there. See p. 245.

Carpets

FRIENDSHIP STORE
17 Jianguomenwai Dajie

One whole salon of the Friendship Store is devoted to carpets of all styles; I happen to be more attracted to needlepoint carpets and less afraid to buy them because I know they are new and there's less room for being cheated. My needlepoint carpet was not inexpensive, but it's gorgeous—western (almost English, a series of flowers)—and sooo chic I can barely stand to walk on it. See p. 245 for more on Friendship store.

Cashmere & Pashmina

ZHU XUE YI
No. 21 Xiushui Market Second St.

This small stall/shop is on the side street attached to the market at Silk Alley; you will find it easily, despite this sounding rather vague. When you get here, you either show this copy of the book or say you were sent by Chet and the guys at the Palace Hotel; they speak English here.

Now then, I am not going to tell you this is the best pashmina in the world or that you even still want to buy pashmina; I am going to tell you that Chet did the legwork for you and therefore there is an established flat price, so that you don't have to bargain. That price is 480 yuan ($55!).

KING DEER CASHMERE
9 Jianguomen Dajie

This tourist store, which sells all kinds of souvenirs and stuff, is a block from Silk Alley and a block from China World Hotel, so it's not inconvenient. It is very, very touristy and tour-group oriented.

MONGOLIAN CASHMERE
Jianguomen Dajie (CK)

I accidentally found this store (there's no such thing as an accident?) while looking out my bedroom from a Club Horizon room in the China World Hotel (that means it was a very high floor). It's unlikely you would spot this store otherwise, although perhaps your taxi would pass it. I'm not sure if it's worth going to in the long run because I'm not convinced Chinese cashmere is a super buy, but this is a hoot.

OK, the store is a private club—there are two prices on each item, the off-the-street price, and the discounted price that you get if you join the club. It costs about $25 to join; you can sign up immediately and use the discount immediately and your membership is good for 1 year. Now you have an excuse to come back to Beijing in a few months.

The store is rather large and modern, with two salons filled with displays and stock, and sales help that speaks many languages. They are even quite willing to help. They seem to get a lot of business travelers buying for spouses back home.

The selection is so large that you can pick from classical (boring) cashmeres, fashion cashmeres, and even ugly cashmeres. Prices are reasonable, maybe even the best in town, but this isn't Scottish cashmere either. If you buy a lot you can bargain on rounding down the price. They take credit cards. The store is a lot of fun and does feel like a big adventure.

If you're up for the thrill of it, you can get here by metro and then cross the street (which is like a highway and there are no lights, so good luck) or walk from Friendship Store and Silk Alley (again you still have to cross the street) or take a pedicab, if you can get the address written for you in Chinese. You still have to cross the street.

FRIENDSHIP STORE
17 Jianguomenwai Dajie

Boring selection of cashmere; possibly all right if you are the kind of person with a good eye or who gets lucky at places like this. See p. 245.

SILK ALLEY
13 Jianguomenwai Dajie

The first listing in this section is a store in Silk Alley that I was specifically sent to by my friends Chet and Kevin who used to live in Beijing. There are many more stores and stalls in Silk Alley that sell pashmina and cashmere—some on a seasonal basis, others: all year-round. Just be careful you know what you're getting with anything you buy in Silk Alley.

Department Stores

WANGFUJING DEPARTMENT STORE
255 Wangfujing

Happy days are here again: a true 1950s-style department store that's been renovated as such. I love it, if only because it makes me laugh. I also use it as my local one-stop shopping source from the Palace Hotel—I've bought luggage here and all sorts of things. Glam it is not, but it's not Shanghai Number One either—they do try harder. The fountains out front are a hoot.

PARKSON
101 Fuxingmennei Dajie

Famous name in Chinese retail. There's a supermarket and crafts department (not together). Parkson is located in the Xidan Shopping Center to the west of Tiananmen. I think the Forbidden City is more fun.

LUFTHANSA SHOPPING CENTER
9 Beisanhuan Longlu

I will not tell you this is a good mall or even lives up to its local reputation. I did, however, have a great time here. There's an antiques center across the street from the Kempinski Hotel; the mall has a department store that has everything you could want or want to stare at.

Emergencies (Medical)

It's possible that the doctor is only in for guests of the **Palace Hotel,** but when I got sick and knew I was on the verge of pleurisy, and asked the concierge to send a bellboy to Wangfujung to get me some cillin drugs, I was incredulous when he told me that the hotel had an English-speaking doctor in the house and to head upstairs. The doctor was wearing a white coat; his English was better than my Chinese. He gave me some Chinese pills (looked like Drixoral to me) and, after I insisted, an antibiotic. I paid about $10 for the visit and $2 for each of the medicines. I even got to charge it to my room. The man saved my health.

The **Beijing United Family Hospital,** 2 Jiangtai Lu, is in the Chaoyang district, not far from the Beijing Hilton—I have not been there, but knowing about it gives me comfort. They offer western medical care on outpatient and in-patient basis; there is 24-hour emergency room service; you can arrange an in-hotel visit by a doctor. May you never need to know. May your house be safe from tigers. You can visit their web-site: www.beijingunited.com. Call ☎ 8610/6433-3963.

FRIENDSHIP STORE
17 Jianguomenwai Dajie

I have chosen to classify this as a department store because it simply sells everything—it's one of the best one stop shops in Beijing and also one of the best stores in Beijing. I can't say I rely on their sense of fashion, but the store has a supermarket, a branch of Starbucks, a bookstore, a luggage department, and three floors of selling space. You name it, they sell it.

Here's the fun part. Every time I have bought anything here, especially a high-ticket item, I have asked for and received a 10% discount.

BEIJING MEDICAL DEPARTMENT STORE
153 Wangfujing Dajie

I am not Dr. Kalter's daughter for nothing—show me a place where you can buy prescriptions, play with the over-the-counter drugs, practice Chinese medicine, have your blood pressure taken (free), and touch prosthetic devices and I am a happy camper. Two blocks from the Palace Hotel. Also, see box on medical emergencies.

Fakes

I cannot condone fake merchandise, but I can tell you that it's pretty easy to find in Beijing, although as China joins the World Trade Organization (WTO), it is expected that there will be a crackdown.

You can buy anything from illegal copies of videos, CDs, and computer programs to fake Louis Vuitton, Tag Heuer, Fendi, and much more. The Louis Vuitton is often not on display and must be asked for in a whisper.

The best place for a wide selection of fake anything is the Hong Qiao Market; watches are on the ground floor, and leather goods upstairs before you get to the antiques and crafts.

What I call the Palace Strip is a line of stalls between the Palace Hotel and Wangfujing—in this strip there are also a few dealers who sell fakes.

Flea Markets

BEIJING CURIO CITY
Dongsanhuan Nanlu

Whoaaa, how to explain this—I went several times so I could be accurate, because the first time, I stayed 5 minutes and walked out, deciding that I hated it and you would too. Then I thought it over. The "lobby floor" is really tacky and frightened me. Then a local friend told me there were some good places. So I returned and spent several hours here and decided it wasn't bad at all, which is much the secret of shopping in China. (What things look like isn't reliable.)

What I hated is the atmosphere, the immediate ground-floor selling space—the market is in the lobby and the mezzanine levels of a modern building and resembles an ugly hotel lobby. Also, the place is very touristy—prices are high, many vendors speak English (a bad sign), and the place simply has no soul. However, once you get into the recesses of the ground floor, or up on the other levels, it really isn't bad at all. There are a million better places to shop in Beijing.

That said, it's a good one-stop shopping place if it's the best you can do, or you hate the real China. There is a shipping desk in the lobby—naturally it was closed each time I visited.

THE P MARKET (PUNJIAYUAN)
Huaweiqiaxi Nan Dajie

Let's get the technical stuff taken care of first: Many guide-books report this as a "Sunday only" affair. That is wrong. The market is held on both Saturday and Sunday. I have attended both days; there isn't much difference in the flow of either day. At approximately 10am, suddenly the market is mobbed. From 8:30 to 9:55am it's a pleasure.

Now then, the market is 14km from city center; you take a taxi south and are suddenly there. It cost me about 60 yuan to get there. I don't know what I was expecting, I just know that my first seconds of arrival did register disappointment. That's because all I saw were gates and what appeared to be an industrial park or dumping zone. Once I saw all the merchandise, I was delirious with glee. So don't judge a flea by its entrance.

The market is not as large as I was expecting, although everyone I ever spoke to told me it was vast. It consists of open dirt ground, covered with blankets from which vendors sell their wares; aisles under rows of corrugated tin rooftops, from which more vendors sell their goods; and a series of tiny shops in the walls that surround the compound in a U shape. Many of the official alleys are devoted to a type of goods—scrolls, ephemera, crafts, jewelry, and so on.

Bargaining is expected. Some of the stuff is fake (really!). Few dealers want American dollars, so have cash on you. They don't take credit cards.

Prices range from good to better to you've-got-to-be-kidding giggle lows. I bought two porte-mirrors (a matched set) for $30. How could I leave them behind?

You will have the time of your life. Bargain hard and carry a tote bag or back pack for carrying smalls. Dress down; bring small bills; consider having a donkey and a porter to carry your buys.

LIANGMAQIAO MARKET
49 Liangmaqiao Lu (across from Kempinksi Hotel)

This is a very low-key market, but I find it charming. It is made up of a series of rows, each filled with shops or stalls or whatever you call it in strips or motels of dealers. The entrance isn't too inviting and you cannot go too early in the morning. I was there at 11am and not all dealers were open.

In the far back, to the right-hand corner, I found the best dealer of ancestor paintings I have found in China. There is also a furniture showroom that ships. In fact, there are several furniture showrooms.

Although not my number-one choice for antiques that you have to, must go to, this is a lot of fun and is especially good for those staying at the Kempinski or the nearby hotels.

CHAOWAI MARKET
Chaoyangmenwai Dajie

If you trust me, you will forget that every guidebook and taxi checklist has this market listed. Just forget it; absolutely forget it.

Foodstuffs

CHINA WORLD SUPERMARKET
Basement, China World Hotel

I think this was a branch of Hong Kong's Wellcome but has now changed hands and is marked CRC; no matter. It's fun. It's a rather full-service, western-style grocery store so you can buy snacks for your hotel room, for picnics at the Great Wall, the plane home, the kids or take home packages of international brands with Chinese labels on them.

THE VAGINA MARKET
11 Jianguomenwai Dajie

Excuse the name of this market, obviously I made it up—I don't know the name in Chinese and now I know you'll remember the market and what it sells. (Read on.)

I've never met a foreign supermarket I didn't like—and this one is Chinese so it offers double happiness. You can buy the jelled fruit candies here and all sorts of exciting local products. Yes friends, this is where I stock up on Vagina Cleansing Soap, one of the best gifts I have ever passed out to my friends. Please note this specialty costs 11 yuan, whereas normal soap costs 5 yuan.

The grocery store is almost next door to the entrance to Silk Alley, so you can't miss it.

FRIENDSHIP SUPERMARKET
17 Jianguomenwai Dajie

The supermarket is on the ground floor of the Friendship store. It's a gourmet supermarket with international foodstuffs. Starbucks is nearby, but not within the actual grocery store.

STARBUCKS
Friendship Store, 17 Jianguomenwai Dajie
Sun Dong Centre, Wangfujing

Starbucks has taken Beijing by storm and was a must-do for me—especially since I missed the Shanghai branch, which had opened while I was in Shanghai. While my coffee was a treat, the real fun was to buy Starbucks Beijing coffee mugs.

Wy Lu
Wangfujing

This may be Kmart (it's hard to tell but they appear to sell washing machines upstairs), but the ground floor is a big supermarket with Chinese gourmet and it's wonderful. There are seasonal promotions at the front doors with the appropriate foodstuffs for each of the Chinese festivals, so you can bring your friends just the right eats. The packaging is wonderful; they have traditional Chinese medicine, coffees, candies, jelly fruit cups, and more.

Wangfujing Food Plaza
Wangfujing

Harrods Food Hall meets the new China; many of the gorgeous examples of produce are engineered and have no taste. Other than that, it's great fun to look. I bought many items just for their wrappings; I have no idea what's inside, nor do I care. Until the ants arrive, anyway.

Yaohan Supermarket
Sci-Tech Plaza
22 Jianguomenwai Dajie

Again, this is not worth the schlepp unless you're already in the area—then you will find it great fun. This is a famous Japanese market, quite established in China now.

Furniture

Guang Han Tang
Beijing Classical Furniture Co. Ltd.
Showroom: lobby Kempinski Hotel

This is one of the most elegant, lovely shops in town—its stock has been edited to western taste, probably prices have been too.

Lamps

GEORGE
1 Temple of Heaven Shopping Mall

I love George; I love his shop; I love the lamp I bought there and wish I hadn't bought six lamps in Hong Kong and could have bought more from George. This shop is one of the first ones you will find in the open garden mall part of the Hong Qiao Market (if you are headed south, on the right-hand side.) George seems to speak some English and loves to show off his work. You can spend hours there as he shows you more and more of his creations and dares you to discover how he has wired it. His goods are original, creative, fabulous, and cheap. He also makes the lamps for most of the major hotels in town and is somewhat of a cult icon. Every expat in town knows George. He can arrange shipping. Lamps are sold with the shades but he will reduce the price if you buy without the shade. Creative lamps, with shades, are about $50 each.

Malls

Malls are relatively new to Beijing, most arrived in the late 1990s. They are, as everywhere else in the world, a big hangout for teens and tweens on weekends.

SUN DONG AN
138 Wangfujing

This mall is the pride of Beijing; I mention it first because if this is what's considered the best mall in town, lets all go to Minneapolis. It is a local mall, not a tourist mall like China World. There's McDonald's and Starbucks and lots of crafts stores and CD stores and real people stores, but it is not great. Hmmm, well, it's not even good.

FULL LINK PLAZA
18 Chaoyangmenwai Dajie

Academically, this is one of the more interesting malls, but you might not want to taxi all the way out here just to see it. The mall has everything from good supermarkets to Gucci and a few other western designer firms.

CHINA WORLD SHOPPING MALL
China World Hotel

As you can see from a quick glance at the Big Names section (see p. 240), half the name-brand stores in Beijing are in this mall. There's also a supermarket, bank, and courier offices as well as the hotel lobby shops on the hotel lobby level (which is not actually part of the mall, but while you're there—it shouldn't be a loss).

PALACE HOTEL
8 Goldfish Lane, Wangfujing

This isn't really a mall, it just sort of functions like one—it's like the Galleria in Houston, small and select with only designer stores on three levels of marble floors. There's little that's Chinese about it, except that the prices are sky high. If you have no interest in expensive designer items, go anyway for a quick look because the locals who shop in these stores are so gorgeous that they're worthy of a good long stare.

ORIENTAL PLAZA
Wangfujing

Still under construction as we go to press: will have hotel, mall, and so on.

Markets

HONG QIAO (THE PEARL MARKET)

Take back your poils, I'm not that kind of goil—not since having discovered this market filled with fabulous fake pearls. They have real pearls, too, in fact they've got it all. The so-called market itself is in a modern demi-highrise with about four floors of merchandise. It changed since I was there the first time; on my next visit two floors of antiques and the cafe were closed, so I have no idea which arrangement you will find. Never mind. I suggest this is your first shopping stop in Beijing so you can look over the selection and get a feel for prices. Maggie and I ended up coming back here just about every day.

There is nothing Chinese or even attractive about the building and you will wonder if I have lost my mind. You walk into a room filled with counters of small electronics, past that is a room with counters of dealers who sell watches. Many of the watch dealers have fakes, but they are put away and you must ask for them or find someone who trusts you enough to bring out their selection. Some of these dealers also sell the musical Mao lighters; you can make a deal for lighters if you buy in bulk.

Actually, you can make a deal for anything if you buy in bulk.

Upstairs (there's an escalator), it feels sort of like a cheap department store, but there's luggage if you need some. Then you get to the handbags and again, copies are out but also hidden. The good stuff is put away.

Then you get to the pearl floor, which must have at least 100 dealers selling pearls and semiprecious stones. All sorts of pearls are sold; I tended to give my business to the people who were honest about what they were selling—the "pearls" that I liked (for style and price) were not from oysters but made of crushed shells. Few will tell you this, which is why I gave so much business to Beijing Kaifu Pearl Coral Co. Ltd. (which is right in front of you when you get onto the pearl floor, No. 152, 3rd floor). I did buy from many dealers and was most unhappy with pearls I chose for 150 yuan (after much bargaining) that looked just like those for 40 yuan that other dealers had.

You'll note much advertising of diplomatic visits to assorted stalls—but I don't think Madeleine Albright was born to shop and therefore don't mind that I wasn't impressed by the stall where she bought pearls.

After the pearl floor comes the arts and crafts floor—which Maggie and I both thought was the best place in the city—and then comes the antiques floor. I bought my ancestor paintings here. After much negotiating, some of it done after I walked away and left my Chinese translator behind, I bought two enormous canvas scrolls for about $540. It hurt at the time, but in retrospect, it was one of the best buys of my life.

Silk & Textiles

BEIJING SILK
Qianmen Dajie

This is one of my favorite stores in China and I urge you to poke in, even if you don't want to buy anything—it's very scenic and atmospheric and is smack in the middle of the old fashioned shopping district of Qianmen (right off Tiananmen Square and across the street from the Big Duck restaurant).

Fabric is sold off the bolt in two downstairs salons, clothes are sold upstairs. Forget the clothes (although I did see some factory overruns) and concentrate on the velvets and brocades and gorgeous silks for about $12 a yard, many in unusual fashion colors that you'd expect to find from someone like Giorgio Armani, not Chairman Mao.

ZHANG TEXTILE
China World Shopping Centre

If you adore Chinese textiles and garments, you will go nuts in this store—one of the largest galleries in the world specializing in Chinese antique garments. There's some touristy stuff, but the collection of textile hats and helmets alone is enough to make you weep with joy. Because of China's ethnic diversity, there are a wide range of styles; there are also framed fragments as well as full garments; there are also mandarin rank badges and that old standby, shoes for bound feet.

SILK & COTTON COMPANY
Wangfujing

This store is new, clean, modern, and not at all funky—right on Wangfujing and easy to shop for yard goods or finished scarves and a few clothing items. I bought silk polo shirts (for men) with knit polo collars for $25 each in very soft gray blue shades that my son went wild for—very eurochic (and hand washable). Maggie bought several scarves for gifts.

The silks are about $10 to $12 per meter.

FRIENDSHIP STORE
17 Jianguomenwai Dajie

Silks are upstairs; rather boring but basic.

YUAN LONG
15 Yongdingmenwai

Oh my God. This was one of the adventures of the trip, and one I did for you so you wouldn't have to do it. The store is touristy (but that doesn't mean they don't have some things of interest); the parking lot is filled with taxis and tour buses, guides are licking their fingers, waiting for their kickbacks. It's way off on the edge of downtown on the southern part of the city, not that far from the southern gate of the Temple of Heaven, but too far to be worth considering.

I asked my taxi driver to take me to Beijing Silk but he drove me here instead (gee, I wonder why) and I was frightened because it was so far from anything familiar—or just plain anything. If I wasn't laughing so hard, I would have hated the whole terrifying experience.

The store sells a little of everything (while they have you trapped) and has an excellent Chinese costume department—all reproductions and very, very expensive ($500). Other than that, it is not a good store and the system is disgusting. If you are taken here, expect to be taken.

Weddings

Beijing does not have as many wedding studios as Shanghai, but there are several and they are conveniently located in the

Dongsi shopping area, which is alongside the Palace Hotel, not that far from the St. Regis and about 2 big blocks from Wangfujing. To know how it all works, see this section in the Shanghai chapter.

ONE PERFECT DAY IN BEIJING

I have no tour for you here for several reasons—a lot of visitors, especially first-timers, are on tours to begin with and have little time to themselves. Also, as noted, where you end up shopping is very much related to where your hotel is and how bad the traffic is and what's near the important cultural sights that you came to see. I'd say the perfect day in Beijing would include the Hong Qiao Market and the Lily Street, with maybe a stroll on Wangfujing and certainly with dinner at the Big Duck and a chance to shop the stalls across the street in the Qianmen district. This then allows you a pedicab tour through Tiananmen Square after dinner, and voilà, one perfect day.

Size Conversion Chart

WOMEN'S CLOTHING

American	8	10	12	14	16	18
Continental	38	40	42	44	46	48
British	10	12	14	16	18	20

WOMEN'S SHOES

American	5	6	7	8	9	10
Continental	36	37	38	39	40	41
British	4	5	6	7	8	9

CHILDREN'S CLOTHING

American	3	4	5	6	6X
Continental	98	104	110	116	122
British	18	20	22	24	26

CHILDREN'S SHOES

American	8	9	10	11	12	13	1	2	3
Continental	24	25	27	28	29	30	32	33	34
British	7	8	9	10	11	12	13	1	2

MEN'S SUITS

American	34	36	38	40	42	44	46	48
Continental	44	46	48	50	52	54	56	58
British	34	36	38	40	42	44	46	48

MEN'S SHIRTS

American	$14^{1}/_2$	15	$15^{1}/_2$	16	$16^{1}/_2$	17	$17^{1}/_2$	18
Continental	37	38	39	41	42	43	44	45
British	$14^{1}/_2$	15	$15^{1}/_2$	16	$16^{1}/_2$	17	$17^{1}/_2$	18

MEN'S SHOES

American	7	8	9	10	11	12	13
Continental	$39^{1}/_2$	41	42	43	$44^{1}/_2$	46	47
British	6	7	8	9	10	11	12

INDEX

Notes

FROMMER'S® COMPLETE TRAVEL GUIDES

FROMMER'S® DOLLAR-A-DAY GUIDES

FROMMER'S® PORTABLE GUIDES

FROMMER'S® NATIONAL PARK GUIDES

Family Vacations in the
   National Parks
Grand Canyon

National Parks of the
   American West
Rocky Mountain

Yellowstone & Grand Teton
Yosemite & Sequoia/
   Kings Canyon
Zion & Bryce Canyon

FROMMER'S® MEMORABLE WALKS

Chicago
London

New York
Paris

San Francisco
Washington, D.C.

FROMMER'S® GREAT OUTDOOR GUIDES

New England
Northern California

Southern California & Baja
Southern New England

Washington & Oregon

FROMMER'S® BORN TO SHOP GUIDES

Born to Shop: France
Born to Shop: Italy

Born to Shop: London
Born to Shop: New York

Born to Shop: Paris

FROMMER'S® IRREVERENT GUIDES

Amsterdam
Boston
Chicago
Las Vegas

London
Los Angeles
Manhattan
New Orleans

Paris
San Francisco
Seattle & Portland
Vancouver

Walt Disney World
Washington, D.C.

FROMMER'S® BEST-LOVED DRIVING TOURS

America
Britain
California

Florida
France
Germany

Ireland
Italy
New England

Scotland
Spain
Western Europe

THE UNOFFICIAL GUIDES®

Bed & Breakfasts in
   California
Bed & Breakfasts in
   New England
Bed & Breakfasts in
   the Northwest
Bed & Breakfasts in
   Southeast
Beyond Disney
Branson, Missouri

California with Kids
Chicago
Cruises
Disneyland
Florida with Kids
Golf Vacations in the
   Eastern U.S.
The Great Smoky &
   Blue Ridge
   Mountains

Inside Disney
Hawaii
Las Vegas
London
Miami & the Keys
Mini Las Vegas
Mini-Mickey
New Orleans
New York City
Paris

San Francisco
Skiing in the West
Southeast with Kids
Walt Disney World
Walt Disney World
   for Grown-ups
Walt Disney World
   for Kids
Washington, D.C.

SPECIAL-INTEREST TITLES

Frommer's Britain's Best Bed & Breakfasts and
   Country Inns
Frommer's Britain's Best Bike Rides
The Civil War Trust's Official Guide
   to the Civil War Discovery Trail
Frommer's Caribbean Hideaways
Frommer's Adventure Guide to Central America
Frommer's Adventure Guide to South America
Frommer's Adventure Guide to Southeast Asia
Frommer's Food Lover's Companion to France
Frommer's Gay & Lesbian Europe
Frommer's Exploring America by RV
Hanging Out in Europe

Israel Past & Present
Mad Monks' Guide to California
Mad Monks' Guide to New York City
Frommer's The Moon
Frommer's New York City with Kids
The New York Times' Unforgettable
   Weekends
Places Rated Almanac
Retirement Places Rated
Frommer's Road Atlas Britain
Frommer's Road Atlas Europe
Frommer's Washington, D.C., with Kids
Frommer's What the Airlines Never Tell Y